Paul Grigaut
March 1990

IRISH PEASANT SOCIETY

IRISH PEASANT SOCIETY

Four Historical Essays

by

K. H. CONNELL

PROFESSOR OF ECONOMIC AND SOCIAL HISTORY
THE QUEEN'S UNIVERSITY OF BELFAST

CLARENDON PRESS . OXFORD
1968

*Oxford University Press, Ely House, London W.*1

GLASGOW NEW YORK TORONTO MELBOURNE WELLINGTON
CAPE TOWN SALISBURY IBADAN NAIROBI LUSAKA ADDIS ABABA
BOMBAY CALCUTTA MADRAS KARACHI LAHORE DACCA
KUALA LUMPUR HONG KONG TOKYO

© *Oxford University Press 1968*

SET BY SANTYPE LIMITED OF SALISBURY AND
PRINTED IN GREAT BRITAIN AT THE UNIVERSITY PRESS, OXFORD
BY VIVIAN RIDLER, PRINTER TO THE UNIVERSITY

JOSEPH PATRICK LAURENCE MCMULLAN
1893–1967
Senior History Master
Taunton's School, Southampton
1921–1954

PREFACE

IN PREPARING these essays, I have drawn much on the invaluable material for Irish social history collected by the Irish Folklore Commission. I am grateful to Professor J. H. Delargy, the Commission's Honorary Director, for permission to work in its archives; and to him, Captain Kevin Danaher, Mr. Sean O'Sullivan, and Dr. Thomas Wall for adding to the pleasure and profit of the process. I am grateful, too, to the Australian National University for bringing me, as a Visiting Fellow in the Research School of Social Sciences, to the enviable environment in which one of these essays was written.

Dr. David R. Nagle, Lexington, Kentucky, roused my interest in ether-drinking and generously agreed to my writing on a subject on which he was working. I am also indebted to Mr. George Thompson and Dr. Alan Gailey, of the Ulster Folk Museum, for circulating a questionnaire on ether-drinking and allowing me to quote from the replies it elicited; to Professor G. W. A. Dick and Miss J. B. Webster for bibliographical guidance; to Mrs. Margaret O'Hara and Professor V. B. Proudfoot for help with the preparation of the maps and chart; to Mr. W. B. Seaby, Director of the Ulster Museum, for permission to reproduce a photograph from the Welch Collection; and, for advice or information, to Professor Norman Gibson, Mr. R. C. Jarvis, Librarian to H.M. Customs and Excise, Dr. M. D. McCarthy, the Reverend Hugh D. O'Neill, Mr. T. P. O'Neill, and the Reverend John Silke.

When planning 'Catholicism and Marriage', I saw it as more than 'historical essay'. But too much in its field has changed since then. Peasant marriage and peasant Catholicism, though agile enough in shaping themselves to a society re-shaped by mass emigration, Famine and land legislation, idled thereafter with the society. But, agile again today, they are adapting themselves to a society bedevilled less by the impropriety of indulgent marriage as a livelier economy brings it in reach; a society whose emigrants settling nearer home, are more frequent emissaries of laxity, 'un-Irish' and 'un-Catholic', more telling evidence that 'Irishness' and Irish souls are limbered as well as 'destroyed' by the outside world, by its journalism and television, by some inkling of its affluence and sophisticated contraception; a society taught by persisting *malaise* that politics is no panacea, tackling emigration with more than words, tackling it not least by loosening Catholicism and loosening marriage; a society, Catholic still, but Catholic less naïvely and less parochially, its priests and laity involved in the outside world, tempted by liberalizing Catholicism abroad to liberalize Catholicism at home, driven to liberalize it as the bright boy, the budding entrepreneur, the dullard's doting mother, wealthier and worldier, see brightening prospects beyond the priesthood—see the increasing blightening, the 'spoiling', of priestly prospects.

Any significance of 'Catholicism and Marriage' is, then, historical rather than contemporary. And its text has profited less than I have myself from comment and criticism, comment in universities within striking distance of Belfast or Canberra whose sociologists or historians asked me to talk on its content; criticism of colleagues in the Irish university world, generous of their time, however sharp, however shocked, in their disagreement. I thank, not least, Professor J. C. Beckett, the Reverend Professor Theodore Crowley, O.F.M., the Reverend Professor Aubrey Gwynn, S.J., Dr. Hugh Kearney, Professor James Lydon, Professor F. S. L. Lyons, Dr. Cornelius O'Leary, Professor Oliver MacDonagh, Dr. Thomas Wall and the Reverend Dr. Conor Ward; I am grateful for the comment and encouragement of Dr. R. M. Hartwell, Mrs. Kate Kearney and my wife, colleagues also in Irish scholarship, if by the rockier roads of external examining or marriage. I thank, finally, the Delegates of the Clarendon Press and Mr. D. M. Davin and his colleagues, for indulging a capricious author who wouldn't include 'Catholicism and Marriage' in this volume; and would, disrupting the publishing process, when the remaining essays were ready for machining. May they be similarly indulgent should a lengthier study emerge, touching on the present, accepting or answering the criticism.

Earlier versions of 'Illicit Distillation' and 'Ether-drinking in Ulster' appeared in *Historical Studies, III: Papers read before the Fourth Irish Conference of Historians* and the *Quarterly Journal of*

PREFACE

Studies on Alcohol; I am grateful to the Irish Committee of Historical Sciences and the Editor of the *Quarterly Journal* for agreeing to their reproduction here.

K.H.C.

INSTITUTE OF IRISH STUDIES
THE QUEEN'S UNIVERSITY OF BELFAST

May Day 1968

CONTENTS

LIST OF FIGURES xiii
I ILLICIT DISTILLATION 1
II ILLEGITIMACY BEFORE THE FAMINE . . 51
III ETHER-DRINKING IN ULSTER . . . 87
IV CATHOLICISM AND MARRIAGE IN THE CENTURY AFTER THE FAMINE . . . 113
INDEX 163

LIST OF FIGURES

Fig. 1: A Connemara Still, *c.* 1890 .   .   *facing page* 5

    2: Location of Illicit Distillation, 1836   .   .   31

    3: Duty collected in the various Irish Revenue Districts on Irish-made Spirits, 1776–7   .   40

    4: Stills of various sizes in the various Irish Revenue Districts, 1822   41

    5: Annual Number of Detections in Ireland, England and Scotland under the Laws for the Suppression of Illicit Distillation, 1830–1956. Rate of duty per proof Gallon on Spirit distilled in Ireland, 1790–1921 44–45

    6: Location of Ether-drinking, 1890 . . . 98

I

ILLICIT DISTILLATION

IN 1661, with the re-introduction of an excise duty on Irish spirit, the struggle between 'parliament' whiskey and poteen was resumed, a struggle in which the rout of the illicit distiller took a couple of centuries, and which, even still, he survives. In this essay an attempt is made to survey the history of poteen-making since its heyday in the late eighteenth and early nineteenth centuries. Much in these years fostered the industry. Between the establishment of Grattan's parliament and the ending of the wars with France there was probably some mitigation of the lot of the peasantry: they had, it may be, rather more money to spend; and inclination, like the scarcity of alternative opportunities, persuaded them to spend it on drink. The demand for spirit was further increased by the growth of population; and as grain was more widely grown in Ireland the distiller's raw material was more readily available. These factors, however, encouraged the licensed, no less than the unlicensed, distiller: it was, it seems, ill-conceived excise regulations that specially favoured the poteen-maker. The original duty on Irish spirit was 4d. a gallon; it had reached 1s. 2d. by 1785 and climbed steeply during the wars to 6s. 1$\frac{1}{2}d$. in 1815[1]—when parliament whiskey was selling for nine or ten shillings a gallon.[2] The exchequer, of course, was hard-pressed; but it was questionably wise to increase so substantially the price an impoverished people was asked to pay for parliament whiskey; a people, moreover, whose social life was hinged to cheap drink; who knew how to make poteen, and were not notably law-abiding.

[1] *Fifth Report of the Commissioners... Collection and Management of the Revenues arising in Ireland...*, Parl. Papers, 1823, VII, p. 111; *Seventh Report of the Commissioners of Inquiry into the Excise Establishment*, Parl. Papers, 1834, XXV, p. 66; 'The Distilling Industry in Ireland', in *Ireland Industrial and Agricultural*, ed. W. P. Coyne (Dept. of Ag. & Tech. Inst. for Ireland, Dublin, 1902), p. 495. [Parliamentary Papers abbreviated to P.P. in later refs.]
[2] *Select Committee on Illicit Distillation in Ireland*, P.P., 1816, IX, p. 148/141.

So large a duty was an obvious encouragement to the distiller who escaped it; but he was further helped by excise regulations designed to lessen the evasion of duty in the licensed distilleries; so much did these regulations hamper the legal trade that its produce, if not bad, was unpalatable to many an Irish consumer; and as the fiscal arrangements forced out of business (or out of legal business) many local stills, their customers, remote from the surviving licensed distilleries, turned to the poteen-maker.[1]

Early in the nineteenth century most poteen seems to have been made from malt.[2] But malt, while producing an excellent liquor, was a treacherous material to the illicit distiller; he grudged the time and the space needed for its proper preparation; it was risky for him, too, to get it dried or ground by a miller.[3] Continuously, then, malt has been supplemented, and sometimes supplanted, by raw grain.[4] And by the end of the century, grain, whether malted or not, was being displaced: less was grown in the areas of illicit distillation, and if the materials of poteen had to be bought, there were alternatives, making a less palatable liquor, but doing so more cheaply, and with less trouble and risk to the distiller. Molasses was widely used by the 1880s, and then, or soon afterwards, sugar, treacle, and porter:[5] more recently 'almost anything' is said to be

---

[1] These points are more fully argued below: see pp. 35-42.

[2] *Committee on the Distilleries in Ireland*, P.P., 1812–13, VI, pp. 9, 11; W. Shaw Mason, *Statistical Account ... of Ireland* (Dublin, 1816), ii, 395; H. Dutton, *Statistical Survey of the County of Galway* (Dublin, 1824), p. 368; *Seventh Report, Commissioners of Excise*, P.P., 1834, XXV, p. 377.

[3] Irish Folklore Commission, MS. 227, p. 165; *Seventh Report, Commissioners of Excise*, P.P., 1834, XXV, p. 446. [Irish Folklore Commission abbreviated to I.F.C. in later refs.]

[4] There was some feeling that if raw grain alone were used the spirit would be poor in yield as well as flavour (*Select Committee on ... extending the functions of the constabulary in Ireland to the Suppression or Prevention of Illicit Distillation*, P.P., 1854, X, q. 451). The malt might be made from barley or oats, and both grains were used raw: barley may have been more commonly used in Ulster and oats in Connaught (Mason, op. cit., 1816, ii, 395; *Fifth Report, Revenue arising in Ireland*, P.P., 1823, VII, p. 84; *Seventh Report*, 1834, op. cit., pp. 377-8; *S. C. on Illicit Distillation*, 1854, op. cit., q. 1282; I.F.C., MS. 1458, p. 23). One of the advantages of barley was that it was the first grain to ripen, and the distiller might therefore hope to 'have a "run" or two before the still-hunting season really sets in' (Hugh Dorian, 'Donegal 60 Years Ago', MS. in the library of St. Columb's College, Londonderry; photostat copy in the library of the I.F.C., 1890-6 (?), p. 345). I am grateful to the authorities of St. Columb's College for permission to quote from this important document.

[5] A. I. Shand, *Letters from the West of Ireland* (1885), p. 15; Dorian, op. cit., 1890, p. 334; Coyne, op. cit., 1902, p. 500; I.F.C., MS. 1540, p. 2.

ILLICIT DISTILLATION

distilled—including potatoes, rhubarb, apples, blackberries, and currants.[1]

In the traditional poteen-making there were three processes, malting, brewing, and distilling. Malting was begun by steeping a sack, partly filled with grain, in a bog or stream; or it might be buried in a dunghill. When the grain had swollen, the sack was removed and the contents, thickly spread out, perhaps in a loft, or under the distiller's bed, perhaps in an empty house or underground cave.[2] Wherever it was put it required the 'nicest, cleanest and most skilful handling': carelessly managed, it might turn sour, or acquire some other unwelcome flavour, and taint the poteen.[3] The skill in malt-making lay in ensuring that the grain sprouted evenly; this was done by turning it over with the hands, very carefully, once or twice a day.[4] After some ten days, this stage completed, the malt was ready for drying and grinding. Sometimes it was dried in a miller's kiln, but more commonly in a rough furnace, erected for the purpose.[5] Smoke, a constant worry to the illicit distiller, was particularly likely to give him away while he was drying his malt: in Glen, co. Donegal, accordingly, the distillers aimed at having malt ready early in July, 'when all the police are taken off

---

[1] I.F.C., MS. 227, p. 167; 1102, pp. 333, 338; *The Gael*, New York, Nov 1904, p. 365. I am grateful to Dr. Thomas Wall for referring me to this issue of *The Gael*. I have come across only recent evidence of the use of potatoes in making illicit spirit; Dr. Salaman, too, gave a recent recipe, but quoted no evidence in support of his presumption that as early as the eighteenth century the Irish turned to the potato for their drink as well as their food (R. N. Salaman, *The History and Social Influence of the Potato* (Cambridge, 1949), p. 264 and n.2).

[2] E. Wakefield, *An Account of Ireland, Statistical and Political* (1812), i, 730; *Committee on Distilleries*, P.P., 1812–13, VI, p. 11; *S. C. on Illicit Distillation*, P.P., 1854, X, q. 267; Shand, op. cit., 1885, p. 15; Dorian, op. cit., 1890, p. 344; I.F.C., MS. 1458, p. 455.

[3] Dorian, op. cit., 1890, pp. 344–5. But some distillers were not over-meticulous: two, working on a lake-island in Donegal, were said to have been 'half-naked, squalid, unhealthy looking creatures, with skins encrusted with filth, hair long, uncombed and matted, where vermin of all sorts seemed to quarter themselves and nidificate.... The whole area of the island was one dunghill composed of fermenting grains; there were about twenty immense hogs either feeding or snoring on the food that lay beneath them; and so alive with rats was the whole concern, that one of the boatmen compared them, in number and intrusiveness, to flocks of sparrows on the side of a shelling-hill adjoining a corn-mill' (Caesar Otway, *Sketches in Ireland* (2nd ed., Dublin, 1839), p. 65).

[4] Dorian, op. cit., 1890, pp. 344, 346; *S. C. on Illicit Distillation*, P.P., 1854, X, q. 267.

[5] *S.C. on Illicit Distillation*, P.P., 1854, X, q. 269; Dorian, op. cit., 1890, p. 347; I.F.C., MS. 1458, p. 43.

to Derry to put down the riots there'.[1] Querns might be used for grinding, but more frequently this was done by a miller—in co. Cavan, indeed, early in the nineteenth century many millers were said to be employed almost exclusively by the illicit distillers.[2]

The equipment needed for brewing was a vat in which boiling water was poured over the malt; some means of heating the water (usually the still was used); and barrels in which the liquid might ferment. When the wort (the mixture of water and malt) was sufficiently cool it was transferred to the barrels. Boiled hops might then be added, and perhaps also some slices of soap.[3] Yeast, too, was needed. Usually it was available as the sediment fallen to the bottom of the barrel in some previous brew. In co. Longford there was a belief that a sod of turf would serve for yeast, and some distillers used the same piece, time after time, hanging it in the chimney when not in use.[4] But sometimes, especially at the beginning of a season, if yeast were hard to come by, the distiller might send to some distant colleague: his was a friendly profession; no member 'would refuse or deny an article belonging to the trade'.[5] Once the yeast had been added to the wort, the mixture had to be kept from contact with the air—lest undesirable yeasts should be introduced: sometimes this was ensured by putting a layer of bran or chaff on top of the fermenting liquor—it was kept afloat, presumably, by the rising bubbles, and fell to the bottom of the barrel when the fermentation had finished.[6]

The process of fermentation, if left to work itself out, might take as much as three weeks, and, ideally, the pot-ale (the fermented liquor) was left to settle for a week or more before being distilled.

---

[1] W. R. Le Fanu, *Seventy Years of Irish Life* (1893), p. 273.

[2] *Committee on Distilleries*, P.P., 1812–13, VI, p. 23; *S.C. on Illicit Distillation*, P.P. 1854, X, qq. 269, 478; Dorian, op. cit., 1890, p. 319.

[3] 'They don't know any reason [for putting in soap] but that it "cuts it"' (Dorian, 1890, op. cit., p. 352). At a later stage in spirit-making, both licensed and unlicensed distillers might put soap into their stills, with the object, it seems, of 'keeping the barm down' in rapid distillation, and so preventing the still from 'running foul'. And soap—as well as vitriol—might be added to poteen and parliament whiskey to please the customer who considered that 'a bubble at the top' was the mark of a strong whiskey (*Fifth Report, Revenue arising in Ireland*, P.P., 1823, VII, pp. 86, 44); Samuel Morewood, *Inebriating Liquors* (Dublin, 1838), p. 673; Alfred Barnard, *The Whiskey Distilleries of the United Kingdom* (1887), p. 10).

[4] I.F.C., MS. 1458, pp. 23–24. Yeast, presumably, was needed the first time turf was used, but afterwards sufficient might be deposited on the turf.

[5] Dorian, op. cit., 1890, p. 354.   [6] I.F.C., MS. 227, pp. 166–7.

A Connemara Still, c. 1890 (Welch Collection, Ulster Museum)

ILLICIT DISTILLATION

But the private distiller, always fearing detection, was apt to hasten his processes: sometimes, too, he believed that cutting short the fermentation improved the spirit; and he was reluctant to keep pot-ale too long on his hands, for 'it was thought to be more intoxicating than porter, and people would come with straws and reeds, anxious for a surreptitious draught'.[1]

There were four parts to the distilling apparatus: first, the vessel in which the pot-ale was heated; second, the 'head,' a tight-fitting cap to this vessel, from which protruded, third, the 'arm', a pipe which led to the fourth part, the 'worm', a coiled tube, submerged in water, from which the spirit emerged. It was, of course, important that the parts of the still should fit tightly: this might be ensured by the use of dough or porridge, or a 'simple cement' made from clay and horse-dung.[2]

For the first distillation the still was filled with pot-ale, and the product was known as 'singlings' or 'first-shot':[3] singlings was said to be a harsh, potent spirit, unsafe to drink, but a useful antiseptic and good for pains when used as a rub.[4] It was allowed to run until it would no longer ignite, then the liquor left in the still was poured away (or kept as cattlefood), and the still cleaned out.[5] The second distillation began when the still had been filled with singlings—possibly with the addition of a little pot-ale kept back from the first distilling, or with some nitre and 'burnt coals' (charcoal), intended to improve the clarity of the spirit.[6] The distillate this time was 'the real precious stuff'. The first keg-full was thought to be the best: the very first noggin-full might be earmarked for the fairies, and left for them on a wall, or sprinkled on the ground; commonly, in Donegal, it placated Red Willy, the fairy with power over the excise, capable of leading its agents astray

---

[1] *S.C. on Illicit Distillation*, P.P., 1854, X, qq. 267, 450; Dorian, op. cit., 1890, p. 353; I.F.C., MS. 1458, pp. 23, 456. Before the Famine, Donegal distillers are said to have sold much pot-ale (known as 'kilty') for a few pence a gallon (Sean Ban MacMenamin, 'Life in co. Donegal in pre-Famine Days', *The Donegal Annual, 1954-5* (Co. Donegal Historical Society), p. 3).

[2] The sealing material was known as 'lute' or 'luting'. I.F.C., MS. 227, p. 169; 1480, p. 177; Dorian, op. cit., 1890, p. 355.

[3] W. Carleton, *The Emigrants of Ahadarra* (1848), p. 34; I.F.C., MS. 1458, p. 457.

[4] Ibid; Dorian, op. cit., 1890, p. 354; Patrick Macgill, *Maureen* (popular ed., n.d.), p. 274. Columb Ruagh, Macgill's distiller, sold 'fossaid' or 'foreshot' (the early distillate, chemically different from the later) for sprains, hacks, and cuts (p. 106).

[5] I.F.C., MS. 227, p. 170.   [6] Ibid., p. 171.

or bringing them to the still.[1] Sometimes the doublings was distilled again to make a very strong spirit, 'limpid as still water', and expensive; but by the 'nineties this 'double-refine' was less frequently made, part of the price of the harrying of the private distiller.[2]

Poteen was seldom allowed to mature, not, at least, by the distiller:[3] his capital was too slight, and the longer he kept his spirit, the greater the risk of theft, as well as of detection. Many of his customers, moreover, liked their whiskey 'hot all the way down': rather than fade its early fire the distiller might enliven it with vitriol; or entrust it to one of the itinerant craftsmen who offered 'their services at a certain rate for adulterating spirituous liquors'.[4]

Besides poteen there were two other usable products of distillation: 'grains' (the residue of the malt after fermentation), and 'barn [or burn] beer', or 'burnt pot-ale' (what was left in the still when the singlings came to an end).[5] These by-products were prized as cattle-food: at one time, indeed, a man bringing a cow in good condition to a Donegal fair was liable to be suspected of illicit distillation.[6] When the distiller had cattle of his own he was said to be loth to part with the waste; though, if he sold it, it might bring him a third or more of the cost of his grain.[7] Sometimes, however, the waste was an embarrassment, incriminating evidence to be hastily buried.[8]

[1] I.F.C., MS. 171, pp. 502; 227, pp. 170, 172; 846, p. 104; 1215, p. 433; 1220, p. 64; Dorian, 1890, op. cit., p. 357. I am indebted to Mr. Sean O'Sullivan for the reference to Red Willy.

[2] Shand, op. cit., 1885, p. 14; Dorian, 1890, op. cit., p. 357.

[3] But a Tyrone distiller reckoned to keep his spirit in the moss for some months: he scooped out a hole for the keg, taking away the loose material, but leaving 'a good top scough' as a hinge; he chose a site on rising ground and drew off the matured spirit with a 'medical tube' (I.F.C., MS. 1220, pp. 61–62). A Sligo gentleman, similarly, used a stomach-pump to draw poteen buried in his garden (J. Binns, *The Miseries and Beauties of Ireland* (2 vols., 1837), i, 329).

[4] *Fifth Report, Revenue arising in Ireland*, P.P., 1827, p. 68; *Tales of the R.I.C.* (Edinburgh, 1921), p. 144; *Report from the Select Committee of Inquiry into Drunkenness*, P.P., 1834, VIII, q. 795. 'Corduroy' was a term of praise for a spirit which left a roughness on the tongue and palate: 'mild spirit is, with the mob, of low repute' (ibid.).

[5] Ibid.; I.F.C., MS. 227, p. 174. There was also 'fence' or 'dross'—what was left in the still when doublings was made; this, reputedly, was no good for anything (I.F.C., MS. 1221, p. 176).

[6] *S.C. on Illicit Distillation*, P.P., 1854, X, q. 732.

[7] *Seventh Report, Commissioners of Excise*, P.P., 1834, XXV, p. 405; *S.C. on Illicit Distillation*, P.P., 1854, X, p. 263, qq. 731–2.

[8] Wakefield, op. cit., 1812, i, p. 730.

ILLICIT DISTILLATION 7

There seems to have been no great difficulty in getting the vats and barrels needed for brewing: in the 1850s an empty American flour-barrel could be bought in Donegal for a few pence; an old herring-barrel might be used, a flax-seed cask, or a sugar hogshead.[1] The still, in its traditional form, was less readily come by. An all-copper apparatus was thought to make the best poteen.[2] But not every illicit distiller dared, and could afford, to make quality his main concern; the cost of copper was a deterrent, the more so as the apparatus might at any time be seized; copper stills, too, were heavy, troublesome to carry off in a pursuit by the revenue officers.[3] Tin, cheaper and lighter, was probably also more readily worked by the travelling tinkers and braziers who made and repaired most of the stills.[4] Early in the nineteenth century it was said that stills were usually made of tin in part of Donegal, in Sligo, Cavan, and Mayo: and even in Inishowen, the classic poteen country, tin was generally used by the 1880s—though not always for the worm, the part most likely to taint the spirit.[5]

Stills varied greatly in capacity: some held no more than 10 gallons, others as much as 80.[6] Early in the nineteenth century a good copper still, complete with head, arm and worm, might cost six or eight guineas; by having the still itself made of tin, a couple of guineas might be saved.[7] Cheaper models—some with copper worms—might be had for thirty or forty shillings, or even

---

[1] *Fifth Report, Revenue arising in Ireland*, P.P., 1823, VII, p. 79; *Seventh Report, Commissioners of Excise*, P.P., 1834, XXV, p. 400; *S.C. on Illicit Distillation*, P.P., 1854, X, q. 254.
[2] Wakefield, op. cit., 1812, i, 729; W. H. Maxwell, *Wild Sports of the West* [1834] (Gresham, Dublin, n.d.), p. 134.
[3] *Committee on Distilleries*, P.P., 1812–13, VI, p. 12; *The Gael*, New York, Nov 1904, p. 363.
[4] *Committee on Distilleries*, P.P., 1812–13, VI, p. 12; Maxwell, op. cit., p. 134; *Seventh Report, Commissioners of Excise*, P.P., 1834, XXV, p. 400; *S.C. on Illicit Distillation*, P.P., 1854, X, q. 245; I.F.C., MS. 227, p. 176; 1220, p. 63. The worm might be made by filling a copper tube with sand, heating it, and twisting it round a bush (ibid.).
[5] *Committee on Distilleries*, P.P., 1812–13, VI, pp. 12, 22; *Fifth Report, Revenue arising in Ireland*, P.P., 1823, VII, p. 79; Maxwell, op. cit. p. 134; Dorian, op. cit., 1890, p. 355.
[6] *Committee on Distilleries*, P.P., 1812–13, VI, p. 12; *S.C. on Illicit Distillation*, P.P., 1816, IX, p. 96.
[7] Wakefield, op. cit., i, 729; Mason, op. cit., ii, 1816, p. 166; *S.C. on Illicit Distillation*, P.P., 1816, IX, pp. 148/144; *Fifth Report, Revenue arising in Ireland*, P.P., 1823, VII, p. 79.

less.[1] By the 1880s a traveller in Inishowen said, surprisingly, that a still cost as much as £20; but some forty years later the price was put at £3. 10s. 0d.[2]

Today—as no doubt in the past—makeshift apparatus is sometimes used for distilling. Empty tar-barrels, milk-churns, oil-drums, and potato-pots have all been pressed into service; the worm, at some risk of poisoning, may be made of lead piping:[3] it has been demonstrated, indeed, that a complete still may be made from a kettle and a mug.[4]

In illicit distillation the producer's liberty, as well as his profit, hinged on his choice of a site; and this decision was peculiarly trying, because the safest site was rarely the most profitable. The still must be set up on some spot that was inconspicuous and inaccessible to the police, but one, nevertheless, where the distiller and his party might assemble their materials and apparatus without undue inconvenience. A scattered local population was an asset: the police were unlikely to be stationed nearby; there would be fewer people to congregate at the still, and fewer outlets for news of its activity. Peat and water must be to hand—and running water was of great help, especially in keeping the worm continuously cold. If the smoke could be screened—by working in a ravine, for instance, or by steep rocks—so much the better.[5]

Clearly, the private distiller required much from his site. But sites nearly perfect might be found or created. A hole in a bank near a river had much to commend it; or a cave at the foot of a cliff where spring-water gushed out: and there was Carleton's deep cave, running 'under the rocks which met over it in a kind

---

[1] *Committee on Distilleries*, P.P., 1812–13, VI, p. 22; *S.C. on Illicit Distillation*, P.P., 1854, X, qq. 141, 245.

[2] Shand, op. cit., 1885, p. 15; I.F.C., MS. 227, p. 176.

[3] I.F.C., MS. 227, p. 190; 1458, p. 456; 1102, p. 336; Macgill, op. cit., p. 272.

[4] A kettle of a kind commonly used in co. Longford is partly filled with fermented liquor, and a pint mug is stood inside it; the spout of the kettle is sealed, and its lid is turned upside-down, with the nipple descending into the mug. The kettle is then put on the fire; the vapour condenses on the lid and drips into the mug (I.F.C., MS. 1458, pp. 457–8). Mr. Sam Hanna Bell has pointed to the pressure stove—smokeless and readily adjusted—as an 'inestimable boon' to the private distiller ('In Search of the Mountain Dew', *Erin's Orange Lily* (1956), pp. 56–57).

[5] E. Chichester, *Oppressions and Cruelties of Irish Revenue Officers* (1818), p. 31; *S.C. on Illicit Distillation*, P.P., 1854, X, qq. 244, 1298; Dorian, op. cit., 1890, p. 350; Shand, op. cit., 1885, pp. 14–15.

of Gothic arch: a stream of water fell in through a fissure from above forming... a subterranean cascade in the cavern'.[1] A subterranean workshop might be found ready-made as a souterrain or scooped from the bog.[2] And 'when distillation might be truly considered as almost universal, it was customary for farmers to build their outhouses with secret chambers and other requisite partitions necessary for carrying it on.' 'Several of them had private stores built between false walls, the entrance to which was known only to a few, and many of them had what were called *Malt-steeps* sunk in hidden recesses and hollow gables, for the purpose of steeping the barley, and afterwards of turning and airing it.'[3]

But luckiest of all were the island distillers: on the Inishkea islands, for instance, when rising winds made it perilous to venture from the Mayo coast, the inhabitants put their stills to work. And if, afterwards, the police made a raid, the islanders loaded stills and poteen on their curraghs and took them out to sea; the crew of any boat on which the police concentrated their pursuit simply dropped their cargo overboard and made their escape.[4] These islands, indeed, enjoyed 'a sort of prescriptive privilege to sin against the ordinances of the excise': every process in poteen-making was given its due time, and the product was of such 'superior excellency' that these 'gifted islanders are worthy of being canonized'.[5]

Not every distiller found a site naturally shielded from the police, and his own organization might have to make good its deficiency. He might put his trust in the deterrent effect of ridicule: the booby-trap, for instance, which caused the policeman, thinking he was stepping on firm ground, to plunge knee-deep

---

[1] *S.C. on Illicit Distillation*, P.P., 1816, IX, p. 53; [A. Blenkinsop] *Paddiana; or Scraps and Sketches of Irish Life* (1847), i, 102 ff.; Carleton, *Ahadarra*, op. cit., 1848, p. 33; I.F.C., MS. 1245, p. 577; Emily Bowles, *Irish Diamonds* (1864), p. 73.

[2] E. Estyn Evans, *Irish Folkways* (1957), p. 119; C. R. Weld, *Vacations in Ireland* (1857), p. 33.

[3] W. Carleton, 'Bob Pentland; or the gauger outwitted', in *Tales and Stories of the Irish Peasantry* (Dublin, 1846), pp. 52–53. A fisherman, falling through the fern-covered bank of a Wicklow river, says he found himself 'face to face with an ancient weather-beaten crone' in her distillery (Weld, 1857, op. cit., p. 33).

[4] *Letters from Ireland, 1886*, by the Special Correspondent of *The Times* (1887), p. 121.

[5] Maxwell, op. cit., 1834, pp. 119, 134. See also [Mrs Blake] *Letters from the Irish Highlands of Cunnemarra* (2nd ed., 1825), pp. 156–9.

into manure; or the rope, hidden at the lake-side, which hauled in, not the expected still, but a dead dog.[1] He might station *videts* on roads approaching the still, or place *cordons* of children in the neighbouring hills[2]—sentinels whose warnings were transmitted with 'wonderful celerity': 'sometimes a sharp, peculiar whistle conveyed the unwelcome intelligence, at others the sounding horn, or if the enemy approached at night, a line of fiery torches shot off along the hill-side.'[3]

Systematic bribery sheltered many a still from molestation. The gauger, Wakefield reported, 'receives a regular rent from all the stills within his district': the 'surest safeguard' of the Sligo distiller is to keep the constable, or confidential agent employed by the revenue officer, in constant pay. 'This man, or one of his family, pays regular visits to the distillers in the parish, and gets from a crown to ten shillings from each of them, in proportion to what they have on hands.'[4]

As a last resort (certainly until the reorganization of the revenue police in the mid thirties) the distiller commonly tried to out-arm or out-man his opponents: until then, poteen was made by 'gangs of 60 or 80 men in the glens and fastnesses; gangs of men that were so ferocious that it required armed men to cope with them, and even then it was the case with the military frequently that they were defeated by those smugglers'.[5] In two or three square miles of Erris, co. Mayo, nearly 200 distillers were said to be constantly at work, summer after summer. Their site, bounded by mountains and sea and approached by only two passes, was well-suited to defence. In 1815, nevertheless, a party of excise-men,

[1] Dorian, op. cit., 1890, pp. 340–1.
[2] Shand, op. cit., 1885, p. 15; Mason, op. cit., ii, 1816, p. 394; A. W. Long, *Irish Sport of Yesterday* (n.d.), p. 33.
[3] 'Maghtochair', *Inishowen: its History, Traditions and Antiquities* (Londonderry, 1867), p. 116; Isaac Weld, *Statistical Survey of the County of Roscommon* (Dublin, 1832), pp. 114–5n.
[4] Wakefield, op. cit., 1812, i, 730; Mason, op. cit., ii, 1816, p. 394. To assist the revenue was a perilous matter. In 1817 an Inishowen family, supposed to be informers, narrowly escaped with their lives when their house was burned down (*Magistrates' Reports (Ennishowen)*, P.P., 1818, XVI, 13 Oct 1817). Some years earlier a Clare man, thought to have informed on his distilling neighbours, was used in a 'shocking manner', 'having one of his ears with a part of his cheek cut off, his head shockingly battered, and his body and limbs lacerated all over' (*Ennis Chronicle*, 30 Jan 1792; from the collection of newspaper extracts deposited by Miss Katherine Dillon in the library of the I.F.C.).
[5] *S.C. on Illicit Distillation*, P.P., 1854, X, p. 59.

attended by thirty soldiers, made a raid. The distillers, drilled already by an army deserter, are said to have permitted the troops to make some seizures, but when they were retreating along one of the passes with their spoil, they were subjected to heavy fire by a party much more numerous than they. The engagement continued for much of the day until, eventually, the soldiers' ammunition was exhausted.[1] Between 1808 and 1814 *The Londonderry Journal* reported half a dozen fatalities in clashes with distillers and their sympathizers; on three occasions revenue officers or their escorts were acquitted of murder; a private of the Dublin Militia was killed when 'ferociously assailed by stones' near Buncrana; white-shirted men fired a volley on a party of the Lincolnshire Militia in the Glentaugher mountains; six men of the North Hampshires were disarmed near Stranorloar, and the officer they were accompanying fatally wounded; revenue officers, not infrequently, were 'carried off by the banditti', perhaps in sacks, to work at the stills.[2] Towards the end of the French wars there was talk of a combination of Inishowen distillers, armed with weapons saved from a frigate wrecked in Lough Swilly.[3] No less resourceful were the 'flying mountaineers' who 'left portions of their whiskey scattered behind them, which, new and fiery as it was, was greedily swallowed by the jaded and exhausted soldiers': 'the English militia' 'tumbled down senseless on the heath' to be taken to 'the poor people's cabins, where they lay until they had slept themselves sober'.[4]

Many a peasant had the resources to make an occasional run of a potent, if sometimes unpalatable, poteen; and the amateur's still, no doubt, accounted for most of the output. Occasionally the amateur distiller was well-to-do:[5] but a man without capital suffered no great impediment; he might grow his raw material

[1] *S.C. on Illicit Distillation*, P.P., 1816, IX, pp. 80–81.
[2] *Londonderry Journal*, 6 Dec 1808; 7 July 1812; 18 Aug 1812; 26 Jan 1813; 3 Aug 1813; 15 Mar 1814; 31 Mar 1814; 16 Aug 1814; 23 Aug 1814. For these and other references from *The Londonderry Journal* I am indebted to Mr. Kenneth Darwin and Mr. Brian Trainor, of the Public Record Office of Northern Ireland.
[3] *S.C. on Illicit Distillation*, P.P., 1816, IX, pp. 80–81. See also *Fifth Report, Revenue arising in Ireland*, P.P., 1823, VII, p. 83.
[4] J. Gamble, *Views of Society and Manners in the North of Ireland* (1819), p. 301.
[5] Wakefield, op. cit., 1812, i, 729; Mr. and Mrs. S. C. Hall, *Ireland: its Scenery, Character, etc.* (1843), iii, 487n.

himself, and for a few shillings hire a still from the travelling tinkers who made them, or from some petty capitalist.[1]

There were also men who were illicit distillers by profession, a number by hereditary profession.[2] Some of these, it was said, were 'miserable creatures', 'men of a very low class': they travelled round the country 'charging a shilling a hundred for the grain [they] distil'; a spell in prison they regarded as an inevitable, even a welcome, part of their routine.[3] Teigue O'Gallagher, however, was a professional of a different stamp: 'there is not a man in Ireland lives better than Teigue'; he is 'the only man of his sort in Donegal that eats white bread, toasted, buttered, and washed down with tea for his breakfast'; his sheep 'range on a hundred hills'; 'the roof of his kitchen is festooned with bacon'.[4] Success so striking[5] called for unusual qualifications. By no means the least was an aversion to poteen—or a liking strictly controlled. If the distiller was to exploit the economies of location, he must have an intimate topographical knowledge; and this, too, might help him to evade pursuit. He needed considerable technical skill, for on his ability as maltster, brewer, and distiller rested the repute of his wares.[6] His neighbours were his suppliers and customers, his assistants and spies: a friendly manner, therefore, was essential; nobody must be antagonized, even when dissuaded from congregating at the still. And, unless the distiller was exceptionally

---

[1] *S.C. on Illicit Distillation*, P.P., 1816, IX, p. 39; Mason, op. cit., ii, 1816, p. 395; *S.C. on Illicit Distillation*, P.P., 1854, X, q. 248. In Sligo in 1816 the charge for hiring was said to be from three to five shillings, according to the amount distilled (Mason, op. cit., ii, 1816, p. 395). In Swinford, co. Mayo, early in the present century, when a still was borrowed, a deposit was needed as security against damage or seizure, and a fee of eight shillings was paid, to which was sometimes added half a gallon of poteen (I.F.C., MS. 227, p. 176).

[2] Carleton's Condy Cullen, for instance, 'was descended from a long line of private distillers' (*Tales and Stories of the Irish Peasantry* (Dublin, 1846), p. 275). *S.C. on Illicit Distillation*, P.P., 1816, IX, p. 86; *Fifth Report, Revenue arising in Ireland*, P.P., 1823, VII, pp. 31, 73, 79; Maxwell, op. cit., 1834, p. 134. Shand, 1885, op. cit., p. 14.

[3] *S.C. on Illicit Distillation*, P.P., 1816, IX, pp. 86; *Seventh Report, Commissioners of Excise*, 1834, XXV, p. 401; *S.C. on Drunkenness*, P.P., 1834, VIII, p. 765.

[4] *Sketches in Ireland*, op. cit., 1839, p. 64.

[5] If, indeed, it was to be found except in fiction and in the works of imaginative tourists: the inspector-general of the excise in Ireland 'never knew anyone engaged in illicit distillation, and in traffic in illicit spirits, get rich by it' (*Fifth Report, Revenue arising in Ireland*, P.P., 1823, VII, p. 83).

[6] In an itinerant and clandestine trade it was an asset to be cooper enough to dismantle and re-erect barrels and vats (Dorian, op. cit., 1890, p. 351).

ILLICIT DISTILLATION

well-informed on the movements of the police, he must be able to win their tolerance, and (to guard against all eventualities) that of the magistrates as well.

The method by which the private distiller disposed of his product depended, of course, on the scale of his operations. We may presume that the baronet or clergyman, with a still in his kitchen or stable,[1] produced in the main for his own household. There were distillers, too, of humbler rank, who made their own poteen as they grew their own potatoes; and others who would help a friend in need with poteen as with potatoes. But there can be no doubt that in the first half of the nineteenth century poteen-making was one of the few Irish industries whose product might be bought in much of the country and, occasionally at least, in other parts of the British Isles.

It is only to be expected that poteen was readily available in the districts where much was made—in, that is, the seaboard counties from Clare to Derry, together with Cavan, Monaghan, and Tyrone.[2] But (according at least to a deputation of city distillers) illicit spirit was sold in Dublin 'as openly in the streets as they sell a loaf of bread, and nothing is more publicly sold in the streets of London than illicit whiskey is sold in Ireland';[3] in the streets of New Ross it was offered so commonly and so publicly 'that no one wonders at it';[4] it was available also in Belfast and Armagh.[5] From Grean, co. Limerick, it was reported: 'no illicit distillation in the parish, but a sale of that commodity to an extraordinary degree';[6] there were similar reports from country parishes in Meath and Westmeath; Cork and Tipperary; Wicklow, Queen's, and Kilkenny.[7]

Such was the success in the Irish market of the private distiller (or his distributor) that it would be no surprise to find that he ventured beyond it—especially, perhaps, in an endeavour to serve fellow-countrymen who retained in emigration their taste for

[1] Wakefield, op. cit., 1812, i, 729.
[2] For evidence that this was the case see below pp. 30–32
[3] *Seventh Report, Commissioners of Excise*, P.P., 1834, XXV, p. 416.
[4] S.C. on Drunkenness, P.P., 1834, VIII, q. 2758.
[5] *Fifth Report, Revenue arising in Ireland*, P.P., 1823, VII, p. 80.
[6] *Poor Inquiry (Ireland)*, P.P., 1836, XXXII, p. 220.
[7] Ibid. pp. 67, 73, 101, 103, 118, 134, 152, 175, 234. These reports may exaggerate the extent of the private distiller's market; those quoted appear to relate to poteen, but some, it may be, refer to untaxed spirit sold by licensed distillers: see below, pp. 38–44.

poteen. Some export there undoubtedly was: in 1810, for instance, a government agent reported that every year, from about March, much spirit was sent from Donegal to Scotland;[1] and some twenty years later an English distiller had heard of much illicit spirit being brought to London from the west of Ireland.[2] But, unless the elusiveness of the evidence is deceptive, only a trivial proportion of the poteen produced in Ireland was consumed elsewhere—because, it may be, of the distributors' lack of enterprise; but more probably because their slender capital was used at home with more profit and less risk; and because, in the Irish quarters of British cities, there were producers as well as consumers of illicit spirit.[3]

It is probable that most illicit distillers—even many with a substantial market—could get their produce at least to a retailer, unassisted by dealer or organized market. But if this were invariably the case we could hardly accept the evidence that poteen was regularly sold scores of miles from the districts in which it was extensively made. This evidence is made credible by accounts of professional dealers in poteen, and of marketing institutions quite as sophisticated as those which facilitated dealings in other peasant produce. In the north of Ireland the 'cadgers', professional distributors of poteen, were a 'common trade' early in the nineteenth century;[4] the regular spirit-dealers, too, 'habitually' drew supplies from the private distillers of Inishowen[5] (and this, it may be, was a more important channel of the distant trade in poteen than the slender evidence suggests). And the poteen-drinkers of co. Cork, (so, at least, their High Sheriff believed) were served by clandestine dealers with a commercial practice much akin to that of their licensed colleagues: 'there are', the sheriff wrote, 'regular agents from counties where they do distil extensively; these fellows, I understand, carry samples and make their bargains for deliveries.'[6]

Certainly, in the early decades of the century there were regular markets where poteen was sold—and its raw material bought—

---

[1] *Committee on Distilleries*, P.P., 1812–13, VI, pp. 9, 25–26.
[2] *Seventh Report, Commissioners of Excise*, P.P., 1834, XXV, p. 276. See also *S.C. on Drunkenness*, P.P., 1834, VIII, q. 2438.
[3] See below: pp. 21–23.
[4] *S.C. on Illicit Distillation*, P.P., 1816, IX, p. 54; *Fifth Report, Revenue arising in Ireland*, P.P., 1823, VII, p. 84.
[5] *Seventh Report, Commissioners of Excise*, P.P., 1834, XXV, p. 424.
[6] *Fifth Report, Revenue arising in Ireland*, P.P., 1823, VII, p. 32.

much as though they were butter or eggs; and until much later there were recognized centres of an entrepôt trade. The markets on which we have most information were on the shores of Lough Foyle, one at Bonifoble (Moville) on the Donegal side, and the other at Magilligan's Point, in Derry. Here grain was brought from the adjacent counties of Derry, Tyrone, and Antrim—even, it is said, from as far afield as co. Down and Scotland. Mostly, according to one observer, this grain was sold, but much was bartered for spirit: and spirit also was sold quite openly—'people', it is said, 'would tell the regular prices.' By about 1813 this trade had been made more circumspect: a revenue cutter was policing the Lough, and the markets themselves had been repeatedly broken up by armed attacks.[1] At Drumshambo, co. Leitrim, a little later, 'it had been not unusual ... to see several hundred kegs of smuggled whiskey brought into the town for sale in open day, at the markets': the people, as the new police interrupted the trade, were reduced to 'despondence and dismay.'[2]

Still, in 1909, the Aran Islands (ill-equipped for distilling because of their lack of turf) were thought to be a centre for the distribution of Connemara spirit to co. Clare, where, in places, there was also a scarcity of fuel.[3] Almost a century earlier, Portstewart and Ballycastle were pointed out as entrepôts of the northern trade. The village of Portstewart 'had great notoriety ... above others in the vicinity, both as a depot for the whiskey run across from Enishowen in small boats, and for tobacco landed from vessels bound into the North Channel.'[4] Ballycastle, a little remote from the main centres of the production of poteen, had the

[1] *Committee on Distilleries*, P.P., 1812–13, VI, p. 9; *S.C. on Illicit Distillation*, P.P., 1816, IX, pp. 87, 98; *Fifth Report, Revenue arising in Ireland*, P.P., 1823, VII, pp. 79–80. There is other evidence that private distillers systematically drew supplies of grain from far afield. According to the writer of an official report of 1810, grain for the Donegal distillers was brought from neighbouring counties, much through Derry city, and more across Lough Foyle; and 'great quantities', he said, were drawn from Scotland—a fact confirmed elsewhere (*Committee on Distilleries*, P.P., 1812–13, VI, p. 26; *S.C. on Illicit Distillation*, P.P., 1816, IX, p. 148/141; *Fifth Report, Revenue arising in Ireland*, P.P., 1823, VII, p. 86). Co. Antrim, at the same time, was specifically mentioned as growing barley for Inishowen, and in the 1820s Clare barley was said to be generally used by the Connemara distillers (J. Dubourdieu, *Statistical Survey of the County of Antrim* (Dublin, 1812), p. 181; Dutton, *Galway*, op. cit., 1824, p. 368).
[2] Isaac Weld, *Statistical Survey of the County of Roscommon* (Dublin, 1832), pp. 114–15, n.
[3] Stephen Gwynn, *A Holiday in Connemara* (1909), p. 89.
[4] *Seventh Report, Revenue arising in Ireland*, P.P., 1824, XI, p. 312.

mercantile facilities needed for its distribution: nearby were saltpans and a colliery, and 'the number of vessels resorting there' afforded such 'frequent opportunities for the conveyance of goods to any part of the kingdom' that the government was urged, in 1824, to station customs officials nearby.'[1]

The way in which poteen was carried from producer to consumer was determined, very largely, by the risk of detection. In Derry, around 1800, this was not over-rated; for spirit, it is said, was brought to the city in open tubs.[2] Much was carried on men's backs, in casks, or 'tin cases'; or a couple of kegs might be put in a large bag and slung over a horse's back.[3] In Donegal, in the 1820s, there were women ingeniously equipped for the poteen-trade: 'they have pockets made of tin, exactly in the shape of a woman's pocket; and a breast, and a half-moon, that goes before them; and with a cloak round them, they will walk with six gallons, and it shall not be perceived.'[4] Similarly in Joyce's country: a local distiller, it is said, ordered from a tinker 'a tin vessel with head and body the shape of a woman'; he dressed it to resemble his wife, and rode to market, his poteen on the pillion behind him.[5]

In the folklore, at least, the coffin has served its turn carrying poteen under the very noses of the police; and, hidden in the Christmas turkey, the odd bottle still escapes the British customs.[6] In the 1820s, if not later, the traffic in poteen was ensured by show of force as well as cunning: gangs of a dozen distillers would come to market, armed with loaded cudgels: on one occasion, some thirty mounted men, carrying spirit in Armagh, were

---

[1] Ibid, p. 311.
[2] *Fifth Report, Revenue arising in Ireland*, P.P., 1823, VII, p. 84.
[3] Ibid; *S.C. on Illicit Distillation*, P.P., 1854, X, qq., 832, 960; 'Maghtochair', op. cit., 1867, p. 121; *The Gael*, New York, Nov 1904, p. 363. 'Gaugers', expecting a haul, were said to provide themselves with pigs' bladders, to be filled if they made a seizure (Dorian, op. cit., 1890, p. 328). Among the many presents given to Carleton's Denis O'Shaughnessy when he was setting off for Maynooth was 'a purse, formed of a small bladder, ingeniously covered with silk'. ' "This will sarve you, sir," ' said his uncle, ' "an' I'll tell you how: if you want to smuggle in a sup of good whiskey—as of coorse you will, plase goodness,—why, this houlds exactly a pint, an' is the very thing for it. The sorra one among them will ever think of searchin' your purse, at least for whiskey" ' (W. Carleton, 'Denis O'Shaughnessy going to Maynooth', *Traits and Stories of the Irish Peasantry* [1843–6], ed. D. J. O'Donoghue (1896), iv, 181–2).
[4] *Fifth Report, Revenue arising in Ireland*, P.P., 1823, VII, p. 85.
[5] [Caesar Otway] *A Tour in Connaught* (Dublin, 1839), pp. 253–5.
[6] I.F.C., MS. 1023, p. 41; and private information.

attended by outriders, some with firearms, others carrying 'loaded whips that would break any scull.'[1]

The provision trade, and above all, it seems, the turf trade, facilitated the distribution of poteen: Dublin in the 1830s was supplied with poteen by the 'factors who dispose of eggs and potatoes for the country people';[2] in the present century, and probably earlier, it is 'hid in the heart of a cart of turf' that poteen has mostly travelled.[3] Much, too, has been moved by sea—in hooker, turf-boat, and fishing-boat—and boats, we may guess, of most kinds that sailed in Irish seas.[4]

Who was served by this extensive and clandestine traffic? Who were the buyers of poteen? 'There is a sort of fancy gentlemen have, viz., a sort of pride, in saying, "I will give you a drop of the mountain dew." '[5] Gentlemen esteemed poteen for its flavour and price as well as for its illegality: they paid well, and there was probably relatively little risk in serving them.[6] Well-to-do gentlemen, however, were not numerous in Ireland; and we may presume that their custom, a tiny proportion of the whole, fell to the more accomplished distiller. His colleagues sold to the less discriminating private customer, and to the retailers of spirits, licensed and unlicensed.[7]

In the 1830s a house rented at under £10 might be licensed for 'comparatively nothing': 'the whole country', in consequence, 'is deluged with low inferior establishments'—continuously in the twenty or so years before the Famine there were some 14,000 of them. The licensees 'have but little property, being most commonly broken-down farmers or petty tradesmen'; they 'have no character to lose, and deal without scruple in the illicit article.'[8]

---

[1] *S.C. on Illicit Distillation*, P.P., 1816, IX, p. 53; *Fifth Report, Revenue arising in Ireland*, P.P., 1823, VII, p. 73.

[2] *Seventh Report, Commissioners of Excise*, P. P., 1834, XXV, pp. 450-1.

[3] Gwynn, op. cit., 1909, p. 89; Seumus MacManus, *The Rocky Road to Dublin* (New York, 1938), p. 120; H. P. Swan and others, *Romantic Inishowen* (Dublin, 1947), p. 121.

[4] *Seventh Report, Revenue arising in Ireland*, P.P., 1824, XI, pp. 311-12; Gwynn, op. cit., 1909, p. 89; I.F.C., MS. 1023, p. 42.

[5] *S.C. on Illicit Distillation*, P.P., 1854, X, q. 456.   [6] Ibid.

[7] *Fifth Report, Revenue arising in Ireland*, P.P., 1823, VII, p. 119; *S.C. on Illicit Distillation*, P.P., 1854, X, q. 960.

[8] *Fifth Report, Revenue arising in Ireland*, P.P., 1823, VII, p. 119; *Poor Inquiry (Ireland)*, App. E, P.P., 1836, XXXII, pp. 252, 385; *Report of the Commissioners of Inland Revenue . . . for the Years 1856 to 1869 inclusive; with some retrospective History and complete Tables of the Duties from their first Imposition*, P.P., 1870, XX, p. 45.

18   ILLICIT DISTILLATION

The more cautious of these licensed retailers might colour their poteen with parliament whiskey[1]—a precaution, we may presume, rarely taken by their innumerable unlicensed competitors: in Limerick 'the sale of spirits in *unlicensed* houses is *very general*'; in Down it 'abounded to a fearful extent'; in Tipperary 'every second house sells whiskey'—and so on, in almost every county.[2] Shebeen-keeping was an itinerant as well as a sedentary trade: 'numbers of portable shebeen houses are taken about to every market, fair or funeral' in co. Down.[3] And in a country with no poor law until 1838, shebeen-keeping was a recognized resource of widows: 'they are considered a sort of privileged persons.' ' "That" ', said a Mayo widow, 'pointing to a whiskey bottle, "is my sole dependence. I have no means on earth to keep my children inside the door with me, but to borrow 1s. from one neighbour or another and buy a drop of poteen to sell again." '[4]

It is hardly possible to describe with any assurance trends in the price of poteen. Costs and risks, demand and supply, all varied widely from place to place and from time to time; and dealers can have done little to steady prices inherently unstable—their resources were too slender; they were impeded by the police, and they were interested, not infrequently, in turning fluctuations to good account. We need many price-records to generalize about so erratic a market: few, however, survive; and some leave us uncertain of the measure or the currency in which they are expressed, of the strength and quality of the spirit to which they relate, and whether the sale was by distiller or dealer.

The data, such as they are, suggest that at the end of the French wars poteen could be had in co. Sligo for 7s. or 8s. a gallon; Donegal spirit sold locally for 6s. or 8s., and for an extra shilling

---

[1] *S.C. on Illicit Distillation*, P.P., 1854, X, q. 960. In 1812 the licensed houses of Ulster were said to sell poteeen so generally that 'they very seldom received legally distilled spirits, but for the purpose of obtaining protection for the illicitly distilled spirits they get in' (*Committee on Distilleries*, P.P., 1812–13, VI, p. 9). In the north of Ireland in the 1830s poteen might be more plausibly disguised because of the introduction of Scotch malt whisky, with, it was said, something of the flavour of the best Inishowen (*Seventh Report, Commissioners of Excise*, P.P., 1834, XXV, pp. 409, 430).

[2] *Poor Inquiry (Ireland)*, App. E, P.P., 1836, XXXII, pp. 329 ff.

[3] Binns, op. cit., 1837, i, 107.

[4] [Poor Inquiry Commission] *Selections of Parochial Examinations relative to the Destitute Classes in Ireland* (Dublin, 1835), pp. 106–7, 111, 123–7, etc.

ILLICIT DISTILLATION

or so in Derry city.[1] Prices fell sharply in the next few years, in consequence, it may be, of falling grain prices and an increasing output of untaxed spirit by licensed as well as unlicensed distillers. In 1823 a gallon of poteen cost 2s. 6d. or 3s. in the mountains, 4s. or 5s. in nearby towns—but as much as 12s. in Belfast. Parliament whiskey, still taxed at 5s. 11½d. a gallon, was selling at the time for 8s. 6d. or 9s.; it was, however, a stronger spirit, and its price should be brought down by about one-third to make it comparable with that of ordinary poteen.[2]

Ten years later the Dublin distillers complained that poteen might be had in the country for 3s.; other witnesses put its price at 4s. or 4s. 6d., the equivalent, one of them calculated, of 6s. or 7s. the imperial gallon at 25 o.p.—less, by a shilling or two, than the wholesale price of parliament whiskey of like strength.[3]

After the Famine, while a gallon of poteen of a sort might be had for 3s. 6d., good barley spirit, at 7s. a gallon, cost fully as much as parliament whiskey, weaker though it was.[4] There are reports of Inishowen selling in the 1880s at 8s. or 9s. wholesale, 14s. or 15s. retail; and of Connaught spirit costing 10s. or 12s. a gallon early in the present century, 8s. a pint during the First World War, and 4s. or 5s. a pint before the Second.[5]

The private distiller more probably sensed than calculated his gains: we have, none the less, various estimates of his profit and loss. In Kilmactige, co. Sligo, according to the rector, a 24-stone barrel of oats sold for 14s. in 1816; but 'well-managed [it] will produce eight gallons of common whiskey which will sell for seven or eight shillings per gallon': to distil this grain was hardly more laborious than to carry it a dozen or more miles to the dealer: it involved some risk and incidental expense, but these were minor deterrents when £3 might be earned instead of 14s.[6] The Select Committee on Drunkenness was told in 1834 that sixteen stone of

---

[1] Mason, op. cit., ii, 1816, p. 394; *S.C. on Illicit Distillation*, P.P., 1816, IX, p. 148/137.

[2] *Fifth Report, Revenue arising in Ireland*, P.P., 1823, VII, pp. 38, 56, 57, 66, 75, 119.

[3] *Seventh Report, Commissioners of Excise*, P.P., 1834, XXV, pp. 401, 430, 432; S.C. on Drunkenness, P.P., 1834, VIII, q. 2761; H. D. Inglis, *A Journey throughout Ireland* (1838), p. 262.

[4] *S.C. on Illicit Distillation*, P.P., 1854, X, qq. 260, 454, 458, 463, p. 263.

[5] Shand, op. cit., 1885, p. 151; *The Gael*, New York, Nov 1904, p. 363; I.F.C., MS. 227, pp. 189-90, 191-2.

[6] Mason, op. cit., ii, 1816, p. 394.

barley fetched 12*s*. as grain, but 27*s*. if distilled—and additional expenses of distilling were about offset by the value of the by-products.[1] According to one estimate of 1854, barley-malt costing £2 5*s*. could be made into spirit worth £3 10*s*.; another gives more details:[2]

Expenditure			Income	
40 stone oats	£4.	2*s*. 6*d*.	About 17 galls.	
Hire of still		1*s*. 6*d*.	spirit at 7*s*. per	
Fuel		6*d*.	gall.	£5. 19*s*. 0*d*.
Yeast		1*s*. 6*d*.	Refuse, pot-ale,	
Profit	£2.	5*s*. 0*d*.	grains	12*s*. 0*d*.
	£6. 11*s*. 0*d*.			£6. 11*s*. 0*d*.

The poteen-maker, an excise official concluded in 1854, could earn a 'clear average profit of 3*s*. a gallon . . . less the trifling cost of peat, fuel and labour'.[3] Forty years earlier, 'after deducting all their losses, expences and risks, together with the bribes paid to Revenue Officers', Donegal distillers were making 'one pound sterling each day that they work'.[4] But not every distiller was able and anxious to take his earnings in cash: 'every idle blackguard', knowing where poteen is being made, 'drops in for a taste'; and friends of the distiller 'think it neighbourly to attend' and drink much—with disastrous effect on the distiller's profit.[5]

Distilling is a simple process, its product appealing, its apparatus and materials readily acquired: in any community, then, a considerable spirit-duty is liable to be accompanied by illicit distillation. Certainly there is no reason to doubt that the trade has had a continuous existence, at least since the early nineteenth century, in England and Scotland, as well as in Ireland.

In England there was less of the extreme poverty which made the cheapest spirit imperative to many an Irish consumer: by the 1830s, indeed, the English were said to be unwilling to buy the simple product of the private distiller, so much had they come to appreciate the 'peculiar description of compound' lawfully sold.[6]

[1] *S.C. on Drunkenness*, P.P., 1834, VIII, q. 2761.
[2] *S.C. on Illicit Distillation*, P.P., 1854, X, qq. 452–4.
[3] Ibid., p. 263. [4] Chichester, op. cit., 1818, p. 31.
[5] Maxwell, op. cit., 1834, p. 282; *S.C. on Illicit Distillation*, P.P., 1854, X, q. 1300.
[6] *Seventh Report, Commissioners of Excise*, P.P., 1834, XXV, p. 38.

ILLICIT DISTILLATION

Public opinion, too, may have been less tolerant of the English practitioner, and the excise more rigorous. On the other hand, England's more substantial spirit duties[1] added to the profit of illicit distilling; its appeal was little dimmed by tax-evasion in the licensed distilleries; and its practice was diffused by 'the increased facility of obtaining knowledge among the lower orders by means of cheap publications'.[2] But the real impetus probably came with the immigrant Irish, familiar, many of them, with the taste of poteen, and experienced in its manufacture: 'almost invariably', in the 1830s, private distilling in England was Irishmen's work;[3] 'the stills are in cellars, and the cellars are inhabited by Irish.'[4]

Paradoxically, this prominence of the Irish helps to account for one of the more striking contrasts between English and Irish illicit distilling. In Ireland it was overwhelmingly a rural occupation. But in England 'it is not at all prevalent in the country'; 'we sometimes, but very rarely, hear of a case of distillation in Devonshire and the cyder counties': it was carried on principally in London, Liverpool, Manchester, and other manufacturing centres.[5] In all of the towns named, and in many of the others, there were colonies of Irish, drinkers and distillers of poteen included.[6]

[1] It was not until 1859 that the spirit duty was made uniform throughout the United Kingdom. The following table shows the duty in the different kingdoms at various dates:

Rate of duty, per proof gallon, on spirit made from corn

	Ireland	England	Scotland
1802	2s. 10¼d.	5s. 4½d.	3s. 10½d.
1810	4s. 1d.–2s. 6½d.	8s. 0½d.	5s. 8¾d.
1820	5s. 7¼d.	11s. 8¼d.	6s. 2d.
1830	2s. 10d.–3s.–3s. 4d.	7s.–7s. 6d.	2s. 10d.–3s. 4d.
1840 & 1850	2s. 8d.	7s. 10d.	3s. 8d.
1860	8s.–8s. 1d.	8s. 1d.	8s. 1d.

(*Seventh Report, Commissioners of Excise*, P.P., 1834, XXV, pp. 20, 42, 66–7; *Report, Commissioners Inland Revenue*, P.P., 1870, XX, p. 9.)

[2] *Seventh Report, Commissioners of Excise*, P.P., 1834, XXV, p. 38.
[3] *Seventh Report, Commissioners of Excise*, P.P., 1834, XXV, p. 253; see also p. 38.
[4] *S.C. on Drunkenness*, P.P., 1834, VIII, q. 4305.
[5] *Seventh Report, Commissioners of Excise*, P.P., 1834, XXV, pp. 39, 253–4, 276, 294.
[6] The urban location of private distilling in England is reflected in the materials used—molasses, treacle, beer, and porter, rather than grain and malt. The English stills seem to have been much the same size as those used in Ireland—commonly in the 1830s of 30–40 gallons' capacity, although occasionally twice as large. And in England, too, spirits were sometimes distributed in bladders or in 'tin cases adapted to fit the body' (ibid., pp. 253–4; *Report, Commissioners of Inland Revenue*, P.P., 1870, XX, Pt. i, p. 27).

Like their colleagues in Ireland, illicit distillers in England supplied publicans as well as private persons; but unlike them they sold substantially to chemists, hat-makers, french-polishers, and other industrial users of spirit.[1] This, no doubt, was another cause of the urban location of the English industry. And it was a factor which made it peculiarly vulnerable to the law. Early in the 1850s, when there had been a sharp increase in the number of Irish living in England, illicit distillation was thought to have become more prevalent. Police activities were increased; but more efficacious was the Methylated Spirit Act of 1855.[2] This cut off the illicit distiller's industrial trade by enabling his customers to acquire, free of duty, spirit mixed with wood naphtha. By 1870 the Commissioners of Inland Revenue conclude that the practice of illicit distillation 'is nearly extinct in England'. It appears to have experienced no subsequent revival: by 1890 most of the detections were 'wretched little cases', and their number ever since has remained small.[3]

In Scotland, as in Ireland, during and immediately after the French wars, illicit distillation was encouraged by steeply-rising duties, and by the outlawing of small stills.[4] In the Highlands it had become so prevalent that legal spirit was said to be seldom drunk: in the whole country, in the early twenties, convictions for illicit distillation exceeded 4,000 a year.[5] The Highland Society and members of the nobility and gentry offered to co-operate with the government in stamping out a practice which they believed to be injurious to the country's peace and prosperity.[6] In 1820 the Duke of Gordon raised the matter in the House of Lords, again offering the landlords' co-operation, on condition that the government made

[1] Ibid.; *Seventh Report, Commissioners of Excise*, P.P., 1834, XXV, p. 8; *Twenty-eighth Report of the Commissioners of . . . Inland Revenue . . . with some retrospective History, and complete Table of Accounts of the Duties from 1869-70 to 1884-5*, P.P., 1884-5, XXII, p. 17.

[2] 18 and 19 Victoria, c. 38. *Report, Commissioners of Inland Revenue*, P.P., 1870, XX, p. 27.

[3] Ibid.; *Select Committee on British and Foreign Spirits*, P.P., 1890-1, XI, p. 39. Between 1891 and 1939 the annual number of detections in England and Scotland together only once—in 1892—exceeded 30 (*Reports, Commissioners of Inland Revenue*, and *Customs and Excise*).

[4] *Seventh Report, Commissioners of Excise*, P.P., 1834, XXV, pp. 20, 42, 66; R. B. Lockhart, *Scotch* (1951), p. 11.

[5] *Two Reports of Woodbine Parish . . . on Illicit Distillation in Scotland*, P.P., 1816, VIII, p. 2; *Seventh Report, Commissioners of Excise*, P.P., 1834, XXV, p. 240.

[6] *Reports on Illicit Distillation in Scotland*, P.P., 1816, VIII, p. 1.

ILLICIT DISTILLATION

it legally possible to produce good spirit on payment of a reasonable duty.[1] Three years later the government complied: the duty was brought down from 6s. 2d. a gallon to 2s. 4¾d; and stills of 40 gallons' capacity might be licensed for £10.[2] Convictions fell away steeply: by the years 1830-3 they averaged fewer than 100.[3] As in England, there were private distillers in some of the Scottish towns, and they, too, suffered from the Methylated Spirit Act.[4] By the 1860s the police annually detected fewer than 20 illicit stills in Scotland; and thereafter this figure was only occasionally exceeded.[5]

The statistics of an unlawful trade are apt to be scarce and unreliable. The main index of the extent and location of illicit distillation in Great Britain and Ireland is the series of figures, continuous from the 1830s, of the number of detections made by the authorities. Detections, of course, fluctuated with more than the industry—with the number and zeal of the police, with the help they were given by the public, and much more. But for all their uncertainty, the figures indicate, too emphatically to mislead, that continuously illicit distillation has been overwhelmingly an Irish, rather than an English or Scottish industry. Thus in the 1830s when there were nearly 700 detections a year in the rest of the United Kingdom, there were seven times as many in Ireland: in the 1870s the Irish figure still exceeded 1000, the English was 15 and the Scottish 5; and as late as the 1930s there were 500 detections a year in Ireland, but only 10 in England and 9 in Scotland.[6]

Why was illicit distilling so much more common in Ireland than in Britain? Many commentators believed that the Irish were peculiarly prone to drink—because of their climate or disposition; because of the monotony of their diet, the wretchedness of their lives, or the scarcity of alternative diversions. But, whatever is thought of this contention, it seems that, at least before the Famine, beer and parliament whiskey were less satisfactory substitutes for illicit spirit in Ireland than elsewhere in the United Kingdom. The prevalence of illicit distillation was only one of the many troubles that beset the lawful liquor trade in Ireland. With other

---

[1] Lockhart, op. cit., p. 12.
[2] Ibid.; *Seventh Report, Commissioners of Excise*, P.P., 1834, XXV, pp. 20, 42, 66.
[3] *Report, Commissioners of Inland Revenue*, P.P., 1870, XX, p. 12.
[4] *Seventh Report, Commissioners of Excise*, P.P., 1834, XXV, pp. 28, 362.
[5] See Fig. 5, pp. 44-5, below, and p. 22, n. 3, above.
[6] See Fig. 5, pp. 44-5, below.

branches of industry it suffered from the elusiveness of capital, and the unfamiliarity of the Irish with money; from the prevalence of unrest, the difficulty of communications and the dearness of coal.[1] The very poverty of the Irish tended to put taxed liquor beyond their reach. And the vagaries of the excise were a provoking infliction: the law dallied between encouraging the distiller to have small stills, and forbidding their use; the continuous wavering of the duties added to the ill-effect of their upward trend; and, most serious it may be, the law tended to make parliament spirit unpalatable.

There were two bases for this last charge: first, that the licensed distiller made an inferior spirit because the malt-duty obliged him to work, very largely, with raw grain; and, second, that until 1823 his product suffered further because the form of the spirit-duty encouraged over-rapid distillation. There can be little doubt that the flavour of parliament whiskey was normally distinguishable from that of poteen.[2] But it would be wrong to attribute the difference entirely to the short-sightedness of the law-makers: even more important, perhaps, was the fact that any malt the licensed distiller used was likely to be coal-dried, while poteen had the 'hogo' of the maltster's turf.[3] Some said that only a degraded palate could tolerate 'the detestable taste of smoke'.[4] But if this were true few Irish palates were not degraded: in the 1830s, indeed, it was maintained that to every Irishman poteen is 'superior in sweetness, salubriety and gusto, to all that machinery, science and capital can produce in the legalized way'.[5] Twenty years earlier illicit spirit was scarce and dear in Belfast: it cost two or three times as much as in Derry, and was consumed principally by 'the better classes, where price is no consequence, but quality is everything'.[6] The grand jury of a western town (so it is said) formally retained the right to drink poteen at its common table, so much did its members

---

[1] S.C. on Illicit Distillation, P.P., 1816, IX, p. 125; S.C. on State of the Poor in Ireland, P.P., 1830, VII, p. 16, qq. 5941 ff.

[2] See for instance: Committee on Distilleries, P.P., 1812–13, VI, p. 7; Seventh Report, Commissioners of Excise, P.P., 1834, XXV, p. 396; Dorian, op. cit., 1890, p. 343. But for the contrary opinion see S.C. on Illicit Distillation, P.P., 1854, X, q. 2321.

[3] Dutton, Galway, op. cit., 1824, pp. 367–8; Seventh Report, Commissioners of Excise, P.P., 1834, XXV, p. 396.

[4] Dutton, Galway, op. cit., 1824, p. 367.

[5] [Caesar Otway] Sketches in Ireland (Dublin, 1839), p. 60.

[6] Fifth Report, Revenue arising in Ireland, P.P., 1823, VII, p. 56.

prefer it to lawful spirit.[1] A Limerick distiller believed that most people wanted the cheapest spirit, irrespective of quality: 'except the dignitaries of the church, the officers of the army and the magistrates of the county, there is not anybody cares a farthing about poteen'; he therefore turned down the suggestion that he should make fine spirit to tempt people from poteen.[2] Some of his competitors, however, thought otherwise, and set to work to make their parliament whiskey resemble poteen.[3] 'The Bush-mill', it was said, 'comes nearer to what is termed poteen than any spirit made in Ireland.' 'There would be a little difficulty where a sample of good poteen was placed and a sample of Bush-mill placed before a gentleman; however good a judge he might be, he would pause before giving decided opinion.'[4]

In Ireland, then, before the Famine, a normal (if not more than normal) demand for drink was inadequately served by the licensed liquor trade; little beer was produced, and parliament whiskey, impossibly expensive to most of the population, was ill-regarded by the rest. There was, in consequence, a great latent demand for a cheap, palatable spirit. The poteen industry was reared on this demand, and on the simultaneous existence of a numerous body of men more than willing to satisfy it.

Their willingness was a symptom of the ailing economy in which they lived. Large families, small holdings, and an elastic rent: until after the Famine these mainly determined the social life of the Irish countryside; they created and made chronic the coincidence

[1] Blake, op. cit., 1825, pp. 158–9n.
[2] *Seventh Report, Revenue arising in Ireland*, P.P., 1824, XI, p. 60.
[3] Dutton, *Galway*, op. cit., 1824, p. 367; *S.C. on Illicit Distillation*, P.P., 1854, X, q. 421.
[4] Ibid. Poteen was commonly thought not only to taste better than parliament whiskey, but to be purer and less harmful—though the unscrupulous distiller sometimes attributed the taste of adulterants to the smoke of his turf (Wakefield, op. cit., 1812, i, p. 729; *S.C. on Illicit Distillation*, P.P., 1816, IX, pp. 75, 82; Chichester, op. cit., 1818, p. 24; Dutton, *Galway*, op. cit., 1824, p. 367). The preference for poteen was probably less marked away from the main centres of its production (*Fifth Report, Revenue arising in Ireland*, P.P., 1823, VII, p. 76). There is little doubt that after the Famine the quality of poteen deteriorated as other materials were substituted for malt (Shand, op. cit., p. 15; I.F.C., MS. 227, p. 165). Eventually, to one connoisseur, 'poteen is just murder—it's the end'. 'No matter what anyone tells you about the fine old drop of the mountain dew, it stands to sense that a few old men sitting up in the back of a haggard in the mountains with milk-churns and all sorts of improvised apparatus cannot hope to make good spirits' (Brendan Behan, *Brendan Behan's Island* (1962), p. 126.).

of poverty and idleness—incompatible though these might have been in a happier environment. In most peasant families far more labour was available than was used; while families remained intact, with tiny holdings their one source of income, only a labour-intensive farming might occupy the idle and mitigate the poverty; but while rent remained elastic the appeal of hard work, at best, was equivocal. Short, therefore, of prizing their poverty and idleness, people were interested in subsidiary occupations that might add to their income. And of these, poteen-making was by no means to be despised; by-employment of any kind was scarce enough, and much of it (lace-making, knitting, and the like) appealed more to over-worked women than to under-worked men; that illicit distillation was a clandestine occupation was all to the good, for its earnings were less readily estimated and annexed by the landlord; that it was a risky occupation was no great deterrent; there was, indeed, some shred of the patriot's glory for the man who cheated the excise, and the imprisonment he risked necessarily worsened neither his own condition nor (when neighbours were sympathetic) that of his family.[1]

But some peasants were driven to illicit distillation even more insistently than by their need of a supplementary income: poteen-making, to them, was the alternative to eviction, a condition of retaining the status of land-holder. Rent was not necessarily stretched to the full when it absorbed the margin between the produce of a holding and the subsistence of the tenant's family. On occasion the landlord's demands were met only if the earnings of industry were added to those of the land—for some, that is to say, only if they made poteen. More commonly, no doubt, rents might be paid only if the price of grain were inflated by the private distillers' demand.

Much evidence suggests that before the Famine many people looked upon poteen-making as their only chance of making ends meet. In 1816, for instance, a Sligo rector said that even if distilling were made a felony, the poor of his parish would not desist: it was the only means they had of paying their rents, and (as they said)

[1] Many private distillers, an excise collector pointed out in 1834, 'would almost as soon be in prison during the winter season as at their own cabins: they fare much better... they have a sufficiency of potatoes, oatmeal and milk, and have good warm bedding'. He thought they did not feel the least disgrace in being in prison, and that friends and neighbours would support their families (*Seventh Report, Commissioners of Excise*, P.P., 1834, XXV, pp. 401–2, 405).

'they might as well hang as starve'.[1] In Leitrim at about the same time a land agent reported to his employer that private distillation was *'the only means* they ever made use of to pay rents'.[2] In Donegal, too, it was the prevalence of illicit distillation that allowed much barren land to be rented at up to three guineas an acre.[3]

The economic appeal of illicit distillation tended, of course, to be strong in districts able to grow grain, but unable economically to send it to orthodox markets. Where the alternative was transporting a sackful of grain, perhaps on horseback, perhaps for a score of miles, the distiller might reduce it to a cubic foot of spirit, together with the waste: for the spirit there might be a local demand, and the waste, fed to cattle, provided for transportation.[4] Thus, in Mayo, according to Alexander Nimmo, the civil engineer, 'the only encouragement to agricultural pursuits ... is by conversion of the grain into whiskey; for this is the only shape, I might almost say, in which the agricultural produce of the country can be carried out'.[5] When drained, the 'flats' in the mountains of Galway and Clare produced oats fit for seed; but—as a local landlord admitted to a parliamentary committee—'the roads being so bad, we put it to the purpose of illicit distillation'.[6] In Donegal 'the only markets for grain in all the mountain region are the private distilleries whither the common tenantry convey all their barley for sale';[7] but when stores were set up, by 'English capitalists' or by Lord George Hill, distilling it is said, diminished.[8]

---

[1] Mason, op. cit., 1816, ii, p. 394.

[2] F. S. L. Lyons, 'Vicissitudes of a middleman in county Leitrim', *Irish Historical Studies*, ix, 1955, p. 310.

[3] *Fifth Report, Revenue arising in Ireland*, P.P., 1823, pp. 73–74. In a Mayo parish in the 1830s 'illicit distillation prevails, and generally, in consequence, enables persons engaged in this traffic to pay high rents' (*Poor Inquiry (Ireland)*, App. E., P.P., 1836, XXXIII, p. 23). In Monaghan, small farmers were obliged to distil 'to enable them to satisfy the rapacity of their landlords' (ibid., p. 371).

[4] *Devon Commission*, P.P., 1845, XXI, p. 32; *Seventh Report, Commissioners of Excise*, P.P., 1834, XXV, p. 405.

[5] *Second Report, S.C. on the State ... of the Labouring Poor in Ireland*, 1819, reprinted P.P., 1829, IV, p. 104.

[6] *S.C. on Public Works in Ireland*, P.P., 1835, XX, q. 2375.

[7] J. McParlan, *Statistical Survey of the County of Donegal* (Dublin, 1802), p. 43. See also *Poor Inquiry (Ireland)*, P.P., 1836, XXXII, pp. 11, 34, 302, etc.; and *Seventh Report, Commissioners of Excise*, P.P., 1834, XXV, p. 404.

[8] Ibid. p. 404; *Devon Commission*, P.P., 1845, XXI, *1055*, qq. 28–32. In the parish of Feakle, co. Clare, 'before the improvement in the roads, distillation prevailed to a great extent; at present it is trifling' (*Poor Inquiry (Ireland)* P.P., 1836, XXXII, p. 160).

Primarily, then, the wretchedness and precariousness of living conditions explain the extent and persistence of poteen-making: it was the poverty of the peasantry more than their love of mischief that made them try their hand at distilling; and poverty, if it did not add to the consumption of spirits, made parliament whiskey an impossibly expensive substitute for poteen. The industry, favoured by poverty, was fostered, of course, by the natural features of much of the country; and also by the sympathy widely felt for the illicit distiller.

Poteen-making provides a striking example of the proverbial reluctance of the Irish to accept the law's definition of an offence. Continuously the illicit distiller has enjoyed something of the respect and sympathy due to an important and much-tried functionary: the excise officials lament that he bore none of the malefactor's stigma;[1] and in fiction it is the gauger who is outwitted, the distiller who has the last laugh.[2] It is not surprising that the general public connived at, and encouraged, illicit distillation. In the heyday of the industry, and where it was most prevalent, almost all of the local population had a pecuniary interest in its well-being, the interest of distiller or distributor, or grower of grain;[3] and in, and beyond, these districts, the poteen-maker was cherished for the sparkle he brought to social life. He benefited, too, from the widespread distrust of the government—and from its obverse, sympathy for its intended victim: at best of times the State in Ireland was vouchsafed a grudging co-operation, but when it played the spoil-sport it could count on full-blooded opposition.[4]

[1] S.C. on Illicit Distillation, P.P., 1854, X, qq. 783, 1348, 1710.
[2] See 'Bob Pentland; or the Gauger outwitted', and 'Condy Cullen, or the Exciseman defeated', in W. Carleton, *Tales and Stories of the Irish Peasantry* (Dublin, 1846); W. Carleton, *The Squanders of Castle Squander* (1852), (Ch. iv); 'Still-hunting' in [A. Blenkinsop,] *Paddiana* (1847), i; 'Dinny Monaghan's last Keg', in 'Mac' [Seumas MacManus], *The leadin' Road to Donegal* (n.d. [1896]).
[3] S.C. on Illicit Distillation, P.P., 1816, IX, 126; *Fifth Report, Revenue arising in Ireland*, P.P., 1823, VII, p. 79; S.C. on Illicit Distillation, 1854, X, q. 783.
[4] Thus in 1834 an excise collector attributed a recent increase in illicit distillation in part to the perturbed feeling in the country; in consequence 'individuals have thought they might take the law into their own hands with more impunity than they used to do' (*Seventh Report, Commissioners of Excise*, P.P., 1834, XXV, p. 376). But other witnesses before the same committee pointed out that in the most disturbed counties there was relatively little illicit distillation (ibid. pp. 381, 410).

ILLICIT DISTILLATION

Nor was it only his humbler neighbour who abetted the illicit distiller. Before the Famine some of the clergy certainly denounced his malpractices.[1] But others were more tolerant, and private distillers, in consequence, profited from clerical patronage, or suffered from clerical competition.[2] The clergy's dues and tithes, like the landlord's rent, were swollen by the trade in poteen:[3] it was alleged, indeed, that an Achill friar earned the greater part of his living by blessing illicit stills[4] and that malt was stored and spirit distilled in Erris chapels:

> A house contrived a double debt to pay,
> A still by night, a place of prayer by day.[5]

Continuously, no doubt, there were landlords who opposed illicit distillation: they believed, for the most part, that cheap spirit demoralized their tenants, making them idle and careless, and they treated its manufacture in consequence as an 'eviction crime'.[6] Characteristically, however, the landlord was interested less in the well-being of his tenantry than in the level of his rents. Ultimately, the prosperous, responsible tenant may have brought in most rent; but the landlord's commitments, like his traditions, made him scornful of the ultimate: and immediately (we have seen already) many a tenant paid his rent only because he, or his neighbour, made poteen. There is no doubt that many landlords realized this, and used their influence—even in the administration of justice—to foster the industry and shield it from its oppressors. Galway landlords, it is said, commonly accepted poteen in lieu of rent:[7] 'if there were 50,000 troops,' one of them boasted, 'they would not be able to put it down, for it is a benefit to the landlord to keep it up.'[8] In 1812, according to an official report, the

---

[1] *Fifth Report, Revenue arising in Ireland*, P.P., 1823, VII, p. 80; *Poor Inquiry (Ireland)* P.P., 1836, XXXII, p. 179; 'Irish Clergyman' [J. Spencer Knox], *Pastoral Annals* (1840), pp. 81–111.
[2] Wakefield, op. cit., 1812, i, 729; *Seventh Report, Revenue arising in Ireland*, P.P., 1824, XI, p. 60.
[3] Gamble, op. cit., 1819, p. 302; [Caesar Otway], *Sketches in Erris and Tyrawly* (Dublin, 1841), p. 361.
[4] B. W. Noel, *Notes of a short Tour through the midland Counties of Ireland in the Summer of 1836* (1837), p. 19.
[5] *Sketches in Erris and Tyrawly*, 1841, op. cit., pp. 346, 362.
[6] *Committee on Distilleries*, P.P., 1812–13, p. 25; Chichester, op. cit., 1818, pp 31–32; *S.C. on Illicit Distillation*, P.P., 1854, X, q. 1171; Dorian, op. cit., 1890, pp. 341–2; Le Fanu, op. cit., 1893, p. 275.
[7] *Seventh Report, Commissioners of Excise*, P.P., 1834, XXV, p. 396.
[8] *S.C. Public Works in Ireland*, P.P., 1835, XX, q. 2376.

landlords' unwillingness to co-operate was the chief obstacle to stamping out private distilling:[1] twenty years later they were described as the 'roots of the evil';[2] and as late as the seventies they were chided by the excise, who contrasted their attitude with the 'cordial co-operation' of most of the Scottish proprietors.[3]

It can hardly be disputed that magistrates and juries were sometimes unduly reluctant to convict men charged with illicit distillation. Many of those who administered justice had a landlord's or a consumer's interest in poteen-making; they were reluctant to enforce unpopular legislation, or afraid of the consequences; and some of them, having received presents of poteen, felt that 'a kindness deserves a kindness'.[4] Frequently, then, although 'magistrates privately cry out against illicit distillation . . . in their judicial capacity [they] strain every nerve, and sometimes go beyond the law of doubt to acquit the smuggler': they 'study, if possible, to find some loophole or some flaw, in order to allow them to escape'.[5] Juries, too, might be over-indulgent; and in Donegal, in the 1820s, it was said 'we could not get a jury . . . that were not for the most part smugglers'.[6]

'Does illicit distillation prevail in your parish?' This was one of a series of questions which the Poor Inquiry Commission sent in 1836 to prominent residents up and down the country. Some 1500 replies[7] provide a detailed—and seemingly authoritative—account of the location of poteen-making. The map on p. 31, based on this information, shows that, while illicit distillation was common in the seaboard counties from Clare north and west to Derry, there was little south of a line drawn from the mouth of the Shannon, through Limerick, to Newry. Other evidence shows that in the previous and following two or three decades poteen-making was also very largely confined to these same counties; and that

[1] *Committee on Distilleries*, P.P., 1812–13, VI, p. 25.
[2] *The Times*, Dublin correspondent, 22 Apr 1834.
[3] *Report, Commissioners Inland Revenue*, P.P., 1870, XX, p. 28.
[4] *Seventh Report, Commissioners of Excise*, P.P., 1834, XXV, pp. 376, 380, 401; Dorian, op. cit., 1890, p. 336.
[5] *Poor Inquiry (Ireland)*, App. E, P.P., 1836, XXXII, p. 252; *Report, Commissioners of Inland Revenue*, P.P., 1870, XX, p. 160.
[6] *The Charge of Judge Fletcher to the Grand Jury of the County of Wexford* (Dublin, 1814), p. 10; *Fifth Report, Revenue arising in Ireland*, P.P., 1823, VII, p. 83.
[7] *Poor Inquiry (Ireland)*, Supplement to App. E, P.P., 1836, XXXII, pp. 1–393.

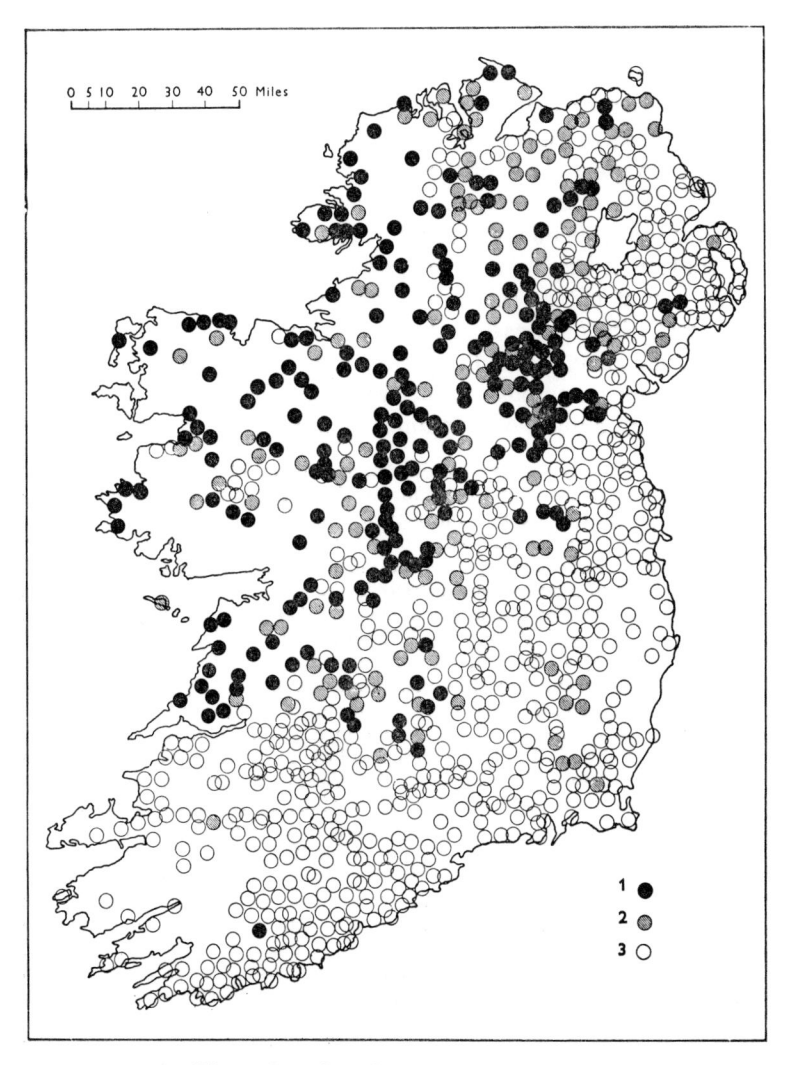

Fig. 2: Location of illicit distillation, 1836
(Copied from an original map prepared by Captain Kevin Danaher)

Key: 'Does illicit distillation prevail in your parish?'
1. 'Yes'.
2. 'Slightly' or 'Occasionally'.
3. 'No'.

(*Poor Inquiry* (*Ireland*), Supplement to App. E, P.P. 1836, XXXII, pp. 1–393)

into the present century, as the industry has decayed, it has only occasionally been detected beyond this area.[1]

Granted that the illicit distiller was a common figure in Ireland, it is no wonder that he was active in Connaught and western Ulster: he was protected by the difficulty of communications with and within great tracts of these areas; there, not infrequently, his was the best price for grain; turf and water were plentiful, and poverty was endemic, the poverty that made light of the risks of his trade as it heightened the appeal of its product. The puzzling thing is that poteen seems to have been made only occasionally and locally in south-eastern Ulster, in Leinster, and Munster.[2] It is true, of course, that in this section of the country the towns were larger, more numerous and better placed for serving the British market: communications, commonly, were easier, the police more

[1] I have seen only one piece of dissenting evidence of seeming authority: in 1823, according to the High Sheriff for co. Cork, 'in the wild and mountainous parts of the south of Ireland, illicit distillation is carried on to an enormous extent' (*Fifth Report, Revenue arising in Ireland*, P.P., 1823, VI, p. 32). But in the same year it was officially reported that illicit distillation was confined almost entirely to certain mountainous districts in the following eight counties (listed in descending order of importance): Donegal, Cavan, Leitrim, Mayo, Clare, Sligo, Monaghan, and Tyrone (*Fifth Report, Revenue arising in Ireland*, P.P., 1823, VII, p. 118). Colonel Brereton recalled that in 1836, when he agreed to reorganize the revenue police, he made inquiries 'of every person who could give me information'. 'I found there was no illicit distillation in the county of Kerry, none in the county of Cork, none in Kilkenny, none in Waterford or Wexford, very little in Limerick; there was little in the county of Carlow. The illicit spirit tried to find its way over the Wicklow mountains, to get sold in Dublin . . . but we quickly put this down' (*S.C. on Illicit Distillation*, P.P., 1854, X, q. 33). In 1854 the chairman of the Board of Inland Revenue prepared a map showing the stations of the revenue police. The force was concerned solely with the suppression of illicit distillation; its disposition, therefore, showed 'where it is apprehended there is the greatest danger of illicit distillation'. 'If a line be drawn between Dublin and Limerick,' the chairman pointed out, 'we have only, in fact, two parties south of that line. . . . Illicit distillation can scarcely be said to exist south of the Shannon, or south of the Liffey; it prevails chiefly in the parts of Derry and Tyrone, in Donegal, in Fermanagh, in Sligo, Galway, and part of Clare. We have no party south of Carlow. It has occasionally happened that a party has been pushed to the southward for, perhaps, a week or a fortnight, when we had intelligence that illicit distillation prevailed in any particular locality, but no party has been permanently stationed, I may say, south of the Liffey, or south of the Shannon, since the formation of the force'(ibid, qq. 6, 8). Between 1946 and 1955 the guards in the 26 counties made 775 seizures under the illicit distillation acts: of these only 52 were in counties other than Galway, Mayo, Sligo, Leitrim, Cavan, and Monaghan. (Information kindly supplied by Dr. M. D. McCarthy, Director of the Central Statistics Office, Dublin.)

[2] With the exception of co. Clare.

ILLICIT DISTILLATION

effective, and the corn-merchant less niggardly. But factors such as these make an unconvincing explanation of the elusiveness of the illicit distiller in the wilder parts of Leinster and Munster, particularly in the great tract of country west of the road from Cork to Listowel. Here, in Kerry and west Cork, topography and the rural economy were as accommodating to the private distiller as in Donegal or Connemara: there were mountains in plenty to conceal his operations and impede his pursuers; turf and water were abundant, and grain no more precariously grown than farther north; the people, we must presume, had no unnatural aversion to drinking or to breaking the law; and they were poor enough, many of them, to choose the cheapest liquor, and to need a subsidiary trade, even one carrying the risk of imprisonment.

How can we account for the elusiveness of the private distiller in the mountains of west Cork and Kerry? 'There is not, nor ever was, illicit distillation [around Parknasilla, but] smuggling was formerly extensively practised.'[1] Well-equipped though this whole area was for poteen-making, did it, then, have an even readier source of spirit? Smuggling certainly was prevalent[2]—but of tobacco far more than liquor:[3] spirit, we may presume, was smuggled for the consumer of some sophistication (and solidity); his neighbours, it may well be, could rarely afford contraband brandy or rum; and it is incredible that they should have consumed it in quantity unremarked—or so it seems—in the travellers' tales, the statistical surveys, and the excise reports.[4]

Smuggling and illicit distillation, moreover, were complementary, not alternative, occupations. Between Sligo and Lough Swilly (notoriously distilling country) smuggling 'is carried . . . to an extent unequalled on any other part of the coast'.[5] At Teillin, co. Donegal, some 14,000 half-bales of tobacco were said to have been landed in nine months—at a saving of some £182,000 in duty; but 'illicit distillation is also carried on to an extent that I certainly

[1] *Poor Inquiry (Ireland)*, App. E., P.P., 1836, XXXII, p. 211.
[2] *Tenth Report, Revenue arising in Ireland*, P.P., 1824, XI, pp. 309, 363.
[3] Thus in 1823 (according to the Controller-General of the Preventive Water-guard of Ireland) 'it is tobacco that is mainly smuggled: also tea and spirits, but not in large quantities' (ibid., p. 363; see also pp. 309, 312).
[4] Latocnaye, however, went into a number of cabins in Connemara, 'and asked, straight away, for brandy or claret without finding any surprise to be expressed' (*A Frenchman's Walk through Ireland, 1796–7* (trans. John Stevenson, Belfast, n.d.), p. 164).
[5] *Tenth Report, Revenue arising in Ireland*, P.P., 1824, XI, p. 309.

would not have credited had I not been an eye-witness of it'.[1] And 'the people of Inishowen were smugglers and distillers from their cradles'.[2]

In west Cork and Kerry, it seems safe enough to conclude, the illicit distiller had neither succumbed nor graduated to smuggling: whiskey—though it may have yielded some ground to beer[3]—had been ousted by no foreign spirit. That the whiskey was not locally produced, Alexander Nimmo attributed to the marketing of butter: 'in the southern mountainous tracts in Cork and Kerry', he said, 'there is no distillation of illicit whiskey carrying on; the ground is there under pasturage, and the produce chiefly butter'.[4] Poteen, it is true, was mostly made where a deficient rent was excused neither by the remoteness of markets, nor the wretchedness of roads: many a peasant, that is to say, distilled his grain so that he might market it more readily on horseback—or on his own back. But, Nimmo implies, within range of Cork, butter was a marketable product, comparable with poteen in value for bulk, and the more attractive because its producer was spared the alarms and penalties of illicit distillation. It is a plausible theory, undoubtedly relevant to our problem; but it explains only partially the ineffectual appeal of distilling in the less accessible parts of Cork and Kerry. 'The butter of Kerry is almost entirely conveyed by land-carriage to Cork, at the distance of from fifty to seventy miles.'[5] Not

[1] Ibid.
[2] Ibid., p. 313.
[3] There are some indications that by the early nineteenth century the substitution of brewed for distilled liquor had proceeded farther in co. Cork than elsewhere in Ireland. Thus it was said of co. Cork in 1810 that the 'love of liquor is daily taking a more favourable turn: porter has become a powerful rival to whiskey'; in a southern barony, the increased use of porter had been apparent even before the 'suppression' of the distilleries, and 'had experienced so rapid an augmentation since that date that there has been very little injury to agriculture' (H. Townsend, *Statistical Survey of the County of Cork* (Dublin, 1810), pp. 564–5). Around Carrigaline, at about the same time, the people were said not to be addicted to whiskey-drinking; and in the twenties porter was still thought to be ousting spirits in co. Cork—though more because of poverty than anything else (Mason, op. cit., 1816, ii, p. 131; *First Report of the General Board of Health* (Dublin, 1822), pp. 100 ff.). We need, of course, fuller information, and from farther afield, to be certain that Corkmen were, in fact, ahead of their compatriots in forsaking spirits for beer. And even if this should be demonstrated, it might have been a consequence, as much as a cause, of the rarity of local poteen.
[4] *Second Report, S.C. on Labouring Poor*, 1819, P.P., 1829, IV, pp. 104–5.
[5] *S.C. on Employment of the Poor in Ireland*, P.P., 1823, VI, p. 189.

infrequently it was the peasants themselves who made this double journey of a hundred or more miles, and made it without lodging on the way.[1] It was not simply the pull of the Cork butter-market that made them tolerate so much inconvenience; they must also have lacked a readier source of income—poteen-making, that is, was less rewarding than farther north.

'The ground', Nimmo said, 'is under pasturage.' If, in fact, it were shortage of grain that restrained the would-be distiller in Cork and Kerry, this need have been no insuperable obstacle: grain, in these southern areas, might be grown as readily as farther north; but if, as was the case in Donegal and Connemara, local supplies should have proved inadequate, they could have been readily supplemented.[2] But we cannot, I think, agree that lack of the raw material was the real deterrent to distilling in the south-west. As early as 1810, even 'from Glangariffe westward, some places excepted that skirt along the margin of the bay, to the furthest extremity of the Durzey islands, [where] the ground is coarse, mountainous, and rocky beyond description, population, however, even here has made great advances, and with it the tillage necessary to its wants';[3] twenty years later, in Traghenackmy, a mountainous barony in Kerry, 'land formerly grazing, has been converted into tillage'.[4]

Beyond Limerick and Cork, we have argued, topography and the rural economy favoured illicit distillation: it was restricted neither by the prevalence of smuggling nor by the scarcity of grain.

---

[1] Ibid., p. 23.

[2] A witness before a select committee of 1854 was asked if he thought that proximity to the great corn-market in Cork was a deterrent to illicit distillation in the mountains of Kerry and Limerick. 'It may be in one way,' he replied, 'but in the other it ought to be an assistance to it, from the facility with which the corn can be purchased to distil from' (*S.C. on Illicit Distillation*, P.P., 1854, X, qq. 1276–80).

[3] Townsend, op. cit., 1810, p. 393.

[4] *Poor Inquiry (Ireland)*, App. F., P.P., 1836, XXXIII, p. 283. Wakefield thought that the 'principal reason' for the extension of illicit distillation in Fermanagh and adjacent counties was the facility with which people could get corn ground and dried—a consequence of the prominence of oatmeal in the local dietaries (op. cit., 1812, i, pp. 728–9). I think he exaggerates. Nor, in all probability, was any sparsity of mills in the south and east a major deterrent to private distilling: in the north there were millers working almost exclusively for the poteen-makers (see above, p. 4); there were distillers making shift with querns and home-made kilns; and there was no reason why any southerner remote from mills—and even from supplies of grain—should not have made from potatoes an adequate spirit.

ILLICIT DISTILLATION

Butter, to some extent, was sent to market instead of poteen: but more important in explaining the concentration of private distilling in the north and west was the fact that public distilling was as effectively confined to the south and east.

The intending distiller was by no means insensitive to many of the natural and economic deterrents to industry west of the Shannon and in much of Ulster: particularly, it may be, he felt the dearth of capital and the cost of coal. None the less, had the policy of the excise been attuned to Irish conditions, licensed distilling might have been more widely diffused: the difficulty of communications made room for small distilleries serving local markets; and the history of poteen-making shows that such markets were common, impoverished though the Irish were, and unfamiliar with the use of money. It was, in fact, legislation designed to lessen the evasion of duty in the licensed distilling industry that led to its extreme concentration in the south and east.

By the 1770s the licensed distillers were well-placed for defrauding the revenue: they numbered more than a thousand;[1] many of them, inevitably, worked in a small way, often in remote parts of the country, and mostly (it may be) they were men of little substance and no great honesty. The administration, naturally enough, was concerned by its loss of revenue—the more so with the sharp increase in the spirit-duty after 1785.[2] Forgetting (as it too often did) that Irish problems sometimes needed Irish remedies, it sought 'to draw the trade as in England into the hands of persons of respectability and capital':[3] even if the substantial distiller should be no more wary of breaking the law, his lapses, it was hoped, would be more readily detected—for the revenue would have fewer stills to supervise; more of them (proportionately) would be in the towns, and all would be obliged to distil slowly because of the size of their apparatus.[4] From 1779, accordingly, no still holding less than 200 gallons might be licensed; and beyond

---

[1] *Fifth Report, Revenue arising in Ireland*, P.P., 1823, VII, p. 40.

[2] 'It is impossible', Wakefield pointed out, 'for the most rapid writer or printer to keep pace with the progress of the distillery laws in Ireland. Those made in one month, are seldom those of the next' (op. cit., 1812, i, p. 729). In the following paragraphs I have examined only superficially this complicated subject.

[3] *Fifth Report, Revenue arising in Ireland*, P.P., 1823, VII, p. 112. See also Chichester, op. cit., 1818, p. 3.

[4] *Fifth Report, Revenue arising in Ireland*, P.P., 1823, VII, p. 111.

this point the rate of duty varied inversely with the size of the still.[1]

There is no doubt that this reorganization of the industry bore with peculiar severity on the west and north: there capital and enterprise were hard to find, even for the most promising projects: they were unobtainable for the folly of setting up a large distillery to serve a local market—which it would share, in all probability, with a host of unlicensed competitors. Nor did the discrimination against the remoter districts cease in 1809–10 when, once more, stills of any size might be licensed, and the larger stills no longer qualified for remission of duty. Since 1791 (in the endeavour to secure at least a minimum revenue) the spirit duty had been levied, not on the distiller's actual production, but on what was regarded as a reasonable output for the size of still he was using.[2] On the scale of duties current after 1810, small stills promised to pay well—but only if, by rapid and continuous working, they produced something approaching their maximum output.[3] Licensed distilling, then, needed, as before, substantial capital and a substantial market; and, adding to the disabilities of the west, it needed also the intense heat that only coal could give.[4]

There is statistical and literary evidence of the effect of this excise legislation north and west of the line from Limerick to Belfast. In 1777 29 per cent of the spirit-duty was collected in this

[1] From 1804 to 1806 no still containing less than 500 gallons might be licensed; in 1807 the former limit of 200 gallons was reintroduced, and the restriction was abandoned two years later. The following table (ibid., p. 124) shows how the rate of duty varied with the size of the still:

Percentage rebate of duty on stills of various sizes

Capacity of still, in gallons	500–999	1000–1499	1500+
1779	3	6	
1781	5	10	
1785	8	16	
1806	nil	8	16
1810	nil	nil	nil

[2] Ibid.

[3] In 1812, according to the inspector-general of excise, a 66-gallon still was required to pay a monthly duty of £373. 15s. (*Committee on Distilleries*, 1812–13, VI, p. 12).

[4] 'Where the fuel is only turf or peat, which is the case in the north-west of Ireland, it is impossible a still can be worked off with the same expedition or advantage' (*Fifth Report, Revenue arising in Ireland*, P.P., 1823, VII, p. 25). The excise, however, made allowances in favour of turf-burning distilleries, which, in the opinion of a Dublin distiller, fully offset their disadvantages (ibid.).

area; but the stills licensed there in 1822 accounted for only 15 per cent of the total capacity.[1] In Donegal 'the rash attempt made to assimilate the collection of the Irish distillery revenue to that of Great Britain' meant that 'men who would gladly have contributed to the increase of the public Revenue' distilled illicitly, because they did not have the capital needed to comply with the law.[2] And in co. Clare, towards the end of the eighteenth century, there had been 'from 50 to 100 malt-houses at full work, and several small distilleries'; but by the 1820s it is reported: 'not a single malt-house or distillery is now at work in this extensive county. The revenue laws have swept all their establishments away . . . . One five-hundred gallon still in the city of Limerick, supplies the consumption of duty paid spirits in the counties of Clare, Limerick, great part of Kerry, and Tipperary.'[3] The excise, too (at least in co. Clare), was dealing around 1800 with illicit distilleries of considerable size: in 1789, for instance, in a raid on a single still-house at Ogonnelly, parts of five stills were seized, and 'several thousand gallons of pot-ale and singlings' were spilled; and three years later, also at Ogonnelly, 'six extensive distilleries' were raided, with the loss, once more, of some thousands of gallons of singlings.[4] Clearly, the excise was stamping out no ephemeral cottage industry: it was struggling, more probably, with the remnants of an established industry, recently outlawed.

The excise, then, made distilling on a small scale unlawful, when local circumstances in the north and west made it unprofitable on a large scale. The private distillers of these districts benefited, of course, by the cost of bringing parliament whiskey to their local customers. But elsewhere the mere availability of taxed whiskey was hardly the main deterrent to illicit distillation. More probably, what made private distilling unrewarding in the east and south was the superior resources of the public distillers nearby for defrauding the revenue. It was a vain hope of the excise that a small number of substantial licensees would have neither the will nor the opportunity to evade the spirit-duty. On the contrary, their wealth enabled them to buy, at a handsome price, the complicity of the revenue officers; and they were urged to do so by the nature

---
[1] See Figs. 3 and 4, pp. 40–41.
[2] Chichester, op. cit., 1818, p. 3.
[3] *Fifth Report, Revenue arising in Ireland*, P.P., 1823, VII, p. 26.
[4] *Ennis Chronicle*, 12 Feb 1789, 30 Jan 1792; from the collection of newspaper extracts deposited by Miss Katherine Dillon in the library of the I.F.C.

of the duties, their extent and administration. Thus in the early 1820s the distillers 'can afford to bribe largely, and they do so to an incredible extent': the formidable duties tempt them to bribe 'at such a high rate, as no virtue yet found in an excise officer can withstand'; so complex is the administration of the excise that it 'places the distillers so much in the power of the officers, as necessarily to lead to undue intimacy between them'. But the worst abuse seems to have arisen from the principle that the duty a distiller paid varied, not according to his output, but according to the time for which his still was lawfully at work: 'by this means the legal distiller is himself systematically made an illicit trader to the amount he can force from his retort beyond the government charge; to increase this *surplusage* a most ardent fire is kept under the still, during the entire operation';[1] 'for one gallon made for the King, another is made for the Queen'.[2]

That the licensed distillers did, in fact, avoid paying duty on much of their output was admitted by spokesmen both of the excise and of the distillers. According to the Commissioner of Excise, writing in 1823, it was agreed 'both by officers and traders that one-fifth at least (it may be said a much greater proportion) of the spirits made under [the present regulations] get into consumption without payment of duty, and without the possibility of the officers detecting and bringing it to charge in the distillery'. The Commissioner pointed out that the stills then in use might 'work with much greater rapidity than is generally taken into account', and that, in consequence, the duty might be evaded on much more than one-fifth of the product. That this was, in fact, the case is made more plausible by the evidence, before a royal commission, of Robert Haig, a member of a deputation of Dublin distillers. 'Legal distillers', he said, 'can make one-third more than they are charged with ... they can make up to one-half more'. 'This practice', he went on, 'is universal in the trade': the clandestine spirit could undercut taxed spirit by 2s. or 2s. 6d. a gallon; without it, he and his colleagues 'could not have met the private distillers'.[3]

Quite possibly, then, the line from Limerick to Belfast marks,

[1] *Fifth Report, Revenue arising in Ireland*, P.P., 1823, VII, pp. 29, 31, 111, 27.
[2] Rev. John Edgar, professor of divinity in the Royal College, Belfast, *S.C. on Drunkenness*, P.P., 1834, VIII, q. 759. 'In civilized districts', according to the same witness, 'larger quantities of spirituous liquors are usually sent out without paying duty from licensed than unlicensed stills' (ibid., q. 807).
[3] *Fifth Report, Revenue arising in Ireland*, P.P., 1823, VII, p. 112, 45-47.

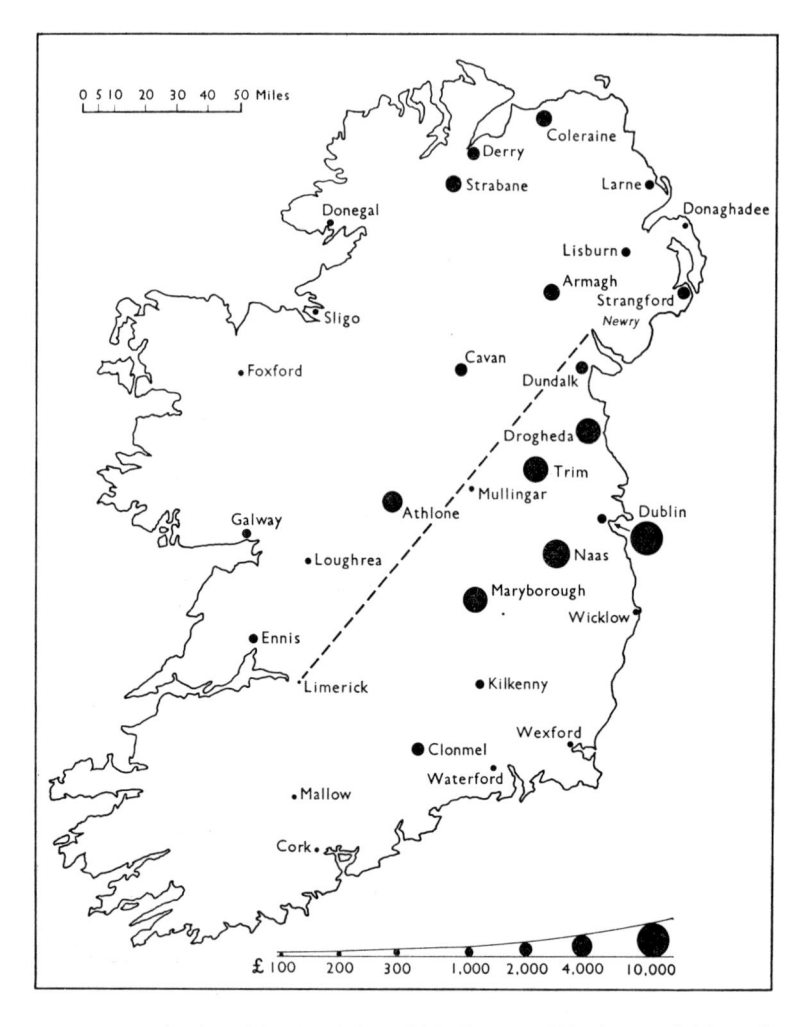

Fig. 3: Duty collected in the various Irish Revenue Districts on Irish-made spirits, 1776-7
(*Journals of the House of Commons of Ireland*, XVIII, 1776-8, pp. 200-1)

ILLICIT DISTILLATION

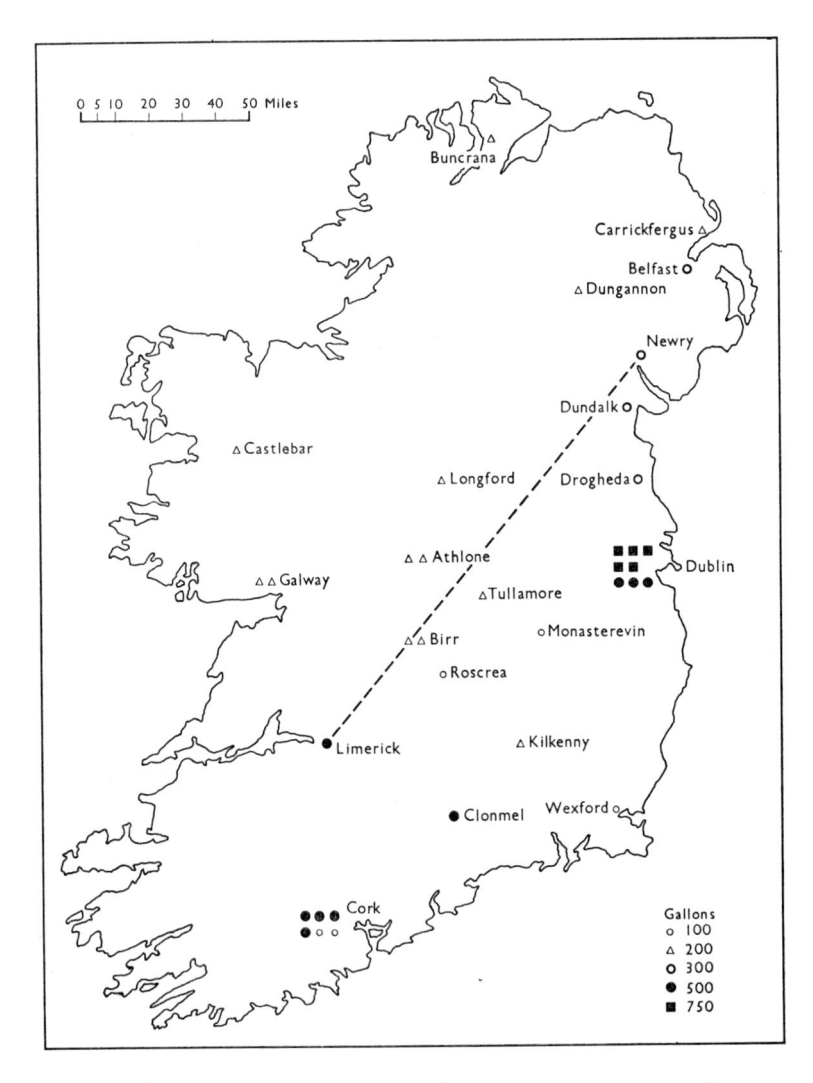

Fig. 4: Stills of various sizes licensed in the various Irish Revenue Districts, 1822
(Fifth Report, Revenue arising in Ireland, P.P., 1823, VII, p. 117)

not the extent of an industry, but the division between two patterns of industrial organization. To the north and west illicit distillation was mostly a peasant industry, harassed by the excise and practised in people's homes, or premises less pretentious. But to the east and south (certainly in the 1820s) much spirit was sold, unlawfully and untaxed, by the licensed distillers—capitalist employers in an urban, 'factory' industry. These were men of real status, tolerated by the excise for their bribes, but favoured also as products of its own policy—a policy not without merit when their competitors (and likeliest successors) were private distillers whose entire output escaped taxation.

The chart on pp. 44-45 shows, over more than a century, the number of illicit stills annually detected in Ireland. Detections, we have stressed already, are an uncertain index of the output of poteen. But there is no reason to dispute two general implications of the chart: that until about the 1870s there was a substantial, though fluctuating, number of illicit distillers, and that, thereafter—more decisively in the new century—their number fell away. We may, then, look for some causes of earlier fluctuations and of later decay.

More than anything else, the fluctuations seems to have been determined by the price of grain, the level of the spirit duties, and the efficiency of the police.[1] Distilling, we have seen, might well be a peasant's readiest means of earning money: less poteen was likely to be made when the corn-merchant offered a better price, more when rising spirit-duties tended to advance the price of poteen. Thus, the alarming grain prices of 1800 and 1801 'put a total stop to distilling' in Tyrone[2]—and elsewhere, no doubt, as well. When the price increase is more modest, 'the farmer calculates whether it would not be better to sell his corn, and incur no risk, than to use it for whiskey'. On the other hand, in the depression following the French wars, there was more distilling, 'because they have no market this year for their grain except private whiskey'.[3] Low prices, too, encouraged distilling in districts where

---

[1] Father Mathew's campaign, no doubt, much restricted the making of poteen in the years after 1838. Uncertainty about the yield of their potatoes was said to make people hesitate to distil their grain (*Seventh Report, Commissioners of Excise*, P.P., 1834, XXV, p. 396). And in years when there was not a 'favourable saving' of turf there might also be some curtailment of distilling (*S.C. on Illicit Distillation*, P.P., 1854, X, qq. 345, 1220).

[2] J. M'Evoy, *Statistical Survey of the County of Tyrone* (Dublin, 1802), p. 162.

[3] *S.C. on Illicit Distillation*, P.P., 1816, IX, pp. 37-38.

ILLICIT DISTILLATION

normally it was not widely practised—in Carlow, for instance, and Leitrim and Wexford.[1] After the Famine, with the increasing use of imported materials, the industry was probably less sensitive to the grain market.[2] But this was a development scarcely perceptible in the sixties. The Commissioners of Inland Revenue pointed out that in 1862, when oats sold for more than 14s. 0d. a barrel, the number of illicit stills detected was 1972; but two years later, when oats had fallen to 12s. 8d., detections rose to 3575. With the return to higher prices in 1866 and 1867 the number of detections fell away once more.[3]

The profit of illicit distilling moved, of course, with the level of the spirit-duty. And this was a capricious master—varying one year in three between 1790 and 1860, and varying from some third of the retail price of legal spirit to about two-thirds.[4] In 1823 the duty was halved: now, according to a licensed distiller in Limerick, '[we] can meet the illicit distiller on fair terms'; 'in the last month a demand has come from a number of villages that never took any before'; 'acknowledged illicit distillers have taken to buying their spirit and there is no poteen on sale in Limerick'.[5] In other districts, too, there was a lull in private distilling until 1830, when nearly a shilling had been added to the duty.[6] Four years later, James Jameson was grateful for the removal of this addition: shortly afterwards he had heard of no recent example of poteen being sold in Dublin; much less, he believed, was being made throughout the country, and none at all in some formerly distilling areas.[7] At the same time, around Lurgan, 'the small private stills ... were nearly all put down, not being able to compete at the present low duty'; even on the fringe of Inishowen a Derry distiller noted 'a material check to illicit distillation'.[8] In 1842 the additional shilling was restored once more: again there was 'a

---

[1] *Poor Inquiry (Ireland)*, App. E., P.P., 1836, XXXII, pp. 45, 91, 139.
[2] Coyne, op. cit., 1902, p. 500.
[3] *Report, Commissioners of Inland Revenue*, P.P., 1870, XX, Pt. i, p. 28. Sometimes, even though sound corn were scarce and dear, damaged grain, fit for distilling, might be cheaply available (*S.C. on Illicit Distillation*, P.P., 1854, X, q. 153).
[4] *Seventh Report, Commissioners of Excise*, P.P., 1834, XXV, Pt. i, p. 66, Pt. ii, p. 93; *Report, Commissioners of Excise*, P.P., 1870, XX, Pt. ii, p. 9.
[5] *Tenth Report, Revenue arising in Ireland*, P.P., 1824, XI, p. 59.
[6] *Seventh Report, Commissioners of Excise*, P.P., 1834, XXV, pp. 376, 449.
[7] Ibid., Pt. ii, p. 95.
[8] Ibid., pp. 93, 97.

ILLICIT DISTILLATION

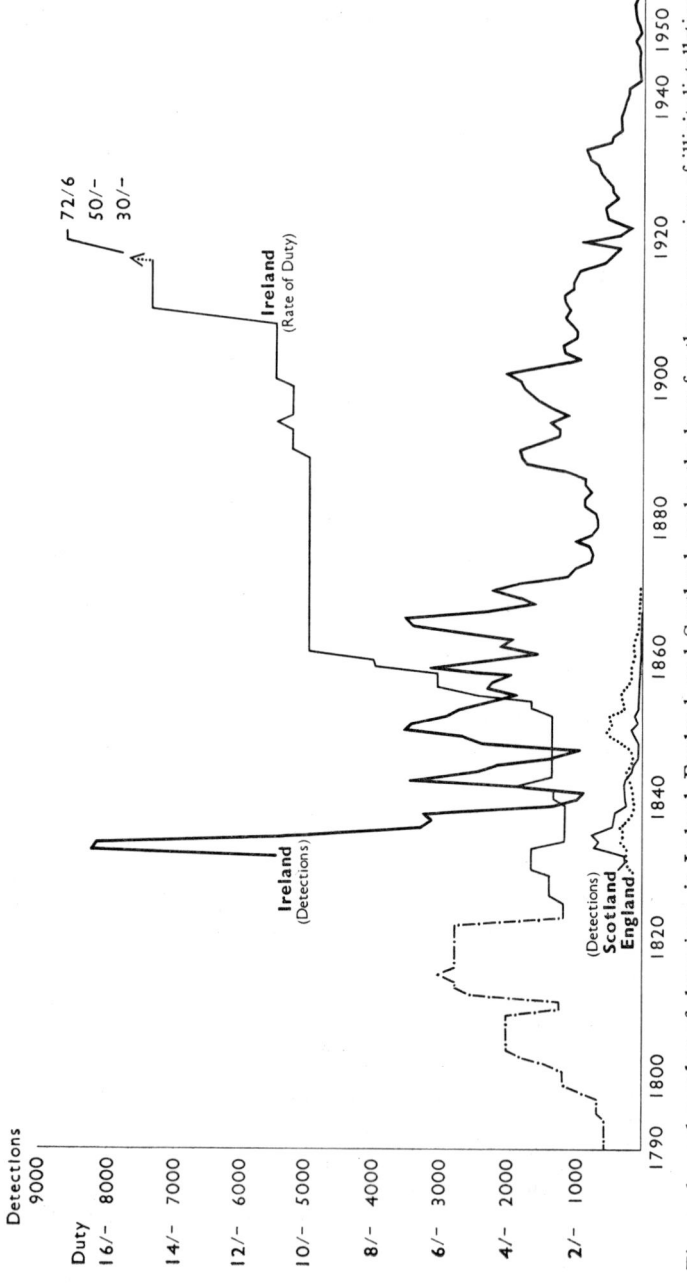

Fig. 5: Annual number of detections, in Ireland, England, and Scotland, under the laws for the suppression of illicit distillation. Rate of duty per proof gallon on spirit distilled in Ireland, 1790–1921

ILLICIT DISTILLATION

Notes:

Detections

(1) No records are said to be available for England and Scotland before 1830, and only imperfect records for Ireland before 1832 (P.P. 1852-3, XCIX, pp. 551, 559, 561).
(2) Years ending, 1830-53, 5 Jan in following year, 1855-, 31 Mar, same year.
(3) In no decade after 1870 were there more detections in England or Scotland than in the eighteen-sixties.

Duty

(1) The duties shown for the years 1790-1823 were levied according to the presumed, not the actual, output of a still: see p. 37.
(2) From 1915, in addition to the duty shown, there was a surcharge of 1s. or 1s. 6d. a proof gallon on spirit not warehoused or warehoused for less than three years.

Detections:

1830-52,	P.P. 1852-3, XCIX, pp. 551, 559, 561.
1853-69,	*Report, Commissioners Inland Revenue,* Pt. ii, P.P. 1870, XX, p. 12.
1870-85,	*Twenty-eighth Report, Commissioners Inland Revenue,* P.P. 1884-5, XXII, p. 150.
1886-1900,	Annual Reports, Commissioners Inland Revenue.
1901-22,	*First Report, Customs and Excise,* P.P. 1910, XXII, p. 31, and subsequent reports.
1923-56,	26 counties, Dr. M. D. McCarthy, Director of the Central Statistics Office, Dublin: Northern Ireland, 1923-39, *Annual reports, Customs and Excise;* 1940-56, Mr. R. C. Jarvis, Librarian, H.M. Customs and Excise.

Duty:

1790-1834,	*Seventh Report, Commissioners of Excise,* P.P. 1834, XXV, pp. 20, 42, 66.
1835-69,	*Report, Commissioners Inland Revenue,* Pt. ii, P.P. 1870, XX, p. 9.
1870-85,	*Twenty-eighth Report, Commissioners Inland Revenue,* P.P. 1884-5, XXII, p. 147.
1886-1921,	Mr. R. C. Jarvis, Librarian, H.M. Customs and Excise.

great increase in private distilling'—so great that in the following year the shilling was again withdrawn.[1]

So much for fluctuations in the poteen industry. Our next problem is to account for its decay. The malignant economy that led to the Famine did not long survive it; within fifty years, where it had not already given way to a milder order, its more vicious features, at least, were softened. The poteen industry, an integral part of the old economy, disintegrated with it. More than anything else its independence of the landlord distinguished the new society. And formerly it was the landlord's exactions, which, directly or indirectly, had set many a still to work: when rent was elastic, a tenant was probably too poor to satisfy lawfully a sharpened desire for drink; the profit of distilling was irresistible, the risk, of little consequence. Socially, by the new century, the landlord was becoming a curiosity, economically, the passive recipient of a dwindling charge; and, as he receded, the peasant acquired new authority; he was made, in effect, the owner of his farm, able to work it as he pleased, to add field to field, confident that his family would profit by his industry. In his farm, therefore (and elsewhere too), the peasant came to have an assured source of income, no less lucrative than distilling; and a man, proud of the newly-won status of landowner, thought twice before incurring the risk of imprisonment.

The ousting of the landlord tended also to reduce the number of private distillers by lessening the demand for their produce. 'Once a man becomes the owner of land he drinks far less.'[2] The

---

[1] *S.C. on Illicit Distillation*, P.P., 1854, X, q. 2063. Most of the evidence quoted in this paragraph comes from licensed distillers—men tempted, it may be, to exaggerate the advantages of lowering the duty on their product.

[2] *Appendix to First Report, Royal Commission on Congestion in Ireland*, P.P., 1906, XXXII, q. 3575. The following table shows the *per capita* consumption of taxed spirits in Ireland (in gallons); foreign spirits are taken into account only from 1901. Spirit drinking, no doubt, declined more sharply than these figures indicate, because they do not include the consumption of poteen:

1857	1·139
1860	1·015
1870	0·923
1880	0·946
1901	1·09
1910	0·63
1922	0·37

(1857–70 from *Report, Commissioners of Inland Revenue*, P.P., 1870, XX, p. 19; 1880, *Twenty-Eighth Report, Commissioners of Inland Revenue*, P.P., 1884–5, XXII, p. 154; 1901 and 1910, *First Report, Commissioners of Customs and Excise*, P.P., 1910, XXII; 1922, *Thirteenth Report*, P.P., 1922, session 2, II, p. 163).

ILLICIT DISTILLATION 47

lazy, improvident tenant-at-will, many other pleasures beyond his reach, had little resistance to drink: but his landowning son might measure its cost by pleasures forgone; he might, indeed, make a bogey of its cost, so luridly did his well-wishers portray it. In some dioceses the Catholic who made or sold poteen incurred spiritual penalties: by the 'nineties, in consequence, private stills and shebeen houses were said to have been virtually eliminated from Donegal[1]—territory where formerly they were probably as common as anywhere. The civil authorities, too, treated the poteen-maker with new rigour. Formerly he had fallen within the province of the revenue police, local men for the most part, 'by no means inveterate haters' of the smuggler.[2] But in 1855 the Royal Irish Constabulary was enlisted in the cause of the revenue:[3] 'they never used snuff, the better to smell out poteen'; 'their manner of searching [was] more shameless and outrageous and... their manner of getting information was at once degrading and base in the extreme'.[4]

The illicit distiller lost ground also to his licensed competitors. By the 'nineties the quality of his own spirit had deteriorated: the more he was harassed by Church and State, the more his workmanship suffered; the less grain that was grown in Ireland, the more he depended on inferior materials. And as poteen became less palatable, parliament whiskey of an improved quality became

---

[1] Congested Districts Board, *Confidential Reports of Inspectors* (*c*. 1894) (in the National Library of Ireland), p. 134. By 1909—in consequence of 'the authoritative act of a very fearless bishop'—'a drop of it could scarcely be found for love or money in all Tyrconnell' (Gwynn, op. cit., 1909, p. 90). Dr. John K. O'Doherty seems to have been the first Catholic bishop to legislate against illicit distillation: in his diocese of Derry (which includes the Inishowen peninsula and eastern Donegal) the distilling and drinking of poteen have been 'reserved' sins since 1892 (they are, that is, sins for which the bishop, not the ordinary confessor, may give absolution). Early in the present century Dr. Patrick O'Donnell, Bishop of Raphoe (western Donegal), although not legislating against poteen-making, told his priests that he wished penitents to be sent to him. Dr. William MacNeely, who succeeded him in 1922, has formally made illicit distillation a reserved sin; so also has Dr. Eugene O'Callaghan, Bishop of Clogher (cos. Fermanagh and Monaghan), since 1943. It seems to be generally agreed that this legislation has been of decisive importance in all but ending illicit distillation in these three dioceses. (I am much indebted for the information in this paragraph to the Reverend Hugh B. O'Neill, and the Reverend John J. Silke.)

[2] Dorian, op. cit., 1890, p. 335.

[3] *Report, Commissioners of Inland Revenue*, P.P., 1870, XX, p. 28.

[4] Dorian, op. cit., 1890, p. 339.

more readily available. More of it was produced; better communications facilitated its distribution; and people were less resentful of its price as they became more familiar with the use of money. The administration of the excise, moreover, no longer put a premium on the production of bad spirit; by 1883 such was the repute of the Irish distillers that twice as much of their whiskey was sold in Scotland as Scotch in Ireland.[1] Nor, of course, was parliament whiskey the only substitute for poteen: between 1852 and 1885 the consumption of taxed beer per head of the population increased almost five-fold.[2]

In the first year of the present century 2000 illicit stills were detected; since then there have been fluctuations, but never since 1943 has the number of detections exceeded 200. 'The troubles', no doubt, encouraged poteen-making;[3] but the new governments wished their gunmen sober as well as disarmed, and the increase in the number of detections after 1922 may reflect greater vigilance by the police. While the distiller's trade became more precarious at home, the dazzling rewards promised by Prohibition in the United States tempted him to emigrate. During the Second World War, although parliament whiskey was scarce and dear, private distilling seems to have fallen away—presumably because of the difficulty of getting rationed sugar and treacle and of getting a still mended or made.[4] Some years after the return of peace a Dublin newspaper pointed to signs of a revival: poteen of a kind, it said, could be bought for £2 a gallon, one-fifth of the price of taxed whiskey; stills might be owned co-operatively; the distillers had their agents in Dublin; many a small publican did well on the sale of poteen; and when American tourists were about it might earn dollars for Ireland.[5]

[1] *Twenty-eighth Report, Commissioners of Inland Revenue*, P.P., 1884-5, XXII, p. 149. In 1884 Ireland was sending nearly as much spirit to England and Scotland as Scotland was sending to England and Ireland; yet in 1869 experts from Scotland had been nearly four times as great as those from Ireland (ibid.).
[2] In the year 1852 it was 0·09 barrels; in 1885 0·443 (ibid., p. 154; *Report, Commissioners of Inland Revenue*, P.P., 1870, XX, p. 23).
[3] *Tales of the R.I.C.* (Edinburgh, 1921), p. 140. But in Mayo, at least, the Sinn Fein leaders were worried by the abundance of poteen. 'Any men who were now found with stills in their possession by the Sinn Fein police were paraded before the congregation outside the chapels after Mass on Sunday morning, the stills broken up with hammers, the owners heavily fined, and then let go with a warning of much severer penalties if they were found guilty of the same offence again' (ibid., p. 146).
[4] Swan, op. cit., 1947, p. 120. [5] *The Sunday Press*, Dublin, 28 Sept 1952.

ILLICIT DISTILLATION

Until after the Famine poteen-making was no amusing trifle in Irish life: when craftsmanship in Ireland was ill-regarded, her pot-stilled whiskey, at its best, was unexcelled; it was amongst the most widely distributed of Irish manufactures; few industries gave so much employment, none gave more pleasure. The coincidence of wretchedness and gaiety was a commonplace of the traveller: there was pleasure to be drawn from marriage, religion, and the potato; but few pleasures in Ireland were neither heightened nor induced by drink. 'There are no dry bargains',[1] a visitor remarked; fair-day, in consequence, was more evidently a social than an economic occasion. Poteen enlivened the story-teller and his audience, the fiddler and his dancers, the game-cock and his admirers. Birth, marriage, and death were marked by drinking as well as religious duties. Into the present century poteen in Connemara was said to be 'associated in a strange degree with the expression of . . . the religious feelings of the people.' There was plausibility, certainly, in an economic link with religion. At a funeral, for instance, contributions to the priest's collection might be regarded as 'indirect payment' for the poteen drunk at the wake. 'If the "altars" [collections] were discontinued, the copious supply of liquor would cease. The priests understand the relation of the two customs, and some of the young clergy are trying to stop the "altars". At a funeral in a Connemara village, a young curate, disgusted with the drunkenness, threw down the money that had been collected, and told the people that it was the price of devilry.'[2]

By the 1830s, when flax-spinning was largely mechanized, no cottage industry, it may well be, earned more than distilling; in the previous decade—so a Dublin distiller maintained—poteen accounted for half, perhaps two-thirds, of all the spirit consumed in Ireland.[3] A force of more than a thousand officers and men was recruited solely to restrict its production;[4] their diligence—but also the extent of the industry—is shown by the seizure of 16,000 stills in the two years 1833 and 1834; and during the following forty years seizures, on the average, remained between two and three thousand a year.[5]

[1] S.C. on Drunkenness, P.P., 1834, VIII, q. 4651.
[2] Irish Nation, leading article, 17 Apr 1909.
[3] Fifth Report, Revenue arising in Ireland, P.P., 1823, VII, p. 49.
[4] S.C. on Illicit Distillation, P.P., 1854, X, p. iii.
[5] See Fig. 5, pp. 44–45.

The rent of a mercenary landlordism draws on subsidiary earnings as well as the yield of the land; illicit distillation, there is little doubt, allowed the payment of rent out of all proportion to the quality and location of the land. But the subtlety that evaded the gauger served also when rent was due: the making (as well as the drinking) of poteen might alleviate a peasant's distress; the still—or the shebeen—helped him to establish his children;[1] in extreme misfortune, when emigration was unusual and emigrants' remittances unknown, it might be his only resource.

The critics of illicit distillation blamed it for more than excessive drinking: it saddled the country, they believed, with unnecessary taxes; it brought the law and the government into disrepute; 'this baneful practice', a Donegal rector maintained, tended 'to promote dissipation, perjury, rebellion, revenge and murder.'[2] The exchequer, certainly, was a substantial loser: in the early 'fifties more than a quarter of the Irish revenue was drawn from the duties on malt and spirit; yet these duties may have been evaded as often as they were paid—in spite of the expenditure of some £45,000 a year on the revenue police.[3] Nor is there any doubt that other malefactors profited by the poteen-maker's popularity. 'A bottle for the sergeant' and a crown for the revenue officer led on to grosser venality. Warmth, drink, and company, all drew men to the private distilleries: they were the meeting-places 'for all the loose and disorderly characters in the neighbourhood, where half-intoxicated they discuss politics, and regulate rents, tithes and taxes.'[4] Illicit distillation, says a member for Clare, 'is the fertile source of half the crime committed in this unfortunate country.'[5] But criticism might have been more fruitful if some of it were deflected from the poteen-maker to the folly of passing excise legislation that was unenforceable as well as unpopular.

[1] 'When they marry—for Malthus and restrictions upon population are no more recognized in Erris than the Pope is by a modern Methodist—they will obtain a patch of mountain from their patron, erect a cabin, construct a still, and setting political dogmas at defiance, then and there produce most excellent whisky, and add to the "seven millions" considerably' (Maxwell, op. cit., 1834, p. 100). The drinking, as well as the distilling, of poteen was thought to quicken the growth of population—by making people 'less prudent, less wise, less cautious in contracting early and improvident marriages' (James Johnson, *Tour in Ireland* (1844), p. 169).
[2] Mason, op. cit., 1816, ii, p. 166.
[3] *S.C. on Illicit Distillation*, P.P., 1854, X, pp. iii–iv.
[4] *Fifth Report, Revenue arising in Ireland*, P.P., 1823, VII, p. 34.
[5] Ibid., p. 26.

II

ILLEGITIMACY BEFORE THE FAMINE[1]

IN the Irish countryside before—and probably long after—the Famine it was the lucky mother, or likely mother, of an illegitimate child who was not shunned by her neighbours and despised, if not cast off, by her own family. Here and there, it is true, little might be made of her mishap: perhaps too many of her neighbours were in the same boat for any to bear much opprobrium;[2] or they were 'too much reduced and in too great poverty' to register further degradation.[3] There was lurking sympathy, too, for a girl deceived by promise of marriage; and if seduced by a gentleman she might be forgiven, because she had 'weighty reasons for her yielding', or even 'looked up to on account of the money'.[4] In a tolerant parish, by avoiding further lapses, by generally seemly behaviour, she might, over the years, wear down her disgrace.[5] But even the

---

[1] The main source of this essay is evidence collected by the Commissioners for inquiring into the Condition of the Poorer Classes in Ireland, and published in 1835-6. The Commissioners began their enquiries by circulating more than 7500 sets of 'statistical questions' to magistrates, police superintendents, clergy of various persuasions, 'and to such educated persons as have been named as able and willing to give us assistance'. More than 3000 sets of replies were returned, descriptive of 1100 parishes. Replies to questions on illegitimacy were published in Supplement to Appendix A, *First Report of Commissioners for Inquiring into the Condition of the Poorer Classes in Ireland*, P.P., 1835, XXXII, 811–1219, referred to below as 'Supp. App. A'.

The Commission, needing much additional information, and deeming it impracticable or undesirable to obtain it by sending its own members on circuit or by bringing witnesses to Dublin, appointed instead itinerant Assistant Commissioners. They sought persons 'possessing intelligence in tracing the truth, diligence in pursuit of it, patience in examining a variety of persons of different views and impartiality in deciding between different statements'. To depend on Irishmen, they felt, risked partiality or its imputation; to depend on others risked ignorance of the language, feelings, and habits of the Irish. Assistant Commissioners worked, therefore, in pairs, one Irish, one British. The Commissioners, before drafting their assistants' instructions, took oral testimony, and searched private and parliamentary publications for evidence on the condition of the Irish and the causes of that condition. Assistant Commissioners

[2] App. A, 111 (Limerick); 103 (Cork). [3] Ib. 116 (Cork).
[4] Ib. 75 (Carlow); 67 (Galway); 94 (Clare). [5] Ib. 72 (Sligo).

tolerant, drawn into a quarrel, 'always charge her with her shame'.[1]

By and large, however, there was small tolerance of any woman's 'failure in chastity'.[2] There could 'not be a more disgraceful event'; she forfeited 'for life her character and caste'; she was 'despised by her equals', 'slighted and shunned by all her former acquaintances'; no respectable man would be seen courting her; nobody at a dance, it was said, 'will step out with her as long as he can find another'.[3] Her 'stain', moreover, was 'never forgotten': for twenty years it weighed on her family; even her children's children bore some of the brunt.[4] Parents, unusually compassionate, might allow her to live on uneasily at home, her 'frailty ... ever a constant source of bickering and reproach'; but, more probably, ashamed of her and embittered by the disgrace she brought on the family, they turned her adrift.[5]

More (we shall see) than abhorrence and harsh treatment of the unmarried mother lessened the appeal and possibility of premarital sexual adventure. Most unmarried peasant girls, living still with their parents, seem to have been effectively restrained. The reports certainly suggest that unmarried girls, pregnant for the first time,

---

were 'positively required' to probe as deeply as they thought necessary: 'Minute Heads of Inquiry', in a form that 'did not anticipate a negative or affirmative', were intended, not to restrict the assistants' interrogation, but to ensure that 'at each examination no part of the subject, however minute, which was known to be worthy of examination', would be omitted.

To ensure that evidence heard by the Assistant Commissioners would be full, impartial, and fairly reported, they were required, at each local examination, to request the attendance of persons 'from every grade of society', from every religion and political party; to examine each witness in the others' presence, and on the understanding that evidence not contradicted was generally accepted; to record the evidence (with their own observations on it) as it was being given, putting it as nearly as possible in the witnesses' own words; and to send to Dublin the minutes of one examination before proceeding to the next.

In all, the Assistant Commissioners conducted about 120 local examinations, one in each barony of seventeen counties, three of the counties being in Ulster, four in Connaught, and five each in Leinster and Munster. Most of the evidence given to the Assistant Commissioners on illegitimacy appears in Appendix A, *First Report, Condition of the Poorer Classes in Ireland*, P.P., 1835, XXXII, pp. 15–809 and in Addenda to Appendix A, P.P., 1836, XXX, pp. 557–80, referred to below as 'App. A' and 'Add. App. A' (*First Report* ... , P.P., 1835, XXXII, pp. 8–11).

[1] Ib. 71, 72 (Sligo); 108 (Cork); ib., Supp. App. A, 983 (Cork).
[2] Ib., App. A, 91 (Clare).
[3] Ib. 126 (Donegal); 66, 67 (Gal.); 68 (Mayo); 92, 95 (Clare).
[4] Ib. 125 (Don.); 68 (Mayo); 126 (Don.).
[5] Ib. 70 (Roscommon); 108 (Kerry); 52 (Mayo); 126 (Don.); 80 (Kildare); 94 (Kerry).

were mostly servants, living with their employers;[1] they became so, partly perhaps, because they had harsh, unsatisfying lives, somewhat removed from the restraint and consolation of parents, priest, and friends; essentially (to contemporaries) because of the way they were lodged. Thus, in co. Clare, while 'farmers' [unmarried] daughters are rarely known to become pregnant', 'farmers' servants ... are particularly exposed to danger from the promiscuous manner in which such servants, both male and female, are obliged, from want of other accommodation, to sleep together';[2] the wonder, indeed, was 'that it does not happen oftener in consequence of the promiscuous manner in which male and female servants are permitted by farmers to sleep together in barns and outhouses'.[3] Similarly, in Derry, 'women are generally led astray while in service, and there, when their fortune is broken, become careless'; the mothers, in Tipperary, 'are chiefly servant maids in farmers' houses'; mostly, in Limerick, 'farmers' servant girls'; in Cork, 'very often they are servants'.[4] 'Strolling women', vagrants and prostitutes, often driven to the life by bearing one illegitimate child, probably bore many of the second and subsequent illegitimate children.[5]

The fathers, though many seem to have been fellow servants, indoor or outdoor, or soldiers, ranged more generally up the social scale, including farmers' sons, farmers themselves (those, not least, deserted by their wives or widowed),[6] and gentlemen. The 'gentleman's miss' seems to have been a familiar figure up and down the country.[7] Still today, according to the Waterford folklore, a landlord 'taking a fancy to a good-looking girl, would wait till he found her going somewhere alone, then he would take her away on his horse and keep her locked up in his mansion.'[8] 'Laxity of the kind', it has indeed been suggested, 'was the curse of our

[1] Ib. 111 (Lim.); 115–6 (Cork); 93 (Clare).
[2] Ib. 91 (Clare).   [3] Ib. 100 (Clare).
[4] Add. App. A, 566 (Londonderry); App. A, 112 (Tipperary); 111 (Lim.); 105–6 (Cork).
[5] Ib. 67 (Longford); Add. App. A, 565–6 (Derry).
[6] App. A, pp. 105–6 (Cork); 111 (Lim.).
[7] Ib. 103 (Cork); 109 (Kerry); 67 (Gal.); 111 (Lim.); 89 (Long.) etc. Wakefield referred to the 'prevalent custom ... of females of the indigent class, having illicit intercourse with their landlords'. But the practice, he maintained 'in general, is the precursor of a marriage' (Edward Wakefield, *An Account of Ireland, Statistical and Political* (1812), II, p. 579).
[8] Irish Folklore Commission, MS. S1157, 488.

[landlord] class in old days, and caused half the disloyalty and rebellion of the country.'[1]

What became of the unmarried mother-to-be? Failing marriage to the father of her child or somebody else, she might live with her parents, friends or relations; if, unusually, she had the means, she might emigrate;[2] she might go into, or remain, in service; take to begging or prostitution—sometimes supplementing any other income by an allowance from her child's father.

Marriage to the father was perhaps her likeliest fate. Affection apart, she was drawn to it by the difficulty of marrying otherwise, or living peacefully unmarried. The father, too, was persuaded to marry by his own, and his society's, sense of propriety; by priest and magistrate; by the girl's friends; perhaps, even, by his own parents. A negligent father might be cold-shouldered by the girl and her sympathizers, forced to leave the parish,[3] or more sharply brought to heel: unmarried mothers in Kildare were 'continually brought before the magistrates charged with assaulting, breaking the windows, etc. of men' unconcerned by their plight; in Carlow, too, offenders' windows were broken, their houses and haggards burned down.[4] A Galway priest hoped his erring parishioners married 'from a principle of conscience and honour'; he could not deny, however, 'that the influence of the roman-catholic clergy assisted much to bring about this desirable result'; 'in all cases', he said, 'where a single man has seduced a female, whose character was free from any other taint, we use every means in our power to induce him to make the only adequate reparation in his power, by marrying her.'[5] This, no doubt, was near enough the position of most clergy.[6] Some, however, protesting too often that they would celebrate no 'subsequent marriage',[7] had tied their hands when occasion arose; and others, less doctrinaire, would not insist on a marriage threatened with disaster by the physical or mental deficiency of one of its partners, or their social disparity.[8]

'By the influence of a magistrate and a clergyman, any man

---

[1] 'Andrew Merry' [Mildred H. G. Darby], *The Green Country* (1902), p. 189.
[2] App. A, op. cit., 106 (Don.).
[3] Add. App. A, 562 (Long.); *S.C. on State of the Poor in Ireland*, P.P., 1830, VII, q. 1727.
[4] Ib. 79, 80 (Kild.); 77 (Carl.).
[5] Ib. 66 (Gal.).
[6] Ib. 103 (Cork); 106 (Antrim); 50 (Carl.); 70 (W'meath); 113 (Derry).
[7] Ib. 54, 70 (Rosc.).   [8] Ib. 77, 83 (Clare); 50 (Gal.).

ILLEGITIMACY BEFORE THE FAMINE

might be forced into marriage';[1] the magistrate's sanction in such a matter was hardly less telling than the priest's. The girl might name before him on oath the father of her expected child: to the magistrate, her declaration was some safeguard against infanticide; for the girl, it scotched allegations of indiscriminate liaisons and strengthened her claim to marry the man she named.[2] Fathers, too, sometimes yielded rather than risk a magistrate's order for maintenance; and, with rape punishable, and sometimes punished, by hanging, a woman, rightly or wrongly swearing rape, but dropping the charge, might 'marry out of the dock' the man she had named:[3] ' "Please your honour" ', one such girl explained, ' "I intended to have made a hanging business of it." '[4]

A girl not marrying the man by whom she was pregnant was unlikely to marry another—not, certainly, without overcoming one way or another the abhorrence her plight provoked. ' "No man would marry a woman that had a bastard, unless a very forlorn man entirely" ': a soldier sometimes stooped so low; 'some person as profligate as herself'; a man needing money to emigrate; an old man who 'had nobody to wash his linen'; 'an Englishman and a pensioner'.[5] But (so it was said) 'no Irishman would demean himself by such an act.'[6] She might, however, win grudging recognition by 'several years of moral and industrious life', marrying then 'a man for ever after looked upon as having demeaned himself'.[7] But she proved her worth more swiftly and beneficially by money, land, or stock, found by her father, friends, or seducer. ' "In the poverty of this country a small sum of money forms a great temptation" '; ' "the eagerness to procure land is so great in consequence of its being the only source of support to the peasantry, that nothing is so likely to procure a partner for such a girl as the temptation of a small farm" '; ' "if women of that kind had money, they would get husbands flying." '[8]

Thus in co. Clare (and doubtless elsewhere) a girl's relations sometimes made up a dowry 'to induce someone far inferior to her

[1] Ib. 65 (Gal.).   [2] Ib. 118 (Ant.); 104 (Cork); 108 (Kerry).
[3] Ib. 68 (Mayo); 79, 81 (Kildare); 66 (Gal.). In the seven years, 1823–9, 65 men in Ireland were sentenced to death for rape; thirteen were executed (*S.C. on State of the Poor in Ireland*, P.P., 1830, VII, App. (K.1), p. 138.)
[4] App. A, 79 (Kild.).
[5] App. A, 101 (Cork); 123 (Don.); 88 (Long.); 76 (Carl.); 83 (Long.).
[6] Ib. 78 (Kild.).
[7] Ib. 71 (Rosc.).
[8] Ib. 68 (Mayo); 94 (Clare); 88 (Cork).

in condition to marry her'; and the father, now and then, 'gave a much larger sum of money than he would otherwise have given as a portion... to cover up the disgrace of his daughter.'[1] But servant girls, needing rehabilitation more than others, rarely had fathers or friends of much tolerance or wealth. The fortunes, therefore, not infrequently found for them, were found for the most part by their seducers. Such endowment, if the man could afford it, was 'the usual way of getting rid of them'. Thus, making over five cows to his former mistress, a Clare gentleman got 'a young man her inferior in station to marry her'; other erring girls were settled by twenty or more pounds, or by a few acres and a cottage. It took £100 to find a husband for a girl with two children; a Carlow gentleman, giving two brothers a farm apiece, persuaded one to marry his mistress, the other her daughter; and a Westmeath man was 'in the habit of pensioning off women in that way'.[2]

Work, begging, prostitution: of these three resources of the pregnant girl estranged from her family, not otherwise befriended, nor likely to marry, work was the least and least inviting. If, when she became pregnant, she were working in a family with some respect for her and some independence, she might be kept on, 'doing her work as well as she can'.[3] But, more often, she was 'sure to be turned out of doors'.[4] And other employers, in a buyers' market, looked her up and down. No respectable family would take her, though the less respectable sometimes profited by her misfortune; in a Clare report she was given outdoor work readily enough, 'but in consideration of her being somewhat occupied in attending to her child, she is obliged to accept half wages'; and sometimes in Cork she 'gets into a farmer's house, and works for herself and her child, supported without any wages; and she is often a great slave for it'.[5] When potatoes were being set and picked, the girl who could leave her child had the chance of the odd week's work.[6] Failing domestic and farm work, chances of employment were few. When she had weaned her child, or if he

[1] Ib. 94, 92, 93 (Clare).
[2] Ib. 72 (Sligo); Add. App. A, 563 (Meath); App. A, 98 (Clare); 73, 74 (Carl.); 64 (Kild.); 89 (Long.); 87 (Wexford); 67 (Gal.); 77 (Carl.); Add. App. A, 563 (Westmeath).
[3] App. A, 112 (Tipp.).
[4] Ib. 90 (Clare).
[5] Ib. 108 (Cork); 94 (Clare); 103 (Cork).
[6] Ib. 96 (Clare).

ILLEGITIMACY BEFORE THE FAMINE

died, she might wet-nurse a motherless child—but on sufferance: 'a man don't like to give such suck to his child'.[1] She might, too, travel the country with her child, spinning wool, gathering wayside manure, peddling eggs or fish, tobacco or poteen; she might try her hand at extortion, 'threatening to father her child' on 'respectable shopkeepers'.[2] But, hardly making ends meet, she was half beggar already and trainee prostitute.

Begging and prostitution were successive as well as complementary occupations, and the progress might be either way: they 'follow the barracks while they are well-looking and are obliged to beg when they have lost their good looks'; but elsewhere 'those of them who have to resort to begging generally become prostitutes'.[3] The girl, begging her livelihood and her child's, rarely begged at home:[4] ashamed, perhaps, of her plight and the circumstances leading to it, she shrank from former friends; and strangers more readily mistook her for an object of charity, for deserted wife or widow. Harshly treated by neighbours, priest, and parents, the girl taking to begging might already be less restrained by society, religion, and family. In a strange country, her most sympathetic companionship might well be that of girls like herself, before dabbling in prostitution: 'having misbehaved themselves once', moreover, 'they have less shame afterwards'.[5] Prostitution, then, might no longer be the abyss; if alms were sluggish, it might be the only chance for her child and herself. Not surprisingly, therefore, 'most of those females who infest the streets of cities are such persons'; 'almost all prostitution may be traced to that cause'.[6] A priest, in his five years in a Longford parish, knew of 'nine or ten cases where girls gave themselves up to prostitution from downright necessity, after they had struggled a year or two to support themselves and children, and in many cases had resisted tempting offers';[7] and in co. Clare the

> unfortunate creatures ... are first driven from their cabins; they then rear a wretched hovel of sods against some ditch, which, as soon as it is discovered by the farmer on whose ground it is, is immediately pulled

---

[1] Ib. 116 (Cork).
[2] Ib. 104, 105-15 (Cork).   [3] Ib. 111 (Lim.); 118 (Ant.).
[4] Ib. 60-61 (Carl.); 94 (Clare); 79 (Kil.); 74 (Carl.).
[5] Ib. 128 (Derry).
[6] Ib. 84 (W'meath); 74 (Carl.). See also 67 (Gal.); 68 (Mayo); 114 (Ant.); 108 (Cork); 109 (Kerry).
[7] App. A, 562 (Long.).

down to prevent the corruption of his children and his servants: she then goes to another place and finds the whole neighbourhood leagued against her; she is then compelled to lead a wretched and vagabond life, and, gradually rendered reckless by her suffering and by a consciousness of her degradation, she instructs her children in every kind of vice, and ultimately takes refuge in a town, where she soon terminates her miserable existence.[1]

The man by whom a girl was pregnant, if he refused to marry her, probably hesitated also to help her support their child: though he admitted paternity, she had no legal right to filiation payments; at best, a sympathetic court, straining, even disregarding, the law, might induce the man (or his relations) to make some payment. Here and there, it is true, the farmer with a child by a servant treated him as his other children, even when drafting his will: locally, in Derry, father and mother sometimes took the child in alternate quarters; the charitable father, tolerably well off, might voluntarily put the child to nurse or make the mother an allowance; the respectable father, afraid of a scene, or of finding the child on his doorstep, made some payment perforce.[2] Usually, however, the father 'makes every exertion to elude the claim of the mother': 'in the greater number of instances the father evades contributing to the mother of his offspring'; they 'mostly evade'; they are 'generally unwilling'; they 'always neglect them unless compelled'.[3]

That no statute compelled a father to provide for his illegitimate child reflects, perhaps, the sex of the legislators: it shows their unconcern for the least fortunate of children; it suggests a readiness, too, when others bore the brunt, to buttress morality by law. George Nicholls, practised in formulating the legislature's wishes, had no time for an Irish bastardy law: 'Irish females should be . . . guardians of their own honour, and be responsible in their own persons for all deviations from virtue'; 'bastards and mothers of bastards, in all matters concerned with relief of poor, should be dealt with in the same manner as other destitute persons, solely on the ground of destitution.'[4] Or, as it was put by a member of

---

[1] App. A, 93 (Clare). Archbishop McHale believed it ' "frequently . . . happens that the difficulty of supporting herself and child drives the mother to prostitution" ' (Add. App. A, 561 (Gal.)).
[2] App. A, 66 (Gal.); 83 (Clare); 128 (Derry); 75, 78, 97 (Clare); 113 (Tipp.).
[3] Ib. 91, 90 (Clare); 49 (Mayo); 89 (Long.).
[4] *Report of Geo. Nicholls, Esq., . . . on Poor Laws, Ireland*, P.P., 1837, LI, 230–1.

a select committee, witness and interrogator in one: ' "Does not the misconduct of a woman before marriage in Ireland lead to the loss of a husband, and does not the misconduct of a woman in England under the bastardy system lead to the acquisition of one?" '[1] Give her a bastardy law, and Ireland might boast no more that pregnancy was the consequence, not the preliminary, of marriage.[2]

Magistrates, as well as legislators, sometimes upheld the mother's sole responsibility for her child: to lighten her burden would 'give encouragement to crime'.[3] But many, extra-legally, or with questionable legality, sought to ensure some payment by father to mother: they knew, better than the legislators, the people and hardships involved; and some, no doubt, acknowledged that men, as well as women, must be dissuaded from 'crime': 'it is truly heart-rending to see the betrayers often of innocence laugh to scorn and treat with contumely the victims of their passions.'[4]

There were three legal processes which, by allowing them at all or by straining the rules of evidence, sympathetic magistrates used, in effect, to order the father of an illegitimate child to contribute to his support: they might award damages for seduction, questionably proven; they might enforce a promise to help with the child's maintenance, said by the girl to have been voluntarily made by the man; or they might award damages against him for impairing the girl's earning-power by making her pregnant. An action for seduction or loss of wages might bring in some £5, Irish currency. It had, however, to be made by the girl's father or employer, who, even if not estranged from her, might hesitate to appear as her champion.[5] More common were proceedings, instituted by the girl herself, aimed at keeping the man to his alleged promise to help maintain the child.

[1] *Second Report, S.C. on State of the Poorer Classes in Ireland*, P.P., 1830, VII, q. 4141.
[2] ' "Speaking of one of our counties, the county of Sussex, I am quite sure that the present system of affiliating bastard children on the father of them, has promoted prostitution, in a degree which amounts almost to a sanction of the offence" '; ' "Do not the laws of bastardy [in England] lead to many cases of marriage after pregnancy?" "I should be almost ashamed to say, as an English man, how few cases of marriage there are, without that preliminary, in Sussex, among the lower classes of the population" ' (Ib., qq. 1731–3).
[3] App. A, 71 (Rosc.).
[4] Supp. App. A, 1093 (Ant.). The point was made here by a priest, not a magistrate.
[5] App. A, 112, 123 (Derry); Add. App. A, 566–7 (Derry).

Girls' allegations on this score were variously treated: no court, the quarter sessions, or, more often, the magistrates, accepted jurisdiction: they might have heard cases from time immemorial, or begun, or ceased, to do so around 1830.[1] There was diversity, too, in the evidence needed to substantiate a case, in the damages awarded, and in the penalty imposed in default. Magistrates, here and there, made what amounted to local common law of filiation: their cases hinged on the girl's oath, by itself, or borne out by the magistrates' casual knowledge, or by proof of 'intimacy, company-keeping, flirtation or the like';[2] the magistrates (as at Rosscarbery, co. Cork) might presume that a 'natural obligation is imposed on a man of contributing towards the maintenance of his own offspring' and, sure of his identity, might automatically award damages.[3] At the other extreme, of questionably more help to the girl than denial of jurisdiction, 'if [the man] declares he would not believe the child to be his, even if the woman swore, we do not consider we have any power over the man.'[4] Usually, however, the magistrates required proof, not merely of the father's identity, but of some act or promise they might construe as an undertaking to contribute to the child's support—a promise 'obtained at some unguarded moment, at a time when nothing is likely to be refused': 'some act of adoption on his part must be proved, such as having given or promised money'; having sent the girl provisions or arranged attendance at her confinement.[5]

Magistrates, persuaded of an 'act of adoption', assessed damages by various yardsticks—if not by whim or convention. Some aimed, unrealistically, at awarding what the father had promised; others at reimbursing the mother's outlay on the child, at paying her a nurse's wage, or whatever wage bearing and rearing the child had prevented her earning.[6] Awards might be scaled up or down with the magistrates' estimate of the father's ability to pay or the mother's character.[7] Few magistrates ordered any payment against the period before the child was born:[8] some awarded quarterly or

[1] App. A, 67 (Gal.); 70 (Rosc.); 71 (Sligo); 115–16 (Ant.); 92, 96 (Clare); 73 (Carl.); 65 (Gal.).
[2] Ib. 65, 67 (Gal.); 68 (Mayo).   [3] Ib. 104 (Cork).
[4] Add. App. A, 563 (Meath).
[5] App. A, 100, 92, 94 (Clare), 123 (Don.); 68 (Mayo).
[6] Ib. 122 (Don.); 73 (Carl.); 113 (Ant.); 72 (Sligo); Supp. App. A, 1119 Cavan).
[7] App. A, 68, 69 (Mayo); 128 (Derry); 116 (Ant.); 123 (Don.).
[8] Ib. 123 (Don.); 73 (Carl.); 92 (Clare), etc.; but see 66 (Gal.).

ILLEGITIMACY BEFORE THE FAMINE

annual payments for the year, or two or three years, during which they reckoned the child would be at the breast; others, a lump sum, payable, perhaps, in instalments.[1] Lump sums usually varied between £3 and £6; the total of periodic payments, between 30s. and £12 or more. The girl awarded in all £5, Irish currency, was probably relatively lucky.[2] Returning to the magistrates after the birth of a second or subsequent child, she might expect shorter shrift: a woman now of 'injured character', she was perhaps thought more likely to lie, less likely to have been promised help with her child; or, if she were 'considered undeserving, in proportion to the number of her illegitimate children', an award might be scaled down by as much as a half.[3] The risk, or reality, of an order to pay 'wages' was no small incentive to emigration,[4] nor, if the father stayed on at home, could the mother count on getting her award; few courts assumed powers of sending defaulters to gaol, some issued decrees against possibly non-existent goods and chattels, and others took no action.[5]

A neighbour's illegitimacy was no matter of indifference in peasant society. At best—rarely—there was 'not much of a disrespectful feeling' for the illegitimate, or 'mingled feelings of contempt and compassion';[6] more often, however, 'people thought nothing of him', and he was 'generally looked on with great coldness'; 'next to "gauger's spy", bastard is the strongest term of reproach.'[7] 'The stain', in some reports, 'never wears off'; 'it sticks to him through life and to his children and grandchildren for five or six generations.'[8] But in others it might be effaced by 'a long course of good conduct or by the acquisition of property';[9] the 'quiet boy', working hard, might be left in peace—save when tempers rose, and then 'there will be somebody always to remember how he came into the world', somebody to taunt him with 'the

---

[1] Ib. 65 (Gal.); 69 (Mayo); 97 (Clare); 71 (Sligo); 122 (Don.).
[2] Ib., *passim*.
[3] Ib. 92, 96 (Clare); 68 (Mayo); 128 (Derry). But in Antrim she was said to be treated as the mother of a first illegitimate child (ib. 115).
[4] Ib. 68 (Mayo); 113 (Ant.); 73 (Carl.).
[5] Ib. 65, 67 (Gal.); 66 (Mayo); 114, 118 (Ant.); 73 (Carlow); 92 (Clare); Add. App. A, 561 (Kild.).
[6] App. A, 66 (Longford); 87 (Wexford). See also pp. 70 (Rosc.); 128 (Derry).
[7] Ib. 126 (Don.); 82 (Long.). The 'gauger's spy' was the man who helped the excise to combat illicit distillation.
[8] Ib. 98 (Clare); 112 (Tipp.).
[9] Ib. 126 (Don.).

incontinence of his parents'.[1] More decisively, 'the amount of property determines everything'; 'if he be in any way well provided for, all stigma is forgotten.'[2]

In marriage—the regular way to consolidate or advance one's position—the handicap of illegitimacy, and the power of property at least partially to offset it, were plain. The ill-repute of the illegitimate, generally, and with prospective wives and fathers-in-law, reflected more than prejudice: probably reared too hard to be well-favoured physically or morally, he was the more discounted as a marriage-partner for fear of some hereditary taint,[3] or because a family connection, if existent at all, promised little prestige or help on a rainy day.[4] Farmers, therefore, 'would move heaven and earth to prevent their daughters marrying a bastard'—unless he were well-off, when 'a small farmer would not be such a fool as to refuse him his daughter.'[5] But an illegitimate woman, even with money, was looked at askance by the respectable family: 'it would be twice as bad to have a son who should marry a woman so disgraced'; 'decent people would prefer half the fortune without the stain'.[6]

Pregnancy outside marriage was a shameful matter to the girl and her family; it promised a wretched future for the child and herself, and prompted guilty concern in many a prospective father: these four, therefore, had some incentive to arrange an abortion; and, as they were probably the first to know of the pregnancy, they had some chance of doing so undetected. But few illegitimate births seem to have been deliberately forestalled. Of the thousands of witnesses examined for the Poor Inquiry Commission, only two seem to have said the practice was at all prevalent: a Kildare doctor was 'often' asked to induce abortion; and in Derry it was 'frequently' achieved by medicine and over-exertion.[7] Nor does earlier or later evidence suggest any widespread tradition of

---

[1] Ib. 94, 75, 97, 91 (Clare).   [2] Ib. 65 (Gal.); 122 (Ant.).
[3] Ib. 74 (Carl.).
[4] Ib. 118 (Lim.). 'They think much of the clan or family of the party married, and of making numerous connexions by marriage' (Ib. 112 (Lim.)).
[5] Ib. 99, 94 (Clare). See also ib. 72 (Sligo); 126 (Don.).
[6] Ib. 71 (Rosc.); 65 (Gal.). It was harder for a woman than for a man to erase the stigma of illegitimacy: 'a man, no matter what he is at the beginning, can raise himself in the world by his exertions and conduct; but a woman must keep the rank of her birth'; 'a woman will seldom or scarcely ever make a decent match, because she is not able to work her way up in the world as a man can do' (ib. 71 (Rosc.); 95 (Clare)).
[7] Ib. 81 (Kild.); 128 (Derry).

ILLEGITIMACY BEFORE THE FAMINE 63

abortion. Samuel Madden, the patriot landowner, though accusing his people in the 1730s of 'Whoredom and Adultery', thought they were 'very seldom guilty of . . . the horrible Practice of Abortions.'[1] And Wakefield, early in the next century, had 'never heard an instance' 'of attempts to bring about abortions' in Ireland.[2] More recently, the collectors of the Irish Folklore Commission report only odd references to abortion: in Limerick 'there was all kinds of witchcraft practised by people concerning pregnancy and childbirth and I heard of attempts being made to kill the child in the womb'; in Tyrone a herbal concoction known as 'golden rod' was used to induce abortion, and in Antrim there were women who would dose a pregnant girl with soap-suds—women (perhaps it is significant) who were thought to be cursed.[3] Abortion, of course, was no matter for general discussion: the slenderness, none the less, like the tenor, of the evidence probably indicates the rarity of the practice; critics of the Irish were too many and too insistent for all to have been dissuaded by literary convention from exposing what, had they the evidence, they and their readers would have thought utterly reprehensible.

Primitive people the world over are said to have practised abortion;[4] it is widespread still in western countries, in spite of contraception; in France, by the end of the nineteenth century, there may have been nearly as many abortions as live births:[5] it is curious, therefore, that pregnant Irish girls, in an appalling predicament, should have rejected the escape it offered. The girls, mostly Catholic, were members of a society proverbially devoted to its religion—a religion in which abortion is the one excommunicable sin against marriage.[6] But few priests seem to have laboured the enormity of abortion and of the penalty it attracted. Horror of abortion, no doubt, there was, horror, if occasion arose,

[1] Samuel Madden, *Reflections and Resolutions proper for the Gentlemen of Ireland* (Dublin, 1738), pp. 204, 210. Swift, however, thought his 'Modest Proposal' would 'prevent those voluntary abortions, and that horrid practice of women murdering their bastard children, alas, too frequent among us' (Jonathan Swift, *A Modest Proposal* . . . (Dublin, 1729), in *The Prose Works of Jonathan Swift, D.D.*, ed. Temple Scott, vii (Bohn's Standard Library), 1925, p. 208.
[2] Edward Wakefield, *An Account of Ireland, Statistical and Political* (1812), ii, 579.
[3] I.F.C., MS. 1210, 284–5; 1220, 54.
[4] Glanville Williams, *The Sanctity of Life and the Criminal Law* (1958), p. 140.
[5] D. V. Glass and E. Grebenik, 'World Population, 1800–1950', in *The Cambridge Economic History of Europe*, vi, Pt. i, ed. H. J. Habakkuk and M. Postan (Cambridge, 1965), p. 115.
[6] Michael O'Donnell, *Moral Questions*, ed. Sebastian Lee, O.F.M. (1945), p. 135.

bolstered explicitly in the confessional, guardedly in the pulpit. But that occasion arose so seldom suggests that the horror was grounded elsewhere; that perhaps the obverse of the popular esteem and yearning for a large family was horror at procedures that frustrated birth. With most girls marrying and marrying young, with pregnant unmarried women too few and too despised to build their own traditions, the odd unfortunate, though at her wits' end, may have been uninformed of the means, even of the possibility, of interrupting her pregnancy.

Bishop Doyle, appearing before the Select Committee on the State of the Poor in Ireland, answered curiously when questioned on the prevalence of infanticide: 'I know more than an ordinary person upon that subject, but my ministry is such that I think it would be prejudicial to its interest if I were to give the evidence sought for, and, if the Committee would indulge me, I should rather not give it.' He would 'greatly prefer that the Committee would seek for information from a person not a clergyman'.[1] This it does not appear to have done. Fragmentary coroners' statistics, however, as well as evidence collected by the Poor Inquiry Commission, suggest, with Doyle, that infanticide was not altogether insignificant. Returns, from forty-one counties and counties of cities, of inquests held in their areas in 1841 were made to no common form; more than half were admittedly or obviously incomplete, or do not distinguish infant from other victims of murder. Infanticide, therefore, was proven to the coroner's satisfaction in many more than the eighty cases in which we know the verdict may be so classified.[2] Doubtless, too, it was not infrequently committed unknown to any coroner: finding an infant body was not necessarily matter for an inquest;[3] nor, by and large, was the beggargirl's bastard worth much hue and cry.[4] Thus a Galway magistrate believed 'bastard children are more frequently destroyed

---

[1] *S.C. on State of the Poor in Ireland*, P.P., 1830, VII, q. 4577.

[2] *A Return of the Number of Inquests... during the year 1841*, P.P., 1842, XXXVIII, pp. 185–224.

[3] App. A, 111 (Kerry). In the four years, 1831–4, according to returns by the sub-inspectors of police, 2673 children were deserted in Ireland; of the 640 of these found dead, inquests were held on only 407 (*Abstract of Cases of Deserted Children... with the Number of Inquests Held...*, P.P., 1836, XXX, 580). There can be little doubt that the figure for the number of children found dead, like that for the number of desertions, is grossly deficient: see below, p. 65, n. 5.

[4] App. A, 92 (Cork).

ILLEGITIMACY BEFORE THE FAMINE

than is generally admitted; it is a crime very rarely brought to light in this country. There are certainly many children buried in private burial-grounds in this and the neighbouring county, where there is no service performed, and no notice taken of them.'[1] The sub-inspector of police at Tralee believed infanticide 'not uncommon'; a Donegal rector 'very much feared that there were more cases of infanticide than is generally supposed'; they 'frequently destroy them' in Carlow town; and in near-by Tullow (so the rector was assured) 'the increase of infanticide generally has been awful since the closing of the Foundling-hospital in Dublin.'[2] Babies, known or presumed to be illegitimate, were found strangled, smothered, or battered to death; or drowned in drains and canals, bogs and marl-pits, rivers and lakes.[3] But against these forebodings and this evidence (whether because the crime was infrequent or easily concealed) other witnesses, as well placed and more numerous, had never heard of a case or knew only of single cases in three, a dozen, or thirty years; of two cases in eighteen years.[4]

There is little doubt, however, that more desperate girls tried to relieve their plight by infanticide than to forestall it by abortion. Destroying a child was hardly less sinful to the theologians than destroying an embryo: murder, however, more familiar than abortion and sometimes applauded, may have given less popular offence; the means were more accessible to the mother; and, an outcast, perhaps deranged, the actuality of her plight bearing on her child as well as herself, she might feel drawn to use them.

Saving the mother's feelings, if questionably kinder to the child, far more illegitimate children were deserted than murdered.[5] A

---

[1] Ib. 65 (Gal.).
[2] Ib. 110 (Kerry); 59 (Don.); 74, 25 (Carl.). See also 70 (Rosc.); 123 (Derry); 75, 77 (Carl.); 79 (Kild.); 105 (Cork).
[3] Ib. 74, 75, 77, 58 (Carl.); 81 (Clare); 87 (Cork); 70 (Rosc.), etc.
[4] Ib. 65, 66, 67 (Gal.); 69 (Rosc.); 72 (Sligo); 99 (Clare); 109 (Kerry).
[5] According to returns prepared by the sub-inspectors of police for the Poor Inquiry Commission, an annual average of 668 children was deserted in Ireland in the four years 1831–4 (*Abstract of Cases of Deserted Children* ..., P.P., 1836, XXX, 580). There is little doubt that this figure is grossly deficient. Before 1820, when entry was unrestricted, the foundling hospitals in Dublin and Cork admitted between them some 2200 children a year. Those not Irish foundlings were hardly as numerous as the Irish foundlings supported locally, or dying before entering one of the hospitals. Closing the Dublin Foundling Hospital was said to have increased infanticide and reduced desertion; it is implausible none the less, that the number of children deserted fell from probably substantially more than 2200 a year before 1821 to fewer than 700 after 1831.

woman, choosing a spot where she might abandon her child, more probably looked to his safety than her own: foundlings were left in 'conspicuous and well-frequented places'; indoors, rather than by the roadside.[1] Many a bundle was found at the priest's house, the house of a gentleman or magistrate; empty cradles—even an empty tomb—were filled; the child's father might be reminded of his responsibility; or the child, after a night's lodging in town, left in place of lodging money.[2] The mother, leaving her child in the open, might hide nearby—mindful, perhaps, of foundlings who had died from exposure, from attack by pigs or dogs, by rats or water-rats.[3]

Formal responsibility for foundlings lay with the churchwarden of the Established Church, or with the 'overseer of deserted children' to whom his duties were delegated. But some parishes had negligent wardens; others had none, nor (it might be) had they rector or even parishioner of the Established Church.[4] Responsibility here probably fell to the Catholic priest.

The churchwarden was legally empowered[5] merely to find homes for abandoned children of unknown parentage while they remained under twelve months of age, and to pay the foster-mother up to £5, Irish currency, from funds levied by the Protestant vestry on property. Commonly, however, he assumed power, not only to send children to the foundling hospitals in Dublin and Cork,[6] but to make annual allowances of between £3 and £5 for the maintenance in the parish of those up to the age of eight or nine, or even twelve. First, we shall consider the fate of foundlings, probably the majority until the 1830s, sent to one of these institutions; then that of children for whom churchwarden or priest made other provision; or for whom, indeed, there was no provision, save by chance, by some pitying householder.

The Dublin Foundling Hospital, 'one of the most gigantic baby-farming, nursing, boarding-out and apprenticing institutions that these countries have ever seen',[7] was established in 1704 'to

---

[1] Ib. 21 (Rosc.); 26 (Kild.).
[2] Ib. 26 (Kild.); 48 (Ant.); 25 (Cork); 61 (Derry); Supp. App. A, 1053 (Tipp.).
[3] App. A, 26 (Kild.); 62 (Derry). [4] Ib. 35 (Clare).
[5] 11, 12 Geo. III, c.15; 13, 14 Geo III, c.24 (*Second Report, Poor Inquiry Commission*, P.P., 1837, XXXI, 593).
[6] A small foundling hospital in Galway, supported in 1834 by a vestry cess of £62. 10s., had admitted no new inmates since 1827 (*Second Report, Poor Inquiry Commission*, P.P., 1837, XXXI, p. 592).
[7] *Royal Commission on the Poor Laws and Relief of Distress: Report on Ireland*, P.P., 1909, XXXVIII, p. 70.

ILLEGITIMACY BEFORE THE FAMINE

prevent the "exposure, death, and actual murder of illegitimate children"', and to educate and rear them ' "in the Reformed or Protestant Faith, and thereby to strengthen and promote the Protestant interest in Ireland" '.[1] Though financed mainly by the citizens of Dublin, it received foundlings from all parts of Ireland (and some, it is said, from Scotland and Wales);[2] it placed them as speedily as possible with foster-mothers in the country, in whose charge they remained until, at the age of seven or eight, they were readmitted to the hospital to be cared for until old enough to be apprenticed.[3] But, as a parliamentary committee reported in 1826, 'it is evidently the design of Providence that the infancy of children should be superintended by their parents and a great departure from this principle ... will be attended by circumstances of an untoward and perplexing nature.'[4] Such circumstances had become acutely unhappy by the 1790s. In each of the six-year periods 1784–90 and 1790–6 admissions to the hospital numbered between 12,000 and 13,000: deaths there in the earlier period amounted to 31 per cent of admissions; in the later period to 61 per cent—supplemented (in the later period) by known deaths of children sent to the country, amounting to 16 per cent of admissions. In the first quarter of the year 1797, 540 children were admitted, and 454, 80 per cent of admissions, died in the hospital; in the following nineteen days admissions were 116 and deaths 112, or 95 per cent of the admissions. Between 1790 and 1796, 5216 inmates of the institution were sent to its infirmary: three were brought out alive, two, at least, to die soon afterwards. Infirmary patients were dosed indiscriminately with some soothing preparation, but received no other medical treatment. For most of them, it may be, the doctors of the day could do little but see they were kept clean and warm. The physician to the Foundling Hospital, however, never once visited the infirmary during these six years; the apothecary appeared once a year or once a quarter; and the surgeon (or his

---

[1] Ib.
[2] John Carr, *The Stranger in Ireland* (1806), p. 491. 'I once saw at Bangor [Wales], three children who were about to be taken to Wicklow and who were intended to be substituted for children who had died at nurse under the Foundling Hospital at Dublin' (*Select Committee on State of the Poor in Ireland*, P.P., 1830, VII, q. 1727).
[3] *Third Report ... on Irish Education Inquiry*, P.P., 1826–7, XIII, pp. 3–4; Carr, 1806, op. cit., p. 491.
[4] Ib. 3.

deputy) two or three times a week. The patients, scantily and dirtily clad in the clothes they or their fellow foundlings had worn on admission, were put in straw-filled cradles said to be swarming with bugs; and covered with blankets discarded in the nursery of the healthier children. Mondays, Wednesdays, and Fridays, the porter explained, were the burying days: he buried immediately after morning prayers, keeping the bodies meantime in a small house on the burying ground; a regulation requiring the immediate burial of children dying of an infectious disease appears to have been disregarded.[1]

The staff of the hospital attributed the crisis of 1797 to the severity of the season, to heavy admission of venereally diseased children, and to the difficulty of placing children in the country when would-be foster mothers, fearing a French invasion, thought they might not be paid.[2] The crisis, however, like the deteriorating conditions of the preceding years, seems essentially the result of the neglect of the 200 persons 'of first character' responsible for the government of the hospital. Save when paid offices were to be filled, they took little interest in the hospital, and the staff, scarcely supervised, also neglected its duties.[3]

The nine governors to whom management was transferred in 1798, hoping to discourage infanticide, maintained the open door: nobody was to be dissuaded from leaving a child by fear of awkward questions;[4] the job, indeed, could be done anonymously by putting the child in a basket outside the hospital gate, ringing the bell, and walking away. The porter, hearing the bell, rotated the basket to bring the child within the gate and took him to the nursery quarters.[5] A minor profession of 'child-cadger' grew up to bring infants

[1] *Report of a Committee of the House of Commons on the Management and State of the Foundling Hospital, Journals of the House of Commons of Ireland*, 3 May 1797, pp., ccxl–ccxlii; *Eighth Report, Commissioners of the Board of Education in Ireland*, P.P., 1810, X, p. 270.
[2] Ib.
[3] *Third Report . . . Education Inquiry*, 1826–7, op. cit., 4; Edward Wakefield, *Account of Ireland, Statistical and Political* (1812), ii, 423; *Eighth Report, . . . Board of Education*, 1810, op. cit., 270.
[4] *Third Report . . . Education Inquiry*, 1826–7, op. cit., 4.
[5] Wakefield, 1812, op. cit., ii, 423; *Report of a Committee of the House of Commons on . . . the Foundling Hospital*, 1797, op. cit., ccxli. The Church, anxious that children might be left at an Italian foundling asylum without the mothers' identity being revealed, is said to have sanctioned the use of the 'tour' or 'turn-box' in the twelfth century (*Encylopaedia of Social Sciences*, 'Illegitimacy', p. 580).

to the Dublin and Cork foundling hospitals. Its members were employed by churchwarden, rector, or overseer of deserted children,[1] sometimes by the mother herself. William Carleton tells of a woman 'immediately sent for' after an illegitimate birth: she 'received her little charge with a name—whether true or false mattered not—pinned to its dress—then her travelling expenses'; she delivered the child at the hospital, and, returning home with the receipt, was given her fee.[2] Child-cadgers were accused of 'the greatest negligence and inhumanity': some of their charges, fed by the spoon, or not at all, on several days' journey, reached the hospital in a condition 'too shocking to relate', in one instance 'more like a liver than any human thing'; others (it is said) were abandoned on the road—perhaps stripped of their clothing—so impatient were the nurses to collect their fees.[3]

In the nursery quarters, on the advice of the new governors' 'ladies committee', wet nurses replaced the traditional artificial feeding—but with questionable benefit to the children. When Wakefield visited the hospital no nurse was suckling fewer than two infants; some, on occasion, had had as many as five; the nurses, he said, from long familiarity with loss of life, 'thought it the most trivial of all occurrences'; they 'have their feelings

[1] From 1827, in a Mr. James Gibson, Belfast had an active overseer of deserted children. ' "When a child is exposed," ' he explained, ' "I send a pole through the town with the clothes it had on when exposed attached to it, offering a reward of £1. 1s. for private information so as to discover the exposer and £5 if she be prosecuted to conviction." ' The nurse of a deserted child, telling him evasively about questions put to her about her charge, was likely to lose him—when, ' "seeing her gain gone ... and to secure the overseer's interest" ', she would be more forthcoming; or the mother ' "seeing her child gone, she knows not where, will intercede with the overseer" '. Gibson sought, not only to restore deserted children to their mothers, but to forestall desertion, or see that it took place elsewhere than in Belfast. A small gift of money might persuade a mother about to desert her child either to leave Belfast, or proceed against the child's father; though neither court action nor fear of scandal extracted money from the father, the mother, by the time she realized her failure, might have become too attached to the child to desert him. Grateful to Gibson for cutting down their outlay on deserted children, the Belfast authorities gave him between 1827 and 1833 a series of presents of ever-increasing value, amounting in all to £150 (*Poor Inquiry (Ireland)*, App. C, Pt. i, *Reports on the State of the Poor* ... *in some of the Principal Towns*, P.P., 1836, XXX, pp. 39–40).
[2] William Carleton, *Valentine M'Clutchy, the Irish Agent* (Dublin, 1848), p. 36.
[3] Wakefield, 1812, op. cit., ii, 427; *Report of a Committee of the House of Commons on ... the Foundling Hospital*, 1797, op. cit., ccxli; *Third Report ... Education Inquiry*, 1826–7, op. cit., 4, 6; Add. App. A, op. cit., 558 (Derry); *Eighth Report ... Board of Education*, 1810, op. cit., 270.

destroyed and become careless and heedless of the lives of infants committed to their care'.[1]

The child living so long was taken from the hospital by a wet-nurse from the surrounding countryside. Annually thereafter, on showing him in good health at the hospital, she was entitled to a fee of £3, with a bonus of £2 at the end of the first year and another on the child's readmission to hospital. Country nursing was probably the happiest interlude in the foundling's life: the fee, no negligible matter in peasant economy, gave some promise of favourable treatment; and the newcomer, growing with and like his foster-brothers, sometimes assumed their name and as much affection in the home and friendship beyond. Eventually, rather than part with him (and his services), the family might forgo their outstanding fee and bonus.[2]

Foundlings going back to the hospital, under its reformed government, seem to have suffered no great aggravation of the hazards inherent in institutional life in their time. They lived in 'an enormous pile of building', on a 'healthy elevated site': their dormitories were 'spacious and clean'; their chapel 'elegant'; their dining hall 'very noble'.[3] Their food, bread, milk, and broth, supplemented thrice weekly by meat and vegetables, was 'adequate' or 'liberal';[4] the 'cleanliness, order, and regularity' of the institution 'highly creditable'.[5] It was seen, none the less, as a 'mansion of misery'.[6] The children, when Wakefield saw them, mostly 'had sore fingers, scalded heads and inflamed eyes or were afflicted with tumours and ulcers'; 'invariably', a Royal Commission reported in the 1820s, they pined for the affection of their foster mothers and burked at institutional 'confinement and restraint'.[7]

The remaining rigours of foundling life are indicated by figures of admissions, deaths, and discharges between 1796 and 1826. Of more than 52,000 children left at the hospital, 28 per cent died as infants before being sent to the country, and another 2 per cent

---

[1] *Third Report... Education Inquiry*, 1826–7, p. 4; Wakefield, op. cit., ii, 427–9.
[2] John Carr, *The Stranger in Ireland* (1806), p. 491; Wakefield, op. cit., ii, pp. 430–1; *Third Report... Education Inquiry*, 1826–7, pp. 4–5.
[3] Carr, 1806, op. cit., 491; Wakefield, 1812, op. cit., ii, 431.
[4] Carr, 1806, op. cit., 491; *Third Report... Education Inquiry*, 1826–7, p. cit., 13.
[5] *Eighth Report,... Board of Education*, 1810, op. cit.
[6] Wakefield, 1812, op. cit., ii, 431.
[7] Ib.; *Third Report... Education Inquiry*, 1826–7, op. cit., 7.

ILLEGITIMACY BEFORE THE FAMINE

after their return at about the age of 8. Though 26,000, virtually half the number admitted, were returned as having died in the country—nothing having been heard of them for three years—death certificates (entitling the mother to a proportion of her annual fee) had been received for only 16,000; of the remainder, while some, undoubtedly, had died, most may have been retained by their foster families. In all, then, 52,000 children had been admitted and between 32,000 and 42,000—between 61 and 81 per cent of admissions—had died before being due for discharge at about the age of 14. Of 7700—15 per cent of admissions—who left the hospital alive, 1100 had been claimed by a parent; 400 had eloped; 500 had been transferred to charter schools and 5700 apprenticed to a trade.[1]

Like their reduced number, the condition and future of these so-called apprentices told of their unnatural rearing. Discharged from hospital, they were friendless, 'overgrown children', 'a puny and infected race', 'unhealthy from venereal and evil', 'wretched in themselves and a curse ... to society': 'totally unacquainted with the world and totally unfit to deal with others', 'a shipwreck must too often follow'.[2] In Powerscourt, 'a great resort of foundling children', none turned out as badly as they. The foundlings still living with their foster parents in a Wicklow parish were 'not objects of reproach or obloquy', but 'most dreadfully so' if they came back as apprentices.[3] In the Dublin Mendicity Institute, the 'last refuge of the wretchedness of the metropolis', 'those who have been educated in the Foundling Hospital conceal it, because it would be thrown out against them afterwards by their fellow mendicants as a circumstance of degradation; for ... even these poor people have their feelings'.[4] The girls, like their mothers, slipped easily into prostitution. Too despised and too undomesticated to have much hope of marriage, they were unlikely either to hold their own in service. 'Being unfitted for the situations they go to, from the education received, they become victims of the first temptation: they are often destroyed in the places they are sent to'; 'there is no one to call their masters to account for it', and 'they become addicted to vicious pursuits'. The females, in Bishop

---

[1] Add. App. A, 559 (Derry); *Third Report ... Education Inquiry*, 1826-7, pp. 4-6.
[2] Ib. p. 11.
[3] Ib. pp. 4, 11.   [4] Ib. p. 12.

Doyle's experience, 'become corrupt . . . almost without any exception and the boys are unnatural and vicious'.[1]

The governors of the hospital felt it necessary in 1820 to abandon their policy of unrestricted admission. They had long accommodated their full complement of 1200 children returned from the country. In any year, therefore, the number of seven- or eight-year-olds they could readmit was limited to the number of their existing inmates who died or were apprenticed, who ran away or were claimed by a parent. Partly because they had not realized in the past that the number of children annually sent to the country should bear some sort of proportion to the annual number of vacancies in the hospital; partly also because of the growing difficulty in placing children ready for apprenticing, they could admit only a proportion of children due to be returned by their foster parents. The number of children at nurse rose to nearly 9000, an embarrassment to the governors both financially and because of the difficulty of finding homes for so many. They toyed with the idea of sending children to America; a little later they transferred 500 to the charter schools; by offering a higher apprenticeship fee, they hoped more places would be forthcoming. But, tackling the problem also by restricting the admission of infants, they resolved in 1820 that, while they would still freely accept Dublin foundlings, they would take country children only in the summer. Admission was further restricted by legislation of 1822 requiring parishes to provide a fee of £5 with each of their foundlings admitted to the hospital. Parliament, advised that children leaving the hospital were ill-prepared for the world, advised also of the saving (now nearly all to the public purse) its disbandment would involve, decided that it should admit no new foundlings after 1829.[2] The hospital ran down thereafter: the poor law of 1838,[3] charging the Poor Law Commissioners with the relief of destitute children, vested the hospital in them, and they used its premises as a workhouse.[4]

In the years preceding 1820, the final years of unrestricted entry,

---

[1] Ib. pp. 4, 10, 11 ff; *S.C. on State of the Poor in Ireland*, P.P., 1830, VII, q. 4582.

[2] *Third Report . . . Irish Education Inquiry*, 1826–7, op. cit., pp. 8–9; *S.C. Irish Miscellaneous Estimates*, P.P., 1829, IV, p. 132.

[3] 1 and 2 Vict. c. 56, sec. 34.

[4] *Royal Commission on the Poor Laws and Relief of Distress: Report on Ireland*, P.P., 1909, XXXVIII, p. 70.

the hospital was admitting rather fewer than 2000 foundlings a year; by the years 1823–6 the annual intake had fallen below 500; and by 1830 (as we have seen) had ceased altogether. The hospital's restrictive policy was thought to have both increased infanticide and reduced desertion.[1] As the foundlings of much of the country no longer went, as a matter of course, to Dublin, their future appeared more hazardous, their chance of survival more remote. Some mothers, determined to part with their children, might think it kinder now to destroy them; but others, however inconvenienced by their children, or ill-equipped to provide for them, would not abandon them to so uncertain a future. And parishes, as their members were asked to find the admission fee to the Foundling Hospital or provide otherwise for deserted children, became more concerned to discover and prosecute their mothers. Mothers more easily intimidated might now be afraid to desert their children; but others were hardly unaware that there was no similar inducement to search more vigilantly for those guilty of infanticide.

By an act of 1735 the Irish parliament constituted the Governors of the Workhouse of the City of Cork: it endowed them with the proceeds of an additional duty of one shilling per ton on coal and culm landed in the harbour of Cork; and charged them, when sufficient funds had accumulated, to build a workhouse. In the workhouse, opened in 1747, the Governors were to receive from churchwardens of parishes in the city and liberties exposed or foundling children and to have them clothed and educated.[2]

The hospital in Cork, unlike that in Dublin, had no nursery department. It accepted annually at Easter any child certified by a local churchwarden as having been exposed in his parish since the previous Easter. Meantime, at parochial expense, the 'parish nurse' had provided him with a wet nurse, whom the hospital, after the child's admission, reappointed or replaced at a cost of £2. 8s. a year, with a bonus of £1. 1s. if the child seemed at weaning to be well cared for. Thereafter, as dry-nurse, she (or another) was paid £1. 17s. a year, with a further premium of £1. 1s. if the child were in good shape when readmitted to the hospital, in, or about,

[1] *Third Report ... Irish Education Inquiry*, 1826–7, op. cit., pp. 8–11; App. A, 25 (Carl.); 33 (Wex.); 56, 59 (Don.).
[2] *Poor Inquiry (Ireland)*, App. C, Pt. 1, *Reports on the State of the Poor ... in some of the Principal Towns*, P.P., 1836, XXX, p. 28–9; subsequently referred to as 'App. C'.

his tenth year. After some five years' maintenance and instruction in the hospital (at an average cost in the 1830s of something over £7 a year), the child was put to service, or apprenticed—perhaps, if a girl, to millinery or dressmaking; if a boy, to baking or cabinet-making, rope- or umbrella-making.[1]

The hospital in the mid thirties had 1312 children on its books, a third within the walls, two-thirds at nurse in the country; its annual income was nearly £7000, virtually all the proceeds of the coal-tax.[2] Mortality, needless to say, was high. Of every hundred children falling to the care of the parish nurses around 1830, 22 (an implausibly low figure) are recorded as having died before entering the hospital; of the remainder, some 62 per cent died at nurse or in the hospital. Minimal overall mortality by the age of 15, some 70 per cent, compares with a figure of under 37 per cent for both sexes for the first fourteen years of life in the Chester tables.[3]

Cork Foundling Hospital: admissions, deaths, discharges, 1820–33

Ad-missions	Apprenticed or placed at service		Claimed		Died		Eloped	
	no.	% age	no.	% age	no.	% age	no.	% age
3247	516	16	177	5·5	2018	62	536	16·5

Poor Inquiry (Ireland), Appendix C, Pt. 1, *Reports on the State of the Poor ... in some of the Principal Towns*, P.P., 1836, XXX, p. 31. The percentages are of admissions during the period. The number of elopements is a residual figure.

The churchwarden with an eye to the rates might grieve little for the foundling dying before admission to the hospital. The parochial nurse, on occasion, turned a child's death to good account, putting in his place some child she had been bribed to have entered at the hospital; and to counter similar deception by their wet-nurses, the Governors had children branded on admission, the skin under the arm being patterned with puncture-marks, stained with indian ink. It is improbable, however, that infanticide or extraordinary neglect was largely responsible for the severity of mortality. Foundlings, if illegitimate, hardly cossetted before birth or afterwards, suffered further privation when abandoned. But

[1] Ib. 29–31.
[2] App. C, p. 36; P.P., 1842, XXXVIII, p. 181.
[3] App. C, pp. 31–2.

ILLEGITIMACY BEFORE THE FAMINE

most acutely, no doubt, they suffered from institutional life. Foundlings at nurse seem to have been treated much as their foster-brothers and sisters, much as the run of peasant children. Back in Cork, they were installed in 'a large pile of a building, very complete as regards dormitories, schoolrooms, infirmary and chapel': the establishment appeared 'clean and orderly', the children, 'better fed, clothed and educated than those of the peasantry brought up by their parents'. They were, none the less, unprepossessing in appearance, dejected, and unhappy: a local shipowner, giving jobs to a batch of 24, found them, though honest 'unhealthy, idle and indolent'. The odd pupil rose to a clerkship, to teaching school or keeping shop; but 'they generally turn out ill', the girls drifting often to prostitution.[1]

Keeping, and keeping alive, only a fraction of its children, equipping few even of these for reputable living, the hospital was criticised also for encouraging immorality by lessening the unmarried mother's responsibility for her child; for spreading veneral disease, to the 'great confusion' of the family in which the wife, contracting syphilis from her foster-foundling, infected her husband; for saddling brewers, distillers, and coal-burning households with a tax adding six per cent to the price of coal—and for doing so in the supposed interest, not merely of foundlings probably of Cork parentage, but of children whose parents were known, or known to have no claim on Cork.[2]

There is little doubt that the interest of the Governors, or their pity, led to the admission of children whose mothers were known: a Cork accoucheur told of country women, presumably unmarried, coming to Cork to be confined, and putting their babies 'perhaps by bribery' into the hospital. And 'every year' some ten to fifteen two-day-old babies, born to prostitutes in the Cork House of Industry, were made over to the Foundling Hospital—a practice discontinued in 1831, not because the children's mothers were known, but because (so the parish priest insisted) they were Catholics whose children were improperly admitted to a Protestant institution.[3]

More burdensome to the coal-burners of Cork than children whose mothers with a little vigilance might have been identified, were foundlings not (or improbably) of Cork parentage. Some

[1] Ib. 29–33, 37.   [2] Ib. 29, 36.
[3] Ib. 33–34.

country children were abandoned in the city by their parents; more, it may well be, were exposed there a second time, as the parish in which they were originally deserted tried to shift to the Foundling Hospital responsibility for their maintenance: thus, several outlying parishes employed a Mrs Rebecca Clark, at a fee of 10*s*. or £1 per child, to take their foundlings to Cork and abandon them again;[1] the Macroom churchwardens paid a man to take a child to Cork and 'expose him at a gentleman's gate',[2] and a Clonakilty woman, suing the local churchwardens for a guinea for taking a child to the Foundling Hospital, maintained that on a previous occasion they had paid her for similar service a similar sum.[3] The Foundling Hospital 'rendered Cork *the gathering place for all the bastards of the South of Ireland*': that there was substance in this charge is suggested by the average annual admission of 232 children to the hospital between 1820 and 1833.[4] These, if in fact mortality among infants waiting for the hospital to open its doors at Easter was only 22 per cent, were the survivors of 283 children. Now (according to the census of 1841) the average annual number of births in the city of Cork between 1832 and 1841 was 2521—meaning, if the hospital admitted only foundlings born in Cork, that one child of every nine born there was deserted. This was hardly the case: the hospital, there is little doubt,[5] admitted many children, presumably illegitimate, born in the country.

Under the poor law of 1838 the Cork, like the Dublin, Foundling Hospital was vested in the Poor Law Commissioners, who were directed to wind it up. Admissions seem to have ceased in 1838:[6] by 1854 the number on the books had fallen from its maximum of 1485 in 1829 to 46; the coal tax, already reduced to 5*d*. a ton, was to be abolished when provision had been made for disabled foundlings and for employees' retirement allowances.[7]

Even when the Dublin Foundling Hospital accepted all comers, many country foundlings remained where they had been deserted —because, supposedly Catholic, there was resistance to their being

---

[1] App. A, 30, 42, 43 (Cork).   [2] Ib. 119 (Cork).
[3] App. C, p. 34.   [4] Ib., pp. 29, 35, 32.
[5] Some of the children not Cork foundlings were of known Cork parentage; but their number may well have been offset by a deficiency in the rate used above of mortality amongst infants awaiting admission to the hospital.
[6] P.P., 1843, I, p. 101.
[7] App. C, p. 32; *Returns ... of the Cork Foundling Hospital*, P.P., 1854, LVIII, p. 287–96.

reared in a Protestant instutition; because nobody assumed responsibility for sending them on; and because of the cost, the bother, if not the risk to their lives, of sending them to Dublin. What happened to these children, and to the entire body of foundlings, when the hospitals closed their doors?

Churchwardens, as we have seen,[1] assuming power to make an annual allowance for foundlings' support, boarded them out. Such children, in most reports, merged into their foster-families and were treated as affectionately as their own children.[2] In Carlow, they were 'infinitely more moral than children apprenticed out by the Foundling Hospital', and 'much healthier'—because, some said, they were sent to households with cows.[3] Similarly in Derry, the child affectionately brought up generally turned out well—unlike the 'indifferent characters' from the Foundling Hospital, the boys thieves, the girls prostitutes.[4] And in Kildare, though at some disadvantage compared with children reared by their parents, they were 'more strong, more healthy and better in morals' than those from the Dublin Foundling-hospital.[5] The foundling, though tacitly adopted by his foster parents, could hardly expect a share of their land; because of this, as well as his illegitimacy, he seldom married well. Like the boy 'apprenticed' from his foster home he might become farm servant or labourer, weaver, soldier, or emigrant.[6]

The ending of admissions to the Dublin Foundling Hospital in 1831 increased the number of children being boarded out at parochial expense, and led to some questioning of the legality of an annual (as distinct from a single) levy for a foundling's support. Some parishes would contribute only a total of £5 for any foundling's support.[7] His lot became even more precarious two years later with the abolition of the 'parochial cess'. The cess, levied, like the rate for the support of deserted children, by the Protestant vestry on Catholic and Protestant, was devoted exclusively to the costs of services in the Protestant Church.[8] When, after much campaigning against it and the greater grievance, the tithe, the cess ceased to be levied in 1833, vestrymen and landholders were unsure

---

[1] P. 66, above.
[2] App. A, 37 (Rosc.); 24, 25 (Carl.); 26 (Kild.); 62 (Derry).
[3] Ib. 24 (Carl.).   [4] Ib. 74–75, 62 (Derry).   [5] Ib. 26 (Kild.).
[6] Ib. 62 (Derry).
[7] App. A, 18 (Gal.); 22 (Rosc.); 58 (Don.).
[8] James Godkin, *Ireland and her Churches* (1867), p. 134.

(or professed to be) of the legality of the rate for the support of deserted children.[1] It remained in some parishes,[2] and was replaced in others by a charge authorized by grand jury or judge.[3] But 'parishioners [might] object altogether "to pay for another man's sins" '—withholding from their parishes, in consequence, public funds for their foundlings' support.[4] An existing foster-mother might be helped by odd church monies, by a few shillings from the poor box, by kindly magistrate or priest.[5] But commonly she was left, unrecompensed, with 'an infant whose nursing she had undertaken solely as a means of profitable occupation and whom her Christian feelings would not suffer to cast out'.[6] Nor was there much prospect of these parishes boarding future foundlings at public expense; in Kildare, for instance, 'a fine child about three years old was turned adrift in the street when the magistrates could not afford relief'.[7] Deserted children, until formally provided for by the poor law, were left to the kind of *ad hoc* arrangement long made by the priest if the churchwarden neglected his duty, or if the priest wished infants, supposedly Catholic, to be reared in Catholic homes.

The odd child, left at the priest's door, or brought to him, might be cared for by one of the religious orders;[8] but the orders were

[1] Ib. 147; App. A, 38 (Clare).
[2] Ib. 56, 57 (Don.); 18 (Gal.); 48, 49, 50, 51 (Ant.).
[3] Ib. 60 (Don.); 23 (Carl.); 26 (Kild.); 18 (Gal.).
[4] Ib. 19, 20 (Mayo); 34 (Wex.); 62 (Derry).
[5] Ib. 17, 20 (Mayo); 63 (Derry); 22 (Rosc.); 32 (W'meath); 19 (Clare).
[6] *Second Report, Poor Inquiry Commission (Ireland)*, P.P., 1837, XXXI, p. 593; App. A, 46 (Kerry); 46 (Lim.); 55 (Ant.). 'Four years ago,' a Mayo labourer explained in 1835, 'my wife undertook the care of a foundling for 6s. a month; we were regularly paid for the first and second years; the third year, I processed the churchwardens and recovered the amount. £2 is now due to me, and if I had it, it would enable me to release my conacre potatoes. But though I know the churchwarden is accountable to me by law for the money, the law is little protection to me, as I am too poor to pay for it. I worked yesterday for 5d. and have no work to get today, and the expense of filing and serving the process and the attorney's fee would amount to 4s. 6d.' (App. A, 20 (Mayo)). Similarly in Galway, the churchwardens paid two women to whom they had entrusted foundlings, one for a single year, the other for two: 'they then abandoned them altogether, and threw the burden of supporting them upon these miserable individuals, whose abject poverty rendered them fit objects of charitable assistance, but whose benevolent feelings impelled them, up to this day, to share with the infant outcasts their own miserable pittance of potatoes' (ib. 65 (Gal.)).
[7] Supp. App. A, 877 (Kild.).
[8] App. A, 63 (Derry); 19 (Gal.); 33 (Wex.).

poor and few until after the Famine. The priest, like the churchwarden, boarded children out, finding a pound or two a year for their support, which came from his own pocket, from some predecessor's bequest, from collections in church or from door to door.[1]

The foundling, overlooked by priest and churchwarden, might be taken in by some kindly old woman; or passed from house to house, spending a night here, a night there—'they mostly die, it cannot well be otherwise';[2] or people, themselves 'fit objects of charitable assistance', shared with the child they found 'their pittance of potatoes'—until, initiated by an older child, perhaps by the age of four or five, he became a self-supporting beggar.[3]

We have no credible index of the incidence of illegitimacy in peasant society before the Famine. Civil registration was not introduced until 1864. Earlier baptismal registers have been little used by demographers, and the usefulness of data they might yield would be impaired, perhaps decisively, by the tendency of girls becoming pregnant in one parish to bear their babies in another. No less equivocal are the ratios of illegitimate births or baptisms to total births or baptisms which, with some ingenuity, can be constructed for more than fifty parishes from information volunteered, mostly by their priests, to the Poor Inquiry Commission. The ratios range from zero in the handful of parishes in which, though some were of more than a thousand families, no illegitimate birth was said to have occurred in ten or more years,[4] to about 7 per cent in two parishes. Of the 49 intermediate ratios (tabulated on pp. 80-81), 29 were 2 or under; 9 between 2 and 4, and 11 between 4 and 6.

That the incidence of illegitimacy was low; that, for all the pitfalls, these figures may not mislead, is suggested both by later, more dependable, statistics, and by contemporary testimony, champions of the Irish insisting, their critics conceding, that illegitimacy and conduct likely to lead to it were relatively rare in Ireland. Thus to a French traveller in the 1830s 'the Irish are

---

[1] Ib. 17 (Gal.); 46 (Lim.); 45 (Kerry); 35, 36, 37 (Clare); 31-32 (W'meath); 25 (Carl.); 22 (Rosc.); Supp. App. A, 1104 (Arm.).
[2] App. A, 46 (Tipp.); 86 (Rosc.); 17 (Gal.); 46 (Lim.).
[3] Ib. 48 (Ant.); 65 (Gal.).
[4] 'There are instances of parishes in this province, in which there are more than a thousand families in which there has not been one illegitimate child for ten years' (Dr. McHale, Archbishop of Galway, Add. App. A, 561 (Gal.); App. A, 126 (Don.)).

Ratio of Births or Baptisms of illegitimate Children

County and Parish	Source of information in cols. (b), (c), (g)[1] (a)	Total annual baptisms (b)	Annual baptisms of illegitimate children (c)	Population in 1841 (d)	Crude birthrate, 1832–41 (e)	Expected annual number of births (f)	Annual number of illegitimate births (g)	Baptisms of illegitimate children as % of total baptisms (h)	Baptisms of illegitimate children as % of total expected births (i)	Illegitimate births as % of total expected births (j)
Carlow					30					
Barragh	Gent.			3452[2]		104	c. 2			c. 2
Carlow	P.P.		8	9597		288			2.8	
Tullow	n.g.			4478		135	7–8			5.2–5.9
Dunleckney	P.P.			4743		474	6[3]			+1.3
Clare					37					
Abbey, etc.	n.g.			3517		130	—2			—·5
Feakle	P.P.			8744[2]		324	5–8			1·5–2·5
Kildysart	P.P.			5130		190	4			2·1
Killaloe	P.P.			4957		185	3–4			1·6–2·2
Kilfarboy, etc.	R.C.C.			7498						2[2]
Tulla	P.P.[4]		4	7514[2]		278			1·4	
Cork					32					
Macroom	P.P.[4]			7227		231	10[5]			+4·3
Ross-Carbery	P.P.			8839		283	c. 4			c. 1·4
Skull	P.P.		10	11542[6]		369			2·7	
Tracton	n.g.			2959		95	6–8			6·3–8·4
Galway					35					
Kilcummin	P.P.			10824		378	1·75			0·5
Killimore	P.P.			4140		146	2			1·4
Omagh	n.g.			7953		278	2–3			0·7–1·1
Templetoher, etc.	P.P.[4]		2	9742[2]		341			0·6	
Kerry					37					
Dingle	C. of I.C.		—1	14000[2]		518			—0·2	
Kenmare	n.g.	300	c. 20					c. 6·7		
Killarney	n.g.	400	c. 12					c. 3·0		
Tralee, etc.	n.g.			16000[2]		592	30			5·1
Parish near Tralee	n.g.			7000[2]		252	2			0·8
Kildare					30					
Kilcock Union	n.g.			1974		59	c. 3			c. 5·1
Cadamstown Union	P.P.			5000[2]		150	—1			—0·7
Kilkenny					30·5					
Freshford, etc.	P.P.			9220[2]		281	5			1·8
St Patrick's	n.g.			2743[2]		84	4			4·8
St Patrick, Outrath, etc.	n.g.			4981[2]		152	1–1·3			0·7–0·9
Leitrim					36					
Killenumery, etc.	P.P.			7084[2]		265	1·66			0·6

Cols. (a), (b), (c) and (g), *First Report, S.C. on Condition of the Poorer Classes in Ireland*, P.P., 1835, XXXII, App. A, 64–114; Supp. to App. A, pp. 811–1219; Addenda to App. A, P.P., 1836, XXX, pp. 561–8.
Cols. (d) and (e), *Census of Ireland, 1841*, P.P., 1843, XXIV, p. 459 and *passim*.

to total Baptisms or total expected Births

County and Parish	Source of information in cols. (b), (c), (g)[1] (a)	Total annual baptisms (b)	Annual baptisms of illegitimate children (c)	Population in 1841 (d)	Crude birthrate, 1832–41 (e)	Expected annual number of births (f)	Annual number of illegitimate births (g)	Baptisms of illegitimate children as % of total baptisms (h)	Baptisms of illegitimate children as % of total expected births (i)	Illegitimate births as % of total expected births (j)
Limerick					34					
Askeaton, etc.	n.g.									c. 5[2]
Listowel	n.g.			5934						1[2]
Newcastle	P.P.	100–130	6					4·6–6·0		
Shanagolden, etc.	n.g.									c. 5[2]
Londonderry					30·5					
Dungiven, etc.	n.g.		c. 7	10959		328			c. 2·1	
Upper Cumber	P.P. and Rect.		c. 6	7052		212			2·8	
Longford					31·5					
Abbeyshrule	n.g.			3671		116	−3			−2·6
Cloonguish	n.g.			6504		202	3			1·5
Granard	n.g.			10193		316	3–4			0·9–1·3
Kilashee	P.P.			3084		95	2·7			2·8
Templemichael, etc.	n.g.			12410		384	6–8			1·6–2·1
Mayo					37					
Aughagower	P.P.[4]		4·3	11963		443			1·0	
Meath					32					
Moymet, etc.			−1	1063		34			−2·9	
Roscommon					35					
Boyle	n.g.		4[3]	12591		441			+0·9	
Kilkeevan	n.g.		8	2818		99			0·8	
Moore	P.P.		1[3]	4608		161			+0·6	
Sligo					35					
Kilmacshalgan	n.g.			3872		135	1			0·7
Tipperary					34					
Carrick	P.P.	300	10–15	9165				3·3–5·0		
St Mary's Clonmel	P.P.	600	20–30					3·3–5·0		
Westmeath					31					
Killucan	P.P.			9546		296	c. 5			c. 1·7
Moatgrenogue	n.g.			3526		109	c. 4–5			c. 3·7–4·6
Wexford					31					
Monart	n.g.			3712		115	1			0·9

[1] 'P.P.', parish priest; 'R.C.C.', Catholic curate; 'Rect.', Church of Ireland rector; 'C. of I.C.', Church of Ireland curate; 'Gent.', gentleman; 'n.g.', not given.
[2] Figure supplied by informant in col. (a).   [3] Catholics only.
[4] Information specifically said to be drawn from parish registers.
[5] Plus the odd child 'taken through shame to other clergymen to be baptised'.
[6] The population of the parish of Skull was 17,314 and the expected number of births 554. But as the parish priest's figure for baptisms of illegitimate children relates to the two-thirds of the parish for which he was responsible, the other figures are scaled down in proportion.

remarkable for chastity; natural children are rare, adultery almost unknown';[1] to a German in the following decade 'the mass of the people are in the highest degree moral, and the women are more modest than they are to be found in any other part of the world.'[2] To successive English visitors the poor Irish were 'remarkable for their chastity',[3] their modesty 'the subject of remark and eulogy with every stranger';[4] the peasantry were 'signally chaste';[5] 'there are no more innocent girls in the world than the Irish.'[6] Clerical observers, Catholic and Protestant, agreed that the Irish girl's chastity was 'wonderful', 'marvellous', or 'remarkable'.[7] Nor, knowing their districts as no visitor knew Ireland, did local residents demur: 'morality so far as sexual intercourse is concerned is preserved [in a Limerick parish] to a wonderful extent, even among the poorest'; elsewhere in Limerick, priest and rector agreed 'as to the extreme infrequency of a woman being with child at the time of marriage'. In Donegal 'there is scarcely anything known about bastards in the parish'; 'a most extraordinary degree of morality prevails'. The number of bastards in Cork and Limerick, Sligo, Tipperary, and Antrim was 'very small'; bastardy is of 'rare occurrence' in Wexford and Clare[8]—and so on, in more than twenty reports, offset by contrary or equivocal testimony for only four parishes, three, perhaps significantly, in Ulster, the fourth near the barracks of Kildare.[9]

Statistics become available twenty years after the Famine. In the first complete decade of civil registration, 1871–80, illegitimate births in the 26 counties becoming the Republic were 1·63 per cent of total births.[10] In Sundbärg's international table of illegitimacy for the 1890s the ratio for England and Wales was 4·1 per hundred;

[1] G. de Beaumont, *Ireland, Social, Political and Religious*, ed. W. C. Taylor (1839), ii, 35.
[2] J. Venedy, *Ireland and the Irish during the Repeal Year, 1843*, trans. Wm. B. MacCabe (Dublin, 1844), p. 164.
[3] J. Milner, *An Inquiry into certain vulgar Opinions concerning the Catholic Inhabitants and Antiquities of Ireland* (1808), p. 200.
[4] John Carr, *The Stranger in Ireland* (1806), p. 236.
[5] J. E. Bicheno, *Ireland and its Economy* ... (1830), p. 33.
[6] W. M. Thackeray, *The Irish Sketch Book* [of 1842] (1869), p. 119.
[7] Milner, op. cit., p. 200; App. A, 98 (Clare); ib. (Kerry).
[8] Ib. 111–13 (Lim.); 126 (Don.); 108 (Cork); 73 (Sligo); 113 (Tipp.); 121 (Ant.); 88 (Wex.); 95, 96 (Clare), etc.
[9] Ib. 119 (Ant.); 506 (Derry); 561 (Kild.); Supp. App. A, 1100 (Arm.).
[10] Commission on Emigration and other Population Problems, 1948–54, *Reports*, p. 295.

ILLEGITIMACY BEFORE THE FAMINE

that for Portugal, 12·1, was highest; that for Ireland, 2·6, was lowest—though marriage in Ireland was then late by international standards, the proportion of life-long bachelors and spinsters high.[1]

Granted a relatively low level of illegitimacy in the 1830s, with what traits in peasant life would it seem to have been associated? We may assume (if we could not prove) that not only illegitimate births but illegitimate conceptions were few—that the problem is not explained away by the prevalence of abortion, by the number of pregnant girls who married or left the country before their babies were born. Nor can we, at all plausibly, attribute relatively few illegitimate conceptions to an innately weak sexual drive, to relatively widespread sterility or contraception—the people, certainly, showed no reluctance to marry, to marry young and rear large families.

Professor Leontine Young, after studying a group of unmarried mothers in the United States in the early 1950s, argued that few of them 'just happened' to become pregnant. ' "I don't know why, but this is something I had to do" ': the remark of one girl applied to many. The purposiveness of their actions, though they were not consciously planned, was suggested by their following a course of conduct leading in all probability to pregnancy without a husband; by the rarity with which any had used contraceptive devices, though known and available to them; by their seldom toying with abortion; by their contented pregnancy, free of nausea, food fads and odd desires; by their delivering their babies with fewer than average complications. Women normally enough wish to have babies: the wish normally—though not with Professor Young's unmarried mothers—is associated with a desire to have also the child the baby grows into; with feeling for her partner, the desire that he should be her husband, and environmental as well as biological father of their child. Few of the mothers Professor Young studied had been much interested in men: for many their only sexual experience—brief, perhaps, and unhappy—had been that resulting in impregnation. Their idiosyncrasy was that their urge for a baby had been separated from its complement in other women, love for a man. This separation, in an argument of some intricacy, Professor Young associates with infancy dominated by one parent, commonly the mother.[2]

---

[1] G. Sundbärg, *Aperçus statistiques internationaux* (Stockholm, 1908).
[2] Leontine Young, *Out of Wedlock* (New York, 1954), pp. 21–39 and *passim*.

Professor Young's analysis, however valid, hardly applies as closely in a traditional peasant society as in modern America: without contraception, relatively more girls, sexually adventurous but unneurotic, were likely to become pregnant; with little abortion, relatively more became mothers. The made match, spreading after the Famine, was commonly credited with achieving equable marriage, neither father nor mother unduly overborne;[1] if this equability had a longer pedigree, it might have lessened the neuroses and delinquency not improbably associated with unmarried motherhood.

Beyond this, we might make something of the presumably small proportion of resident servants in an impoverished economy of small farms, large families, and neighbourly help: not only in Ireland did servants contribute relatively many parents of illegitimate children.[2] More important, of course, early and general marriage lessened the number of potential parents of illegitimate children—though, not to exaggerate the significance of this, we need more information than appears to be available on the age at puberty. Long lowered, it may be, by good nutrition and an associated early weaning, the age at puberty may have been further reduced in the late eighteenth century as boys and girls more youthfully assumed an adult role: earlier adolescence, though contributing to the youthfulness of marriage, would to some degree have offset its tendency to reduce the number of potential parents of illegitimate children.

Social and economic pressures, too, deterred from conduct likely to result in the birth of illegitimate children. If, as is often said, attachment between parents and children was unusually strong in Irish families, sexuality, tending to divide children from parents, might have roused abnormal guilt, abnormal hesitation. Women, offered few openings save in marriage, were the more likely to conform with the code of conduct proper to unmarried women;[3] the lack of a bastardy law and (until 1838) of a poor law gave further inducement to conformity.[4] We have seen, too, the strength

[1] K. H. Connell, 'Peasant marriage in Ireland: its structure and development since the Famine', *Econ. Hist. Rev.*, XIV, 1962, pp. 513–14.
[2] *Encyclopaedia of Social Sciences*, 'Illegitimacy', p. 581.
[3] Francis B. Head, *A Fortnight in Ireland* (1853), p. 117; Poor Inquiry (Ireland), App. H, Pt. ii, *Remarks . . . by J. E. Bicheno*, P.P., 1836, XXXIV, p. 16.
[4] Ib.; *Observations on the Habits of the Labouring Classes in Ireland suggested by Mr. G. C. Lewis's Report . . .* (Dublin), 1836, p. 12.

ILLEGITIMACY BEFORE THE FAMINE

of the popular disapproval of the illegitimate child and his mother, the bleak lives ahead of them. But the sources of so harsh an attitude towards illegitimacy are not easily traced. Needless to say, it is no universal feature of peasant life. The Welsh in the mid-nineteenth century were more tolerant. In 1847 the chaplain to the Bishop of Bangor, in north Wales, asserted 'with confidence, as an undeniable fact, that fornication is not regarded as a vice, scarcely as a frailty, by the common people in Wales. It is considered as a matter of course.'[1] More recently (and probably in the nineteenth century), the prevalence of pre-marital intercourse and illegitimacy in north Wales suggested that the people did not really think them wrong. The pregnant girl, the unmarried mother, was tolerantly treated. Her own mother commonly took in the child, rearing him as her own. Neither illegitimacy nor having had an illegitimate child was impediment to marriage.[2]

That the Irish took a sterner view is doubtless to some degree associated with their devotion to Church and priest: 'confession is a powerful restraint on immorality'; 'that great terror-striker, the confessional, is before the Irish girl, and sooner or later, her sins must be told'.[3] Similarly, the clergy's close surveillance of their flock, their 'personal inspection',[4] may have been of consequence; so, too, among a people superstitious as well as religious, may have been the religious symbols in their cabins.[5]

Catholicism elsewhere—in Austria, for instance, and Portugal—was associated with no low level of illegitimacy.[6] But, as an Irish priest demonstrated (not simply to his own satisfaction), early in the present century 'Orangeism and illegitimacy go together; ...

---

[1] Quoted by Isabel Emmett, *A North Wales Village* (1964), p. 102.
[2] Ib. 104.
[3] Wakefield, 1812, op. cit., ii, 746; Thackeray [1842], op. cit., p. 119; Harriet Martineau, *Letters from Ireland* (1852), p. 7.
[4] Venedy, 1844, op. cit., p. 164.
[5] The point is made by Paul Vincent Carroll, more extravagantly than might apply when statuary and pictures were harder to come by: bed, to Dillon, the drunken teacher in *The White Steed*, was ' "another prison ... the walls groaning with the pictures of grim saints. St. Anthony of Padua, St. Stephen, St. Paul, St. Michael, with his foot in your throttle. There they are, leaning over, leaning down. You fall asleep by their permission, you dream secretly at your peril. When you awaken, there they are, warders jangling the keys of the eternal puzzle over your head ... Do you think I'd have the nerve to take a woman to bed before that crew?" ' (Paul Vincent Carroll, *Three Plays*, 1944, p. 43).
[6] Sundbärg, op. cit.; *Encyclopaedia of Social Sciences*, 'Illegitimacy', p. 581.

bastards in Ireland are in proportion to the Orange lodges.'[1] An unusual concern with the sins against chastity may have helped Irish Catholicism to keep its people chaste; so, too, may the nature of the relationship between priest and people, the unusual priestly insistence, the unusual popular submission.

Much in the social and economic spheres alone helps to explain the peasant's reverence for Church and priest[2]: long living wretchedly, they needed all the comfort and solace, all the colour and hope that religion might bring. Ties with the Church were strengthened by its sharing the people's suffering under the penal laws; the priests' power was the greater for their being drawn themselves from the peasantry, sharing peasant prejudices, for being, by and large, the only people with the standing and education to act as its leaders. The sharp insistence of the Irish priest on sexual conformity is sometimes attributed to a puritanical, Jansenist, strain brought to Maynooth by its original professoriate in 1795, retained and refined thereafter as vacancies were filled by men of their own persuasion and rearing. And the priests' teaching was the more telling because of their observing, more scrupulously, perhaps, than some of their Continental colleagues, their vows of chastity.

[1] M. O'Riordan, *Catholicity and Progress in Ireland* (1905), p. 272n.
[2] Relations between priests and people after the Famine are discussed below, 'Catholicism and Marriage', pp. 144–61.

III

ETHER-DRINKING IN ULSTER

That any condition of things should arise which should take a nauseous fluid like ether from the pharmacopoeia and laboratory to the chemist and make it the recognised stimulant of any set of men, and that with them it should supplant alcohol—that they should take 'nips' of ether morning, noon and night as they would whiskey and—for anything shown to the contrary—drink good luck or ratify bargains in a glass of ether ... is perhaps without parallel in the history of narcotic stimulants. (H. N. Draper, 'On the use of ether as an intoxicant in the north of Ireland', *Medical Press and Circular*, 30 May 1877, p. 117.)

ETHER, a scientists' curiosity for two hundred years, was brought before a wider public in the eighteenth century when it was marketed as an industrial solvent and for its supposed pharmaceutical virtue.[1] By the 1840s, when its anaesthetic properties were realized, it was already an occasional inebriant on both sides of the Atlantic. Indeed, the pioneer anaesthetists, Clarke in dentistry and Long in surgery, are said to have experimented with ether after observing its effect at social gatherings.[2] At quilting bees in Georgia, where Long was brought up, the girls, when work was finished, might be joined by their young men for a spoon of ether, as well as a dance. In the 1830s, Philadelphia ladies, vaporizing a little ether in a bladder, inhaled it 'for sport' from a tube with a stop-cock. Earlier, young people in Britain and America had

---

[1] The synthesis of 'sweet vitriol' from sulphuric acid and alcohol is said to have been first described by Valerias Cordus (d. 1544): the product was renamed 'ether' by the German scientist Frobenius in or about 1730 (Victor Robinson, *Victory over Pain* (1947), p. 34; A. W. Slater, 'Fine Chemicals', in C. Singer *et al.*, *A History of Technology*, v, *The Late Nineteenth Century* (Oxford, 1958), p. 313).

[2] Slater, op. cit., p. 343; H. R. Raper, *Man against Pain: the Epic of Anaesthesia* (1947), pp. 58–59.

enlivened the occasional evening with whiffs of nitrous oxide. But a bladder of gas was awkward to handle, liquid ether no less effective: the laughing-gas party gave way to the 'ether frolic'.[1]

Such parties hardly involved more than a few people, most of them young, comfortably reared and unusually venturesome, if not neurotic. But later in the century ether-drinkers were more numerous and diverse. The surgical advances facilitated by ether brought it favourably to the public notice. It was more widely distributed as every hospital needed its supply, as photography and refrigeration quickened the industrial demand. Costs of production probably fell, the retail price more sharply, as the alcohol used in its manufacture was freed of duty.[2] And many sought ether the more eagerly as temperance campaigns and fiscal policy put alcohol beyond their reach.[3]

Still, after 1850, there were well-to-do drinkers of ether. The English cases of a distinguished inebriologist were 'persons of education and refinement': all had at some time been alcoholics and they were mostly women; the men were all doctors.[4] A congress of doctors, dispersing at Epsom around 1880, left further evidence of the profession's non-medical interest in ether: among empty bottles of 'Champagne and the great wines' were phials drained of their ether.[5] When feeling depressed, ladies in Germany took their 'Hoffmann's drops' (one part ether to three of alcohol);[6] in France, their *perles d'éther*, gelatine capsules 'beautifully made' to hold 5–10 minims of ether—'the exhilarating effect of one of these little pills on an empty stomach is something marvellous'; as a morning pick-me-up, they were in demand both by the *femmes du demi-monde* and ladies in high position.[7]

[1] T. R. and J. B. Beck, *Medical Jurisprudence* (7th edn., 1842), p. 1068, quoting T. D. Mitchell, *Chemistry*; C. Singer and E. Underwood, *A Short History of Medicine* (2nd edn., Oxford, 1962), p. 343.

[2] Slater, op. cit., p. 300; H. and A. Gernsheim, 'The Photographic Arts: Photography', in Singer *et. al.*, op. cit., v, p. 725; T. N. Morris, 'Management and Preservation of Food', in Singer *et al.*, op. cit., v, p. 46.

[3] See below, pp. 89, 99–102.

[4] N. Kerr, *Inebriety: its Etiology, Pathology, Treatment and Jurisprudence* (2nd edn., 1889), p. 792.

[5] E. Beluze, *De l'Étheromanie* (Paris, 1885), p. 9.

[6] *Lancet*, i (1898), 1568, quoting *Vierteljahrsschrift für Gerichtlich Medicin*.

[7] C. R. C. Tichbourne, 'Ether and methylated spirit drinking', *The Health Record: an Irish Journal of Sanitary Science*, i, (1891), 25–26; Norman Kerr, 'Ether inebriety', *Journal of the American Medical Association*, XVII (1891), 792.

By the nineties the initiated, wanting personal escape or a daring party, looked rather to morphia than ether; now more readily procured, it was pleasanter to take and left no tell-tale smell.[1] But the taste for ether descended the social scale; in half a dozen peasant communities scattered throughout Europe, ether rivalled alcohol as the popular intoxicant; for a while, here and there, it took its place.

In East Prussia—as in Russia and Norway—the spread of ether-drinking was attributed to restrictions on the sale of alcohol. In 1887, when the duty on corn brandy was increased, in Heydekrug, near the Russian border, *Schwefeläther* became the peasants' 'favourite tipple'. This mixture of ether and spirits of wine was sold openly in the grocers' shops; both sexes indulged, the old and young. Their pupils already dosed before lessons began, teachers were 'powerless against the pernicious habit'; roads and markets reeked with the 'mawkish fumes', and peasant carts, travelling the roads, left a 'cloud of ether' floating behind.[2]

In the frontier governments of Russia the sale of vodka in small quantities for immediate consumption was made unlawful in 1896. Though measures had already been taken to check the drinking of ether, it was now so widely substituted for vodka that local doctors pleaded for St. Petersburg's intervention. For some years, however, the government's endeavours were 'almost fruitless': in places, into the present century, ether-drinking was 'extremely prevalent'. At Trossno, for instance, in 1902, six children were killed in an explosion, as a farmer, preparing for his son's wedding, bottled two pailsful of ether.[3]

In 1894 (according to a Lyons medical journal) ether-drinking was increasingly prevalent in France, and responsible for much public drunkenness.[4] Twenty years later the Hungarian Board of Health deplored the habit, brought, it believed, by emigrants returning from the States.[5]

In Britain ether was drunk in 'certain low-class localities' in Glasgow; in Liverpool and Lincolnshire; by textile workers in

---

[1] L. Lewin, *Phantastica: Narcotic and Stimulating Drugs* (trans. from 2nd German edn. by P. H. A. Wirth, 1931), p. 198.
[2] *British Medical Journal*, i (1898), 1033; i (1897), 831; *Lancet*, i (1898), 1568.
[3] *British Medical Journal*, i (1897), 831–2; i (1892), 673; i (1903), 98.
[4] *British Medical Journal*, ii (1894), 960, quoting *Lyon médical*.
[5] *Lancet*, i (1914), 1425.

Bradford and miners' wives in Durham.[1] But nowhere, seemingly, was it matter for great concern. Nor was it a problem in Ireland, save in and around counties Londonderry and Tyrone (whence, it may be, migrants had taken it to Irish colonies in Britain).

Here—if reports can be trusted—in a thousand square miles almost every house had its ether bottle;[2] some 50,000 people, an eighth of the local population, were 'etheromaniacs'. With the occasional tipplers, they annually consumed some 17,000 gallons:[3] to Cookstown alone the railway brought two tons a year.[4] Some local shebeens sold nothing but ether; in others, bottles of whiskey and ether stood side by side.[5] The atmosphere of Cookstown and Moneymore was 'loaded' with ether;[6] hundreds of yards outside Draperstown a visiting surgeon detected the familiar smell;[7] market days smelt 'not of pigs, tobacco smoke or of unwashed human beings';[8] even the bank 'stoved' of ether, and its reek on the Derry Central Railway was 'disgusting and abominable'.[9] 'Enter the humblest cabin and you will see decrepit, white-haired men, tottering and feeble, inane as far as brain power is concerned, who have become the miserable wrecks they are—helpless to themselves and loathsome and disgusting to others—through the long-continued use of ether.' 'What guarantee is there against ether drinking spreading the length and breadth of the land and clouding the spirit and sapping the physique of the finest peasantry in the world?' 'What is the case of Ireland today', *The Times* warned, 'may become that of England or Scotland tomorrow.'[10]

---

[1] *Lancet*, ii (1902), 557; E. Hart, 'An address on ether-drinking; its prevalence and results', *British Medical Journal*, ii (1890), 890; W. Calwell, 'Ether-drinking in Ulster', *British Medical Journal*, ii (1910), p. 389; N. Kerr, 'Ether inebriety', *Journal of the American Medical Association*, xvii (1891), 792.

[2] Hart, 1890, op. cit., p. 885.

[3] *Times*, 27 Mar 1891.

[4] Hart, 1890, op. cit., p. 888, quoting rector of Cookstown.

[5] *S.C. on British and Foreign Spirits*, British P.P., 1890–1, XI, James Clark, inspector, Inland Revenue, q. 3911; letter from Inland Revenue, q. 3175; Kerr, 1891, op. cit., p. 791.

[6] Hart, 1890, op. cit., p. 888, quoting Cookstown doctor.

[7] B. W. Richardson, 'Ether-drinking and extra-Alcoholic Intoxication', in B. W. Richardson, *A Ministry of Health* (1897), p. 325.

[8] *Times*, 27 Mar 1871.

[9] Calwell, 1910, op. cit., p. 388. The Derry Central Railway (opened in 1880) connected Magherafelt with Macfin Junction, south of Coleraine.

[10] *Times*, 27 Mar 1871.

Ether-drinking in Ulster, however highly-coloured the accounts,[1] was threatening enough to be 'cursed by the priest'; denounced by the Synod of the Church of Ireland; investigated and restricted by parliament.[2]

Ether, volatilizing at body temperature, tends to escape as gas on contact with mouth and stomach; and, irritating the stomach, it is liable to be ejected by vomiting. But a ritual was evolved enabling the drinker to retain enough of so elusive a beverage to experience its gratifying effects: after 'renching his gums' (washing his mouth with cold water), he drank a little water, then, quickly, holding his nose, swallowed his ether, following it with more water.[3] The mouthfuls of water, before and after the ether, lessened its burning effect; with nose-holding, they made vomiting less likely; but mainly, no doubt, they delayed volatilization by cooling the mouth and stomach.

The inebriating dose naturally varied with the drinker's constitution and experience. Girls in their early twenties might take a teaspoonful, grown women a little more, men a tablespoonful; a desertspoonful and 'the full of an egg-cup' were normal doses, the 'range of potation' from half a fluid ounce to the three ounces held

---

[1] The sources of any account of Ulster's indulgence in ether are few and not all beyond reproach. Drinkers and dealers, rarely putting pen to paper, were the more reticent about a custom so doubtfully proper; potential publicists—the priests not least—shrank from making their people a by-word; shrank, too, from the realization that they erred beyond local control. When, eventually, public interest was roused, the oddity of ether-drinking invited caricature; and the teetotaller, vesting it with the evils of spirit-drinking, like the publican, fearing for his living, painted it larger than life. But an account of some verisimilitude seems to be possible. The select committee on the adulteration of spirits (*British P.P.*, 1890, X; 1890-1, XI), instructed in the course of its duties to report also on ether-drinking, hardly approached the matter with fixed ideas. Among the witnesses it heard were local clergy and doctors; Inspector Clark, who had spent three months investigating the matter for the Board of Inland Revenue; Mackenzie Ledlie, a professional journalist and *The Times* special correspondent on ether-drinking; and F. W. Pavy, a doctor and a Fellow of the Royal Society, who had questioned every medical practitioner in the supposedly affected area. Other accounts, based on seemingly-searching questionnaires and/or personal observation, were published between 1870 and 1910 by two outside doctors, H. N. Draper and William Calwell, by Sir Benjamin Ward Richardson, F.R.S., the sanitary reformer, Ernest Hart, editor of the *British Medical Journal*, and by Norman Kerr, chairman of the British Medical Association's committee on inebriation.

[2] See below pp. 105-8.

[3] *Times*, 27 Mar 1891; Hart, 1890, op. cit., p. 888; Calwell, 1910, op. cit., p. 388, etc.

by a full-sized wine glass. Every drinker might repeat his dose several times a day. The seasoned toper on each occasion needed a second, even a third, glassful. He might, indeed, take half a pint with no alarming effect; withstand a pint in the heroic debauch, or a steady ten ounces day after day. He scorned, too, the ordinary man's ritual, simply gulping and relishing his ether, increasing his dose to offset the greater loss of gas from his uncooled stomach.[1]

To the novice ether offered no immediate pleasure of palate or stomach. Self-experimenters had difficulty in swallowing it at all: 'the eyes water, the mouth closes on it, and there is an absolute kind of revulsion to the whole thing which seems to shut it out.' The taste was 'highly provocative of vomiting'; so, too, was the contraction of the walls of the stomach as ether irritated the lining. If the ether were retained, its volatilization was accompanied by 'violent eructations', by 'great dissipation of wind', and by a sensation in the stomach variously likened to warmth or burning, to 'a ball of ice', or 'the feeling you have when you grasp a piece of lead'.[2]

In a few minutes, given an appropriate dose, the drinker's pulse quickened, his face flushed, a wave of perhaps hysterical excitement yielded to a calmer mood, and 'he dreamed himself into his personal paradise'. He was in fairyland. Cares vanished in 'blithesome gladness'; his pulse beat with joy, his eye glistened with love.[3] French initiates likened their state to Champagne drunkenness: they were in paradise, listening to delicious music as they danced at the ball and walked on the clouds.[4] In Ireland, too, 'you always heard music, and you'd be cocking your ears at it . . . . Others would see men climbing up the walls and going through the roof, or coming in through the roof and down the walls, nice and easy.'[5]

---

[1] *S.C. on British and Foreign Spirits*, B.P.P., 1890–1, XI, Mackenzie-Ledlie, q. 3217; Pavey, q. 3761; Kerr, 1890, op. cit., p. 544; Richardson, 1897, op. cit., p.329; I.F.C., Murphy, co. Tyrone, MS. 1220, p. 80. Beluze (1885, op. cit., p. 13) and Lewin (1931, op. cit., p. 199) refer to drinkers said to have taken as much as a litre a day. At an inquest in 1962 on a Stoke-on-Trent woman, it was said that she and her husband had each been drinking a pint of ether daily (*Times*, 15 Dec 1962).

[2] *S.C. on British and Foreign Spirits*, B.P.P., 1890–1, XI, qq. 1660, 1729, 3294; Hart, 1890, op. cit., p. 889; A. S. Taylor, *The Principles and Practice of Medical Jurisprudence* (3rd edn., 1883), p. 74; F. E. Anstie, *Stimulants and Narcotics* (1864), pp. 331–2.

[3] *Times*, 27 Mar 1891; Hart, 1890, op. cit., p. 889; *S.C. on British and Foreign Spirits*, B.P.P., 1890–1, XI, q. 3175, etc.

[4] Beluze, 1885, op. cit., p. 25.

[5] I.F.C., Murphy, co. Tyrone, MS. 1220, p. 81.

ETHER-DRINKING IN ULSTER

The erotic appeal of ether was stressed more by Continental than by Irish observers. Elsewhere, men, hoping for 'strange voluptuousness', were rewarded by visions of 'lascivious situations' and 'beautiful women';[1] but in Ireland (where ether-inebriation was a regional more than a personal problem) the drinkers' dreams were said to be 'light' and 'refined'.[2]

In folklore, if not in physiology, the agreeable effects of one day's ether might be recaptured the next, simply by drinking a glass of water.[3] But the ether-drinker's 'luxurious advantage' was that, half-a-dozen times a day, he might pass through 'the drama of intoxication'.[4] Within the hour—in twenty minutes, some said—he might be sober, helplessly drunk, and sober again. Recovering, he was a little depressed, needing a repetition of his pleasurable experience, and denied it by none of the spirit-drinker's headache or vomiting.[5]

The drinkers of ether, like their neighbours, seem mostly to have been Catholic small farmers or labourers, or members of their families. But 'millhands and other operatives' early learned its appeal, and, certainly by the 'nineties, they were joined by 'respectable people'—members, even, of the learned professions. Women, if they took inebriants at all, were thought to be drawn to ether by its cheapness and their greater readiness to forswear spirit, or its unlawful form. Commonly, ailing or fretful children were soothed with ether: they got it, too, from dealers, for odd jobs or an egg or two. 'Smell a man's breath and tell his religion': it was, of course, 'darkly hinted' that ether-drinking was an evil of Romanism. But nothing, an English observer maintained, 'could be more unwarrantable or unfair': 'there are enough and to spare of Protestant ether-tipplers'; the habit, he insisted, prevailed in Protestant Tobermore as in its Catholic vicinity.[6]

Ether is the distillate of alcohol treated with sulphuric acid.

---

[1] S. Levison, *l'Étheromanie* (Paris, 1935), p. 14; Lewin, 1931, op. cit., p. 198.
[2] Richardson, 1897, op. cit., p. 338.
[3] Ulster Folk Museum, 62, Q4, 18, Magherafelt.
[4] Richardson, 1897, op. cit., p. 344; N. Kerr, 'Ether-drinking', *New Review*, iii (1890), 540.
[5] Hart, 1890, op. cit., p. 889; *Lancet*, ii (1890), 627; i (1891), 840; *S.C. on British and Foreign Spirits*, B.P.P., 1890–1, XI, qq. 3245–6, 3259.
[6] *Times*, 27 Mar 1891; H. N. Draper, 'On the use of ether as an intoxicant in the north of Ireland', *Medical Press and Circular*, 16 Feb 1870, p. 118; Kerr, 1890, op. cit., p. 539; *S.C. on British and Foreign Spirits*, B.P.P., 1890–1, XI, qq. 3132, 3146; Lewin, 1931, op. cit., p. 200; Beluze, 1885, op. cit., p. 12n.

Originally it was probably drunk undiluted, but *ether purus*, with its nauseating taste and low boiling point, is hard to ingest and retain, and, maybe, profitable to adulterate. Since ether barely dissolves in water, alcohol was the usual adulterant; the taste and smell of methylated spirit are disguised in ether, but it was probably mixed also with poteen, and with rectified spirit if the manufacturer were also the blender. Alcohol accounted for one part in twelve in one analysis of drinker's ether; for one part in five of a sample procured by a government chemist; the mixture, to one consumer, was 'some kind ev sperrit . . . taken aysier widout wather nor the ayther used to be'. It had the advantage, too, of not coming quite to the boil at body temperature.[1]

Most of the ether drunk in Ireland came from Britain; some, possibly, was made in Dublin.[2] I have seen no suggestion in the literary sources that it was distilled on the spot; the drinker, I presumed, lacked the knowledge and resources to distil at all safely so explosive a liquid. But Mr. W. J. McAuley, a Cookstown chemist, tells me of a tradition that ether was locally made—by adding sulphuric acid to the 'singlings' in the poteen still. Singlings was the distillate of the brewed liquor, returned to the retort for a second, sometimes a third, distillation. Sulphuric acid, familiar in areas of linen-finishing, was used also to enliven poteen: if poteen so enlivened were put in the retort, the early distillate would be ether.[3]

Chemical works in London, Manchester and Gateshead, Edinburgh and Glasgow all seem to have sent supplies to Ireland; the Irish business of some was proportionately 'much larger' than the English. London ether was mostly shipped by the Antrim Ore, the Carron Carrying, and the Clyde Shipping, Companies. Clyde Shipping charged 84*s*. 2*d*. a ton for carrying ether from the London manufacturers to Belfast; but consignors, irked by this inflated rate for explosive deck cargo, transferred much of their ether from its original drums to Winchester quarts marked 'Drugs'.[4]

[1] Kerr, 1890, op. cit., p. 545; 1891, op. cit., pp. 792–3; *S.C. on British and Foreign Spirits*, B.P.P., 1890–1, XI, qq. 1695, 1729, 3218–19; H. N. Draper, 'Ether drinking in the north of Ireland', *Medical Press and Circular*, 30 May 1877, p. 426.

[2] Hart, 1890, op. cit., p. 887.

[3] See above, 'Illicit Distillation', p. 6.

[4] Hart, 1890, op. cit., p. 887; Kerr, 1891, op. cit., p. 791; *Times*, 27 Mar 1891.

ETHER-DRINKING IN ULSTER

Though the larger chemist in Cookstown, Maghera, and Magherafelt might buy from the British maker, the trade was largely controlled by wholesalers in the Irish ports—in Derry and Dublin but mostly Belfast. From Belfast the ether travelled by rail or cart —to some parts by Lough Neagh boat. The railways kept quiet about their ether traffic: the Belfast and Northern Counties— admitting to a carriage of four tons a year—was the only line willing to give a figure to the rector of Cookstown. But official returns would have underestimated the trade; ether was 'smuggled' on trains as on steamers, to travel more cheaply.[1]

Belfast importers dealt mostly with seven towns—Draperstown, Maghera, Magherafelt, and Cookstown in Derry, Pomeroy, Omagh, and Dungannon in Tyrone; and within these towns with doctors, 'druggists and chemists', grocers, and general dealers. Any of these might supply the consumer (to drink on the spot or take away), as well as hawkers, country shopkeepers, and local dealers with no Belfast account.[2]

Some of the regular publicans and shebeen-keepers made no bones about selling ether: 'you can go into a public house, ask for a glass of ether and get it'. Some, indeed, served it willy-nilly— as reinforcement of watered whiskey; perhaps also in 'market' or 'Christmas' whiskey, fast-working, with a 'most fearful and wonderful smell', but unhappy after-effects. Publicans, in general, were chary of the new drink, not stocking it at all, or reserving it for the favoured customer: wiser, some thought, not further to provoke the authorities with a new and suspect trade; nor was there much prospect of profit in an inebriant so cheap and efficacious.[3]

Much of the trade in ether fell, then, to specialist dealers; to grocers and bakers, doctors and druggists. Booths or shebeens selling little but ether were 'scattered' over south Derry; the

[1] Kerr, 1891, op. cit., p. 793; Draper, 1870, op. cit., p. 117; *S.C. on British and Foreign Spirits*, B.P.P., 1890–1, XI, Carter, q. 3116. The Belfast and Northern Counties Railway, originally the Belfast and Ballymena Railway, acquired in 1861 the Ballymena, Ballymoney, Coleraine, and Portrush Junction Railway (R. G. Morton, *Standard gauge Railways in the North of Ireland* (Belfast, 1962), between pp. 18 and 19).

[2] Hart, 1890, op. cit., p. 887; *S.C. on British and Foreign Spirits*, B.P.P., 1890–1, XI, Wilkinson, q. 3154; Calwell, 1910, op. cit., p. 388; Kerr, 1891, op. cit., p. 791.

[3] *S.C. on British and Foreign Spirits*, B.P.P., 1890–1, XI, Carter, q. 3138; Calwell, 1910, op. cit., p. 389; Ulster Folk Museum, 62, Q4, 35; Richardson, 1897, op. cit., p. 327.

tradition of their existence persists today. In some even the moneyless customer was served, the proprietors keeping pigs to feed on the potatoes and meal they received for ether.[1]

Not all the specialists were sedentary traders: hawkers, beggarwomen, and ragmen served much of the casual, country demand, and, making ether so readily available, probably initiated many a new drinker. Their bottles they filled at the chemist's or small shopkeeper's, and emptied for young and old, at the door, in the field or road, accepting in return the odd copper or egg, 'little household articles', or stolen goods; bigger business they transacted at fairs and lodge meetings, at 'balls' and other festive gatherings.[2]

In its hey-day ether was probably sold in most country shops to which drinkers had access; certainly, around Cookstown, the 'wayside little grocers shops' had 'unlimited supplies', 'small poor grocery shops sell it without restriction.' Grocers, bakers, and general dealers all sold it, by the half-pint or pint, for taking away; for immediate consumption, by the wine-glass, with water for the less seasoned drinker. It was sold, too, by most chemists and some doctors, for consumption on or off the premises. On market-days during his apprenticeship in a south Derry 'medical hall', a doctor had sold many a 'dram of ether'— one-and-a-half drachms, he explained, of 'good sulphuric ether'. In the 'eighties, on market and fair days, we hear, 'it is not unusual to see ten to fifteen men and women waiting to be served at the chemist's counter, while the perfume of the place and the whispered "ayther" leave no doubt what is going on.' Doctors, thinking highly of the therapeutic and stimulating effects of ether, 'sold it in draughts over the counter on fair days to anyone asking for it'. Others, short of patients, dealt in it as a side-line, easing their scruples by adding spirits of nitre and calling it a pick-me-up; or brazenly (it was rumoured) selling ether as well as methylated spirit, 'their customers coming in, ordering it, paying for it, and drinking it there, just as they would do whiskies, beer, etc. in a public-house'.[3]

[1] Hart, 1890, op. cit., pp. 886–8; *S.C. on British and Foreign Spirits*, B.P.P., 1890–1, XI, Wilkinson and letter from Inland Revenue, qq. 3154, 3175; Kerr, 1891, op. cit., pp. 791, 793; Ulster Folk Museum, 62, Q4, 18, 20.

[2] Hart, 1890, op. cit., pp. 886–8; *S.C. on British and Foreign Spirits*, B.P.P., 1890–1, XI, qq. 3108, 3132, 3150, 3154, 3235; Kerr, 1890, op. cit., p. 539, 1891, op. cit., p. 793; *Times*, 27 Mar 1891; Calwell, 1910, op. cit., p. 388.

[3] Hart, 1890, op. cit., pp. 886–8; Richardson, 1897, op. cit., p. 328; *Lancet*, ii (1890), 627; *Times*, 27 Mar 1891; Kerr, 1891, op. cit., p. 793; *S.C. on British and Foreign Spirits*, B.P.P., 1890–1, XI, q. 3154.

ETHER-DRINKING IN ULSTER 97

In 1890, according to Mackenzie Ledlie, *The Times* correspondent, the 'infected area' was roughly enclosed by the river and lough shores from Portadown to Kilrea and by lines to Pettigo from Portadown through Lisbellaw and from Kilrea through Dungiven and Strabane.[1] Though Ledlie insisted that he had overstated nothing, the rector of Cookstown ('as I took the initiative in the movement to suppress ether-drinking') complained to *The Times* of his 'gross exaggeration, liable to exposure and contradiction, such that no responsible person could possibly make'.[2] Ether-drinking, he himself believed, was 'very prevalent' only within the area contained by lines from Omagh to 'the north shore of Lough Neagh', one via Maghera, the other via Pomeroy.[3] While Hart also put the 'chief centres' within this smaller area (though none within its western triangle, from Omagh towards Draperstown and Pomeroy), he added an area of lesser prevalence beyond Maghera and Toombridge towards Portglenone.[4] Draper, twenty years earlier, included Omagh as well as Draperstown, Maghera, and Cookstown as principal centres; and he pushed the eastern boundary beyond the Bann and Portglenone into co. Antrim.[5] The select committee asked to enquire into ether-drinking seems to have agreed that it was known throughout the area Ledlie indicated: certainly it incorporated in its report his estimate that it prevailed over some 600,000 acres.[6] Indeed, Ledlie's data (on location, at least) hardly warrant Carter's castigation. He included in his account estimates of the incidence of ether-drinking in various areas: all (unspecified 'miscellaneous areas' apart) in which he thought that at least one person in five took ether, were within Carter's limits; so also were all of the areas (admittedly of varying size) thought to dispose annually of more than 1500 gallons of ether. Beyond this central area, as seems entirely plausible, there were outlying districts where the habit, though it existed, was less prevalent.[7]

The earliest reference I have found to the drinking of ether in Ulster is the account compiled in 1870 by H. N. Draper, an English surgeon, on the basis of replies by gentlemen and clergy, physicians, druggists, and manufacturers of ether to 'a systematic series of

[1] *Times*, 27 Mar 1891.   [2] *Times*, 31 Mar 1891.
[3] S.C. on *British and Foreign Spirits*, B.P.P., 1890–1, XI, qq. 3088–9.
[4] Hart, 1890, op. cit., p. 886.   [5] Draper, 1870, op. cit., p. 117.
[6] S.C. on *British and Foreign Spirits*, B.P.P., 1890–1, XI, p. viii.
[7] *Times*, 27 Mar 1891; S.C. on *British and Foreign Spirits*, B.P.P., 1890–1, XI, qq. 3088–9, 3208 ff.

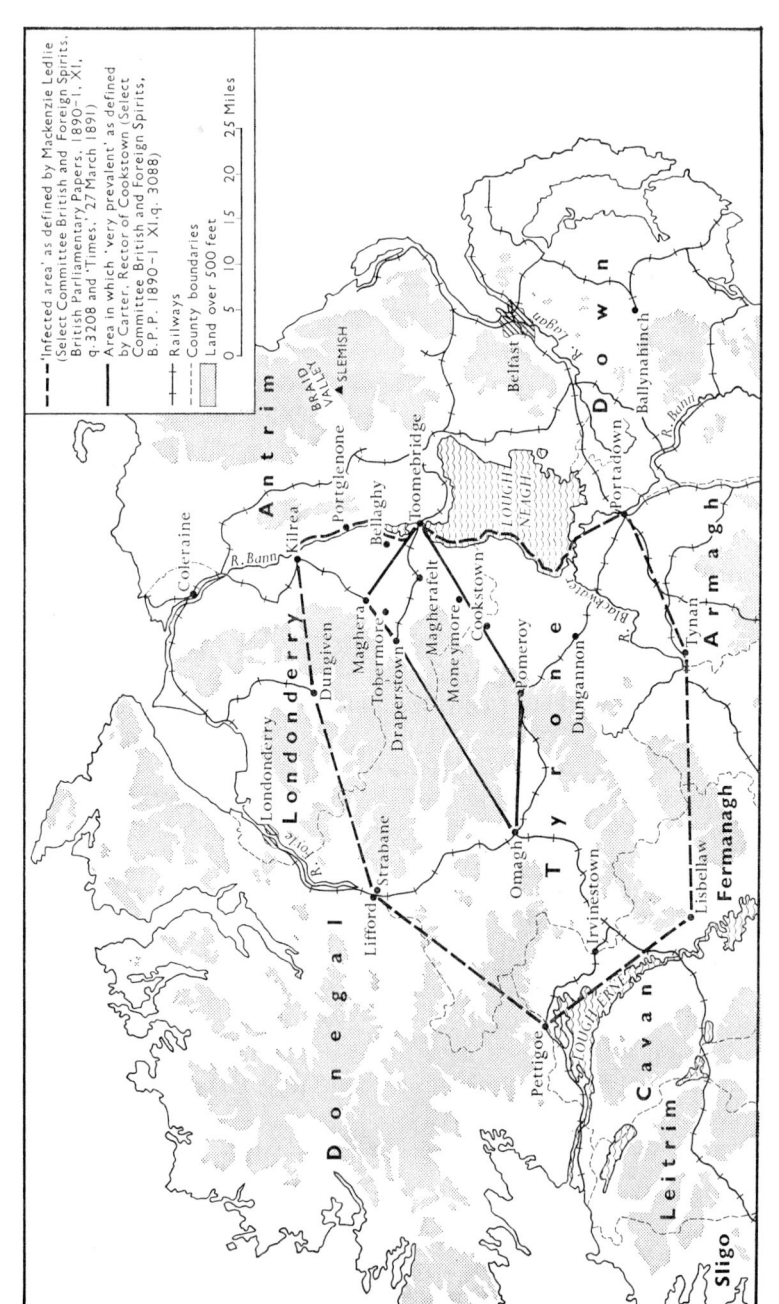

Fig. 6: Location of Ether-drinking, 1890

questions'. Around Draperstown and Maghera, Cookstown, and Omagh, Draper concluded, lived 'a race to whom ether is what koumiss is to the Kalmuck, ava to the South Sea islander, absinthe to a certain class of Frenchmen, and gin and whiskey to their more immediate neighbours'.[1] That ether was well-rooted already by 1870 we can hardly doubt. The method of Draper's enquiry gives some confidence in its results; and their tenor was confirmed within a few years by editorial comment in *The Lancet* and by the testimony of a former medical officer of Tyrone workhouse; and further confirmed in the 'nineties by the recollections of a score of local people.[2]

Less certain is the time at which the custom originated. Surprisingly (since, on his description, it was so widespread by 1870), Draper originally put its introduction at about 1865; but later, on the authority of a friend 'of absolute integrity', traced it back to the 'forties. According to this friend, recently returned from several years' residence in the ether territory, 'the wonderful new drink' first appeared in Draperstown about 1842, spread quickly, reaching Maghera by 1850.[3] No other evidence earlier than the 'seventies suggests so long a pedigree, or shows, even, that it was currently prevalent. But that Draper's friend may not be misleading is suggested by several later, apparently independent, accounts also dating it from the 'forties. Thus, the *fons et origo mali* was variously: the Draperstown doctor who, in the early 'forties, gave ether to newly-pledged abstainers;[4] the unqualified and alcoholic Draperstown doctor who 'a few years' before 1853 made his own progress from alcohol to ether, and encouraged his neighbours to follow;[5] a local doctor who had picked up the habit while studying at Glasgow;[6] or some Draperstown men who had fled from the Glasgow cholera of 1848, bringing with them some of the ether there esteemed as preventive or cure.[7]

[1] Draper, 1870, op. cit., pp. 117-8.
[2] 'It appears that in a district on the border of Tyrone and Derry the habit of ether-drinking has existed for a long period; but it is purely local, does not occur in any other part of the county, and there is no evidence that consumption is on the increase' (*Lancet*, i (1879), 870); W. Parke, 'Ether drinking in the north of Ireland', *Medical Press and Circular*, 13 June 1877, p. 481; Hart, 1890, op. cit., *passim*.
[3] Draper, 1870, op. cit., p. 118; 1877, op. cit., p. 425.
[4] Kerr, 1891, op. cit., p. 791.
[5] Hart, 1890, op. cit., p. 885, quoting Dr. F. Auterson of Magherafelt.
[6] Calwell, 1910, op. cit., p. 388, quoting Dr. Hegarty of Magherafelt.
[7] Ibid., quoting Captain Welch, R.N.

Ether-drinking, then, established in a limited area by 1870, had encroached on it, certainly since about 1865, possibly, more haltingly, since 1845; and it spread within and beyond it over the next twenty years. The drinkers themselves were inclined to attribute their ready acceptance of ether to its medicinal, rather than its inebriating power. Patients with whom alcohol disagreed took it as a stimulant; as carminative it was more welcome to old women than their grandchildren. It was popularly indicated for 'spasms', giddiness, aches, and pains, above all for bronchial and stomach disorders; a spoonful 'cleared the pipes', removed the 'stuffing on the chest', made away with 'wind on the stomach' or 'a smothering of wind about the heart'. 'The immense quantities of wind belched from the stomach after its use' was a process grateful to the drinker, and proof sufficient of ether's virtue: accumulating wind brought discomfort; a dose of ether brought release of wind, and comfort, general and local.[1]

'Perhaps one of the most curious contradictions connected with the spread of the mania for ether is that it has followed closely upon energetic efforts for stamping out ordinary alcoholic intemperance'; but, less obtusely, *'une vice chasse l'autre'*.[2] Needless to say, it was no epidemic of chest and stomach disorders that ether relieved—rather the epidemic craving for a stimulant of a people losing, with their easy access to whiskey, much of their customary comfort and contentment. To the enthusiast, Sunday-closing aggravated the trouble;[3] but, more generally, it was an unforeseen consequence of Father Mathew's campaigning,[4] or of the

[1] Parke, 1877, op. cit., p. 481; Hart, 1890, op. cit., p. 886; *S.C. on British and Foreign Spirits*, B.P.P., 1890–1, XI, Carter, q. 3140; Kerr, 1890, op. cit., p. 539; Calwell, 1910, op. cit., p. 389; Ulster Folk Museum, 62, Q4, 20, 22, 34.
[2] *Lancet*, i (1891), 841; Beluze, 1885, op. cit., p. 12.
[3] *Lancet*, i (1879), 870.
[4] Fr. Theobald Mathew (1790–1856) began his temperance campaigning in 1838. He is credited with administering more than five million pledges to nearly half the adult population of Ireland—with such effect that a taste for music replaced the taste for tippling; that the spirit revenue fell from £1,435,000 in 1839 to £852,000 in 1844; that 20,000 bankrupt publicans left the country; and that the police idled for want of crime. Even the repeal agitation was said to have hinged on Mathew: 'never [so the Liberator is reported] could I have ventured to bring these thousands and tens of thousands of men together, in peaceful agitation, if Temperance had not first spread its soothing blessings among them' (*Dictionary of National Biography*; Kerr, 1891, op. cit. p. 791; J. Venedy, *Ireland and the Irish during the Repeal Year, 1843* (translated from the German by W. E. MacCabe, Dublin, 1844), pp. 34, 173; Austin Clarke, *Twice Round the Black Church* (1962), p. 78).

suppression of illicit distillation. The man, sincerely but rashly pledged to Mathew, took ether as 'consolation for his loss of whiskey'; it was 'liquor on which one might get drunk with an easy conscience'; indeed, not being whiskey, could it intoxicate? Mathew's role is the more credible if (as sceptics concede) it was during his early, extravagant successes that the pioneers turned to ether, and if (as his critics claim) there was nowhere more submission to his appeal than in Tyrone and south Derry.[1] But his role hinges, of course, on whether in fact men turned to ether during and immediately after his campaigning in the late thirties and early forties. As we have seen, evidence that they did is inconclusive; and the attribution to Mathew is less convincing in that, during his early and most influential years, little was known of the anaesthetic and inebriating powers of ether. Its production was limited; its cost high; its taste dissuasive to people used to poteen, able still to get it, and less likely to refuse it as most of their fellow-converts lapsed. But Mathew, not implausibly, depriving the hardened drinker of whiskey, drove him to the doctor who obligingly suggested ether: given several such patients, appreciative of ether and talkative; given their steadfastness to their vow (or their liking for the new drink)—then it may rightly be claimed that Mathew had some hand in making ether available and appreciated, in giving it the foothold that later allowed its speedy diffusion.

By the late 1860s malt and grain, the illicit distiller's traditional materials, were harder to come by; less grain was being grown, and, with the railways, the corn-merchant more readily out-bid the distiller. For a dozen years, too, the Royal Irish Constabulary, less complaisant than the old Revenue Police, had been charged with suppressing illicit distillation; and the parish clergy were less tolerant than of old. None the less, it is hard to believe that as early as the 1860s sheer lack of supplies drove any great number of would-be poteen-drinkers to ether. By the eighties and nineties the argument has more weight: by then the land legislation had curbed rent; it was less necessary to distil to meet the landlord's demands; farming at a fair rent was as likely a source of income as distilling; and a more respectable peasantry, proud of its new-won status, was charier of breaking the law—chary, too, so far as it

[1] Tichbourne, 1891, op. cit., p. 25; Hart, 1890, op. cit., pp. 885–6; Calwell, 1910, op. cit., p. 388; *Lancet*, ii (1890), 627.

was Catholic, of breaking what seemed to be becoming the law of the Church.[1]

Certainly by the closing decades of the nineteenth century, with the sources of poteen drying up and parliament whiskey too dear to take its place, disappointed spirit-drinkers, needing an alternative, turned, many of them, to ether;[2] they turned, however, not as pioneers, but following the now-established local custom. Why, our problem is, did their predecessors take to ether in the sixties? Some few, no doubt, because they found poteen scarce, or its quality worse; most, I think, because ether served more cheaply than poteen their purpose of getting inebriated, and promised what might be a more rewarding as well as a cheaper intoxication.

Favourably publicized and widely distributed, as it permitted the advance of surgery, ether was the more readily acceptable and available as a substitute for alcohol. Its sale, as yet, was unhampered by law; it was cheap, perhaps partly because of its increasing manufacture, essentially because of the Methylated Spirit Act of 1855.[3] Before then, if lawfully made, spirit taxed at 10s. a gallon was needed in its manufacture. To deprive the illicit distillers of the English towns (most of them Irish) of their industrial custom, the Methylated Spirit Act allowed the use of untaxed spirit in the arts and manufactures, providing it had been made unpalatable by the addition of wood naphtha.[4] In consequence, when a quart of rectified ether cost 10s., the methylated product was available for 3s.—a product in no way inferior to the drinker; indeed, rather more soluble in water, boiling at a slightly higher temperature, it was more easily assimilated, and no methylated taint penetrated the pungent taste of ether. Selling, then, for about a penny a tablespoonful, ether offered several bouts of drunkenness for the traditional price of one: with a single penny, the novice drank his fill and—picking his dealer—treated his friend; two-pennyworth, twice repeated, gave the hardened drinker a blissful fair-day.[5]

But, price apart, ether appealed to the man taking spirit for its

[1] See above, 'Illicit Distillation', pp. 46–8.
[2] Hart, 1890, op. cit., p. 886, quoting Ballymoney doctor; *S.C. on British and Foreign Spirits*, B.P.P., 1890–1, XI, p. viii, and Wilkinson, q. 3188; Kerr, 1891, op. cit., p. 791; Calwell, 1910, op. cit., p. 388.
[3] 18 and 19 Victoria, c. 38.
[4] See above, 'Illicit Distillation', pp. 22–3.
[5] *Times*, 27 Mar 1891; *S.C. on British and Foreign Spirits*, B.P.P., 1890–1, XI, p. viii; I.F.C., MS. 1220, p. 80; Hart, 1890, op. cit., p. 887.

effect, the man scornful or unaware of the subtleties of flavour, needing his drink 'hot all the way down', hotter to his hardened body even than poteen, raw and fired with vitriol.[1] Even he might flinch at ether, but there were novel sensations and pleasures ahead: the acquired satisfaction in the tightening of mouth and stomach as he tossed back his glass, the suppressed vomit, the gust of wind. There was pleasure in the admiration of lesser men rejecting or toying with their spoonful; crowning all, was the pleasure of inebriation—achieved for a trifle, achieved in ten minutes, re-achieved without retribution four or five times a day.

More puzzling than the spread of ether-drinking is that it spread only over the area of an average county. The need for a cheaper intoxicant, like the taste for a novel intoxication, was more widespread; elsewhere, certainly, illicit distillation had been more prevalent—and earlier and more successfully suppressed; elsewhere, too, given the demand, ether might have been as readily procured.[2]

A British journalist, approaching the ether country, seeing 'a dreary expanse of low-lying, marshy land', sensed a 'loathsome melancholy'—sensed, one feels, the need for ether;[3] but mountainy men, more than bog-dwellers, were drinkers of ether, the habitat of neither was unmatched elsewhere, nor had their country a monopoly of melancholy.

Doubtless, in more favoured parts, men went on drinking poteen, of much the old quality, at near the old price, until with rising incomes, taxed spirit took its place. Individuals here and there, even localities, found their own alternative inebriants. In places home-made wine and mead were substitutes for poteen—more probably, long-standing rivals. Much methylated spirit was drunk in the late 'eighties and 'nineties in the Braid country, under Slemish mountain; drinkers, later on, were concentrated also round Ballynahinch; they were scattered over Ulster—scattered, indeed, over Ireland. Like ether, methylated spirit was cheap—a pennyworth as effective as sixpennyworth of whiskey; its taste, too, was nauseating, but, dissolving readily in water, it might be taken cold

[1] See above, 'Illicit Distillation', p. 6.
[2] Much of the 'infected area' was isolated yet tolerably served by railways: ether, in consequence, was readily brought in and long drunk without publicity or regulation. But relative isolation within striking distance of a railway was no local peculiarity.
[3] *Times*, 27 Mar 1891.

with sweetened tea, hot as punch, or mixed with cheap, red wine as 'blowhard'.[1] In Belfast, according to the Inland Revenue, 'grogging' was common in the 1890s. Whiskey casks, some brought for the purpose from Glasgow, were partly filled with hot water, vigorously rolled, and left standing for a few days; the 'terrible stuff' that then drained off tested, it was said, the toughest drinker.[2] Locally, in Ulster, there was release in coal gas bubbled through milk, or sniffed at the jet; in Brasso and boot polish, perfume and hair oil; in carbide, paraffin, and anti-freeze; in the 'soup' strained from boiled-up radio batteries—in the spirit, even, preserving diseased specimens in hospitals.[3]

It was, then, no peculiarity of Derry and Tyrone that drove men to ether—no sharper deprivation of poteen, no sharpened poverty or need for inebriation. Ether chanced to be available— sent by the Glasgow cholera, brought by the alcoholic doctor, demanded by Mathew's converts; whatever the reason, ether was locally available; to ether, therefore, people turned. Elsewhere, under much the same forces, twisted by local chance, men (defying God now as well as the revenue) set their stills to work; they craved—or drank—the whiskey they could ill afford; they flaunted, or resented, their temperance; they reached for the boot polish, or drifted off with the tramps and their blowhard.

Ether-drinking was more comforting—and less harmful—than some alternatives; and its merits led to its wider acceptance: from Draperstown in 1842—if that, in fact, was its source—it spread in half a century to Loughs Erne and Neagh, to Strabane and Dungiven, and into counties Antrim, Armagh, and Monaghan. But then it receded, driven back by Church and Law, forsaken

[1] Ulster Folk Museum, 62, Q4, 10 (Drumglass, co. Tyrone); 25 (Layde, co. Antrim), 2 (Mullaglass, co. Armagh), etc.; *S.C. on British and Foreign Spirits*, B.P.P., 1890–1, XI, p. viii and Wilkinson, qq. 3164–6, Clark, qq. 3917, 3922; Ulster Folk Museum, 62, Q4, 1, 3, 7, etc.; Calwell, 1910, op. cit., p. 389.
[2] *S.C. on British and Foreign Spirits*, B.P.P., 1890–1, XI, West, chairman, Board of Inland Revenue, qq. 218, 221 and Williams, collector of customs, Dundalk, qq. 816–19; Ulster Folk Museum, 62, Q4, 1 (Inch, co. Down); 4 (Belfast).
[3] Ulster Folk Museum, 62, Q4, 34 (Belfast, Ballymena); 7 (Ballagh, co. Tyrone); 9 (Cushendun, co. Antrim); 20 (Termoneeny, co. Derry); 35 (Ballycraigagh, co. Antrim); 38 (Strangford, co. Down) etc.; Tichbourne, 1891, op. cit., p. 26. Dr. Stafford Knox tells me that in Londonderry coal-gas intoxication is known as 'pennydrunk'—presumably from the penny put in the meter; and that boot polish to be used as an intoxicant is mixed with hot water and filtered through bread.

by a richer peasantry for other pleasures—those, not least, of seemlier, more palatable inebriants.

' "Et's the threemenj'essest stuff offered, but it's near bet down, for none of the clargy iv any profession'll allow it." '[1] From the time we know that ether-drinking was common, we know also that the Catholic clergy denounced it—though with uncertain success. 'Cursed by the priest' of Maghera in 1869, ' "no Catholic dar' sell it" ': but the same priest, or his successor, proscribed it afresh in the seventies, again in 1889: ' "I publicly from the altar banned it a year ago. Both sellers and drinkers obeyed my proclamation. There is no drinking of it here now [a claim sceptically received]." '[2] In the early eighties, according to the parish priest, ether-drinking, was made a reserved sin in the parish of Cookstown.[3] And, some time before 1877, the priest at Draperstown bought up the local dealers' supplies, returning them at a loss to the Belfast wholesalers. Stocks, however, were built up again, for in 1890 the local priests 'stamped out' the practice once more.[4] Generally, the priests 'in the plague-stricken spots are most earnest and indefatigable in their efforts at suppression'; 'they have done their very utmost.'[5]

Clergy of the Church of Ireland, not inappropriately, seem to have been less active in denouncing a practice mainly of Catholics. The rector of Cookstown, none the less, probably roused Hart's interest in the matter, plied him with information, appeared before the select committee, wrote to *The Times*, and three times persuaded the General Synod of his Church to petition parliament for restrictive legislation.[6]

Illicit distillation, holding its own in endless skirmishes with revenue and police, succumbed eventually with the Catholic Church's attack;[7] but ether-drinking, driven back locally and briefly by the Church, was all but stifled by the first restrictive legislation. The

[1] Draper, 1877, op. cit., p. 426, quoting comments made by a 'labouring man' in 1876.
[2] Draper, 1877, op. cit., p. 425; Hart, 1890, op. cit., p. 889, quoting Rev. Edward Callen, Catholic curate of Granahan and Maghera.
[3] Hart, 1890, op. cit., p. 889, quoting Rev. B. Nugent.
[4] Draper, 1877, op. cit., p. 425; Calwell, 1910, op. cit., p. 389.
[5] Kerr, 1890, op. cit., p. 540; *S.C. on British and Foreign Spirits*, B.P.P., 1890–1, XI, p. xi and Carter, q. 3146.
[6] *Journal of the Session of the General Synod of the Church of Ireland* (Dublin 1888), p. lxxxvii; (1889), p. lxi; (1891), p. lxx.
[7] See above, 'Illicit Distillation', pp. 46–8.

Church's seeming victory over the illicit distiller was partly the result of its belated alliance with the State—given the illegality of poteen-making, its days were numbered when piety overbore the reluctance to inform; the Church, too, mounted its attack when private distilling was already being outdated by the regeneration of peasant society and economy. The clergy grappled earlier, on their own, and in the old society, with ether-drinking; sensitive about their people's failings, preferring their reform by Church rather than by busybodies or State, they made little of ether-drinking in their public pronouncements—leaving allies unroused. They were also criticized for not always indicting drinkers with dealers, and for a piecemeal attack, allowing the faithful to drink with impunity in a neighbouring parish.[1]

Ether, too, mostly brought from outside, was more amenable to State than Church control. Suppliers—of both inebriants—were more rewarding targets than drinkers: suppliers of poteen were the priest's parishioners, subject to his discipline; dealers in ether he might discipline—to find them replaced by others, not of their faith. Producers of ether were beyond reach of the priest, but readily, indeed willingly, regulated by the State. The chemical trades were familiar already with public control: the Irish ether traffic was probably too small to incur ill-will in its defence; nor would defence have been easy—ether was too bulky and too easily identified, the trade too distant, too much of it in country with no feeling for ether.

Until the nineties, with the priests reserving their strictures for the culprits and few doctors much concerned, the outside world knew little of Ulster's peculiar inebriant. Then (thanks not least to Carter and Hart) the clergy of the Church of Ireland, the press, medical and lay, all were roused. Questions were asked in the House; a select committee looked into the matter. Goschen, Chancellor of the Exchequer, after consulting the Board of Inland Revenue and the Royal College of Physicians of Ireland, told the Commons in December 1890 that, by order of the Lord Lieutenant in Council, ether had been 'scheduled' under the Poisons Act of 1870.[2]

---

[1] *S.C. on British and Foreign Spirits*, B.P.P., 1890–1, XI and Carter, q. 3146; Draper, 1877, op. cit., p. 425; Kerr, 1890, op. cit., p. 538.
[2] 33 and 34 Vict., c. 26; Parliamentary Debates (Commons), 3rd series, 134, 25 Mar 1889, 729–30; 349, 1 Dec 1890.

Within months of scheduling (it was reported), the ether trade with Ireland had 'fallen into insignificance'; exports of the firm 'chiefly offending' were down by eighty per cent; sales by local druggists and grocers were 'largely curtailed' or had 'practically ceased'; ether was unobtainable at Maghera, and Biddy-the-knack, a notorious hawker, searched Tobermore in vain. Inspector Clark, investigating on the spot for the Inland Revenue, found that ether-drinking was 'rapidly diminishing': the 'baneful practice', *The British Medical Journal* agreed, 'has been almost, if not quite, suppressed'.[1]

The demand for ether, needless to say, did not dry up as its sale was restricted. Wholesalers received orders in plenty, but most of them refused to execute them, so the drinker, 'complaining of all sorts of pains', pleaded for a doctor's prescription; sought some other inebriant as cheap; or, 'if he really wants it and will run some risk', got his ether by hook or by crook. And, once the initial shock of scheduling was over, new drinkers as well as near-addicts probably found supplies—mostly, maybe, from less scrupulous wholesalers. A clandestine trade was more readily extended because ether had been added to the second part of the Schedule of the Poisons Act; while, therefore, it might lawfully be sold only by qualified chemists and when suitably labelled, it was free of the more stringent regulations applied to the sale of arsenic, prussic acid, and other 'Part 1 poisons'. By the early years of the present century Irish members complained that ether once more—or still—was openly sold: sixteen local doctors knew that it was being drunk in Derry or Tyrone; one, in a shop 'owned by a member of more than one public board', had seen pint and half-pint bottles being filled for market-day—and the job, openly done, seemed 'the usual thing'. In 1910 several juries in and about Omagh and Cookstown formally asked for closer control.[2]

Further regulation, however, was left for the Parliament of Northern Ireland. When the Commons was debating an intoxicating

---

[1] *British Medical Journal*, ii (1891), 759; *S.C. on British and Foreign Spirits*, B.P.P., 1890–1, XI, p. viii and Wilkinson, q. 3178, Clark, q. 3907. But, three months after scheduling, the rector of Cookstown believed sales were 'brisk as ever'; and Mackenzie Ledlie (perhaps loth to lessen the impact of his survey shortly to be published by *The Times*) felt that the practice was increasing (ibid., qq. 3197, 3254).

[2] Ibid., Wilkinson, qq. 3178–84; *British Medical Journal*, ii (1891), 759; Parliamentary Debates (Commons) 148, 26 June 1905, Long (chief secretary); Calwell, 1910, op. cit., p. 387.

liquor bill in 1923, the Minister for Home Affairs, conceding that ether was 'a very dangerous and perhaps very widely used poison', agreed further to restrict its sale.[1] Under the Intoxicating Liquor Act (Northern Ireland),[2] in consequence, drinking of ether, and willing connivance in its being made available for drinking, became offences: dealers might sell only to people over the age of eighteen, known to them, or to whom they had been introduced; they must register particulars of sales of under one gallon.

After four years' experience of these regulations, the then Minister for Home Affairs criticized their 'entire inadequacy': 'this stuff', he believed, 'is sold in very large quantities as a substitute for whisky.'[3] Further restrictions, accordingly, were incorporated in the Intoxicating Liquor and Licensing Act (Northern Ireland), 1927:[4] henceforth, it was unlawful to supply ether, or offer it for sale, except to doctors, dentists, and certain other prescribed users; wholesalers (as well as retailers) were required to keep registers of their sales, and justices of the peace might grant warrants for the search of premises where they thought ether might be unlawfully stored. Only the odd drinker seems to have circumvented the new regulations—an old woman in Tyrone, for instance, with a daughter well placed in an English hospital.[5]

To the critic, the pleasure of drinking ether was ephemeral—pleasurable, indeed, only to the taste it warped; its cost grotesquely great, damaging the drinker's body and mind, threatening his life, imperilling society and posterity. Blindness and digestive troubles were laid at its door, and a 'low brooding melancholy', nervous prostration, sleeplessness, insanity itself. Young girls had to be restrained from harming themselves; adult drinkers, 'made free of their minds', shone their teeth, and laughed hysterically; they shouted, danced, acted like maniacs; suffered, even, convulsions like an epileptic, falling down, writhing and foaming at the mouth. 'The poisonous influence of the destroying agent was shown by an antedated shrivelling up of the living frame': one 'etheromaniac' in his early forties was already 'a wizened, beat, decrepit and tottering old man; a battered and lonely hulk cast up on the

---

[1] Parliamentary Debates (Commons, Northern Ireland), 1st series, 3, cols. 1023, 1222.
[2] 13 and 14 Geo 5 (N.I.), c. 12, 1923.
[3] Parliamentary Debates (Commons, Northern Ireland), 8, 1927, col. 2465.
[4] 17 and 18 Geo. 5 (N.I.), c. 9.
[5] Information kindly supplied by Captain Kevin Danaher.

ETHER-DRINKING IN ULSTER

shores of existence—a hopeless and despairing human wreck'.[1]

These bodily 'evils' of ether-drinking recall the teetotaller's 'evils of alcohol': some thought that, as the brutish pleasure was similar, so too must be the cost; and others, fearing the cumulative effects of the new drink, invented or inflated evils to diminish its appeal. The criticisms are not easily disproved: relatively few people drank ether; they did it, for the most part, when medical research was uncertain, where systematic observation was difficult; and the fact that the heavy drinker commonly had long experience of alcohol made the effects of ether harder to isolate. Significantly, however, medical observers were mostly the milder critics. That the ether-drinker was peculiarly prone to digestive troubles doctors generally conceded; but, one suggested, only the 'hardened toper' suffered acutely, and so long only as he clung to his indulgence. As to ills more grave or lasting, Richardson readily attributed gout, fatty degeneration, paralysis, and cirrhosis to alcohol, but none— nor other organic trouble—simply to ether; nor, in his observation, was it a cause of blindness. 'The aythur is putting the people asthray, an' desthroyin' their heads': clergy and journalists certainly accepted the popular view; so, too, did the odd doctor. Richardson, however, was sceptical, and his doubts were confirmed by physicians from Derry and Tyrone asylums who, though treating patients who took ether, in no case attributed their troubles to its agency. Indeed, mental imbalance in the inveterate ether-drinker was plausibly said to precede rather than follow his addiction. Whether ether, when drunk, was strictly a drug of addiction, was a matter medical observers disputed: most, according to a French inebriologist, felt it was not; but to some, 'addiction was its greatest danger'; the taste for ether was speedily acquired, 'and when acquired the craving was as strong as ever it could be for alcohol.'[2]

[1] Draper, 1877, op. cit., pp. 425–6; Ulster Folk Museum, 62, Q4, 18 (Magherafelt); *S.C. on British and Foreign Spirits*, B.P.P., 1890–1, XI, qq. 3096, 3762; *Times*, 27 Mar 1891; Calwell, 1910, op. cit., p. 389; Kerr, 1891, op. cit., p. 793, 1890, op. cit., p. 543; Hart, 1890, op. cit., p. 889; Richardson, 1897, op. cit., p. 332; Lewin, 1931, op. cit., p. 201.

[2] *Lancet*, ii (1890), 627; Richardson, 1897, op. cit., pp. 335, 345–7; Draper, 1877, op. cit., p. 426; Hart, 1890, op. cit., p. 889, quoting Dr. Hetherington, Londonderry District Asylum; Parliamentary Debates (Commons), 3rd Series, 134, 25 Mar 1889, cols. 729–30, Balfour, chief secretary, quoting physician at Tyrone Asylum (but quoting also report of physician at Derry Asylum that 'insanity in his district is produced in many instances by indulgence in this pernicious habit, combined with other causes'); Levison, 1935, op. cit., pp. 40–41; Kerr, 1890, op. cit., p. 543.

Ether, there is little doubt, is a 'relatively benign poison':[1] compared with alcohol, it is 'far less injurious socially, mentally, and physically'.[2] Organic disease caused by its habitual consumption (so a *Lancet* correspondent believed) 'was exceedingly small compared with the ravages and degenerations which alcohol leaves in its train';[3] Calwell, after questioning every country doctor in Ulster, learned of no single ether inebriate under medical treatment for his inebriety, or its consequences;[4] a French observer commending the Catholic clergy—reasonably enough—for the decline of illicit distillation, commended them also for making 'etheromaniacs' of their alcoholic parishioners.[5]

That ether did little harm, physical or mental, was variously explained: its relative cheapness and immiscibility with water lessened the profit and possibility of harmful adulteration; slowly tolerated by the body, an intake, gently increased, brought a given effect; and since it was nauseating, not beguiling, to take, its smell precluding secrecy, there was the less inducement to use it to excess.[6]

But essentially, it seems, ether's greater potency as an inebriant, its not metabolizing in the body, its lower boiling point and lower solubility in blood as in water, made it less harmful than alcohol. Alcohol, freely entering the blood-stream, pervaded and persisted in all the tissues, working chemical change. But the entire intake of ether, boiling at body temperature, tended to be dispersed as gas; the intoxicating modicum absorbed by the blood was briefly held until excreted, mainly in breath and sweat; unlike alcohol it made no lasting contact with any part, and neither decomposed in the blood nor tended to dehydrate the mucous tissue.[7]

Ether-drinking, though less harmful physically and mentally than the alarmists alleged, was not without risk—the risk, when a man was stupified by ether, of his freezing by the wayside; of his dying from starvation when it too long lulled his hunger; of his being suffocated asleep by the fumes from a broken bottle. It was

---

[1] Levison, 1935, op. cit., p. 40.
[2] Richardson, 1897, op. cit., p. 335.
[3] *Lancet*, ii (1890), 627.
[4] Calwell, 1910, op. cit., p. 389. But when Calwell made his inquiry, ether had been scheduled under the Poisons Act for twenty years.
[5] Beluze, 1885, op. cit., p. 42.
[6] Draper, 1870, op. cit., p. 118; *Lancet*, ii (1890), 627; Beluze, 1885, op. cit., p. 41.
[7] *Lancet*, ii (1890), 627; Richardson, 1897, op. cit., pp. 332, 345; Draper, 1870, op. cit., p. 118.

the more menacing in that the margin between an intoxicating and a fatal dose was uncomfortably small, and in the hurry of so disagreeable a dosing, the odd drop might 'go the wrong way', causing spasm, obstruction and suffocation. Even going the right way, the ether 'would kill or bust you if you didn't rift'—explosive volatilization, too slowly released, might fatally constrict the heart. But the greatest peril was of fire: mixed with air, ether vapour is highly explosive; creeping along the floor, it ignites on contact with flame or fire. The drinker, consequently, must choose the direction of his explosive eructation: 'it wouldn't do to rift into the fire . . . or the flames would travel down your throat.' He must mingle with care the pleasures of ether and tobacco: a farmer at Bellaghy, lighting his pipe, ignited his breath: 'I knew a man that was always dhrinkin' it, and won day after a dose uv it, he wint to light his pipe and the fire cot his breath, and tuk fire inside, and only for a man that was carryin' in a jug of wather wud some whiskey to the kitchen, he'd a lost his life. He just held him down at wanst, as quick as he could, and poured down the wather down his throat.'[1]

Observers of ether-drinking—even leaders of the campaign against it—blamed it for little social evil. The drinker's craving, and the vendor's ready acceptance of stolen goods, led to petty thieving, to husbands' returning from work to find meal and potatoes traded for ether. Some dwelt on the power ether gave 'designing, unscrupulous persons for immoral purposes'. Regular Sunday sessions of Cookstown drinkers were the scene of 'great' (but unspecified) demoralization. Occasionally, ether roused the desire to fight: the odd blow might be exchanged; but the drinker was sober again, or senseless, before he could do much harm. So transient, indeed, was the effect of ether, that, however boisterous the drinker, the constable was loth to arrest him lest he should be sober before being charged.[2]

[1] *S.C. on British and Foreign Spirits*, B.P.P., 1890–1, XI, q. 3101; Hart, 1890, op. cit., pp. 889–90; Beluze, 1885, op. cit., p. 27; Richardson, 1897, op. cit., pp. 345, 350; *Lancet*, ii (1890), 627; Ulster Folk Museum, 62, Q4, 18; I.F.C., MS. 1220, Murphy, co. Tyrone, p. 80; Draper, 1877, op. cit., p. 425. Drinkers, it was said, were brought to Cookstown workhouse almost burned to death by ether; and a Draperstown poor-law guardian told of the explosion of ether in a shop causing four deaths (*S.C. on British and Foreign Spirits*, B.P.P., 1890–1, XI, qq. 3107, 3132).

[2] *S.C. on British and Foreign Spirits*, B.P.P., 1890–1, XI, qq. 3108, 3154, 3091, 3100; *Times*, 27 Mar 1891; Richardson, 1897, op. cit., pp. 336–7; Kerr, 1891, op. cit., p. 793.

IV

CATHOLICISM AND MARRIAGE IN THE CENTURY AFTER THE FAMINE[1]

AN apparent aversion to marriage is perhaps the most intriguing trait acquired—or reacquired—in Irish peasant society under the impact of famine and land legislation. The trend towards longer, if not lifelong, celibacy probably set in with the imminence of famine:[2] it persisted among the people as a whole for the first half-century of civil registration:[3] in 1945–6, on the average, farmers marrying in the Republic of Ireland did so in their thirty-ninth year and married brides of 30, while of male farmers between 65 and 74 one in four was still a bachelor.[4]

[1] Although this *ballon d'essai*, written in 1960–1, is published without systematic renovation, I am aware of the need to return to its argument, method, and implications. Did the Protestant sects, like Catholicism, instil a caution of marriage, theologically aberrant, curious by custom elsewhere, responsive, nevertheless, to the 'needs' of society? Why, and how commonly, are recent ordinands (Protestant, perhaps, as well as Catholic) more tolerant of their parishioners' marrying, irked, indeed, by their protracted engagements and engagements forgone? By what continuous (if contorted) traditon are these modern advocates of marriage linked with their predecessors, belaboured for encouraging the 'criminally early marriage' that plausibly underlay the Famine? Is the Irish novel to be regarded as material of Irish history? material (as in this essay) to buttress and embellish, or material, selected and vaulted, fit to bear a load? These, and allied questions, I hope to discuss elsewhere.

Quotations marked with an asterisk are taken from the recollections, some reaching back into the last century, of Catholics intimately acquainted with their districts.

[2] K. H. Connell, *The Population of Ireland* (Oxford, 1950), pp. 41–6. But see Michael Drake, 'Marriage and Population Growth in Ireland, 1750–1845', *Economic History Review*, 2nd Ser. xvi (1963), pp. 307–13.

[3] Of all women marrying in Ireland in 1864, 18·16 per cent were under 21; the corresponding figure for 1911 was 5·31. In 1864, 71·13 per cent of wives, in first marriages in which both partners specified their ages precisely, were under 25; by 1911, only 51·32 per cent (*Reports of the Registrar-General of Ireland*).

[4] *Reports of the Commission on Emigration and other Population Problems* (Dublin, 1954), pp. 78, 67. In 1946, 24·1 per cent of male 'farmers and relatives assisting' in the age-group 65–74 were single (ib. p. 73).

That your men and youths remain unmated,
And your maids in spinsterhood repining . . .[1]

A charge at the fairy court is treacherous evidence: Merriman's peasants, none the less, were encouraged neither to divide old land nor win new: and if holdings were scarce, marriage was delayed. But even in Merriman's time young people were coming to know more in ugly folk-memory than their own experience how to make shift unmarried: 'the common Irish', at the end of Merriman's life, 'marry very young';[2] 'love lingers only until he can find out a dry bank, pick a few sticks, collect some furze and fern, knead a little mud with some straw, and raise a little hut about six feet high';[3] a generation later, 'they marry when the whim takes them', 'just when they take the notion'.[4] That his predecessors over two or three generations generally married, and married young,[5] makes the new peasant's denial more puzzling. In this essay my main concern is with any tendency of the peasant's Catholicism to initiate or confirm his apparent reluctance to marry.

This, though a significant theme, is secondary. The peasant's wariness of marriage, however moralized or accentuated by Catholicism, was economic in origin. By peasant experience elsewhere, more extraordinary than restricted marriage was the haphazard, happy-go-lucky marriage of the late eighteenth and early nineteenth centuries. In the two or three generations following the 1780s peasant children, by and large, married whom they

[1] Bryan Merriman, *The Midnight Court*, translated from the Irish by Frank O'Connor (1945). Merriman, according to O'Connor, was born about the middle of the eighteenth century and died in 1805. He farmed and taught school in Feakle, co. Clare. In the poem itself the action is dated '178–' (ib. pp. 5–11, 47).
[2] J. Carr, *A Stranger in Ireland* (1806), p. 281.
[3] Ib., p. 152.
[4] J. Binns, *The Miseries and Beauties of Ireland* (1837), i, 57, 104.
[5] As Dr. Michael Drake and others have shown, figures retrospectively collected for the 1841 census do not show that still, in the 1830s, peasant marriage was characteristically of couples in their late teens or early twenties. I do not, however, share Dr. Drake's scepticism about the evidence of a phase of youthful marriage well established by the 1820s by a set of forces inherently unstable, its effect diminishing with the imminence of famine (R. C. Geary, *Studies*, Dec 1950, pp. 492–4; M. E. Ogburn, *Journal of the Institute of Actuaries*, lxxvi (1951), pp. 302–6 [both reviews of Connell, 1950, op. cit.]; Drake, 1963, loc. cit.).

pleased when they pleased. The opportunity to marry in their society was the occupation of land that promised a family's subsistence. Dependence on the potato, ever more extreme, on varieties ever more prolific, reduced the area needed for food. At the same time, rising corn prices and the conversion of pasture to tillage allowed a given rent to be earned on less land. There appeared, in consequence, a margin of land needed neither to sustain the customary population nor to pay the customary rent. An exigent landlordism tended to annex it for rent. But, with the maximization of rent resting now on the maximization of small tillage farms, landlords allowed sons to settle on holdings carved from their parents'. More holdings meant more and earlier marriage, more and larger families: but in the event they underlay not just the extra labour tillage needed, but so sharp a growth of population that subsistence land tended to encroach on rent land. Landlords were alarmed, the more so after 1815 as corn prices slumped; as the small man's endless corn and potatoes exhausted the soil; as there was talk of a poor-law financed by the landlords' rates. 'Consolidate and clear' became their cry. But they had lost the power to do what they would with their own. Their short-lived encouragement of subdivision had shown the peasants how easily and (it seemed) painlessly second sons might be established; and, as these sons married young, soon there were yet more second, and third, sons. Only a minority was drawn or pushed to the Irish towns, to Britain or America. For most, the landlord notwithstanding, provision was made by continued division, facilitated by the potato's bolder trespassing on rent land, by its reaching higher up the mountain and farther into the bog.

Subdivision, earlier marriage, larger families, more subdivision; clearly there was a vicious circle: landlord, economist, and State emphasized its peril; but the peasantry, until disaster was imminent, knew more of its pleasure, the pleasure of unrestricted marriage and a large family; the pleasure, perhaps, of letting the landlord whistle for his rent.

By the decade or two before the Famine the price of this improvident pleasure was brought home to the peasant: many a holding was so reduced, the land so exhausted, that in the aggravating run of bad seasons, there was acute shortage of potatoes: many fathers no longer dared divide; their sons and daughters made up the gathering stream of emigration; their friends, risking life in Ireland, married more circumspectly.[1] Much in the following decades underlined and helped to implement this new hesitancy to marry. Peasant society still, as before the Famine, made the occupation of land the preliminary of marriage: then, certainly in the heyday of division, there was land for all; but now, by and large, there was land only for the elect; and even they, for so rare a prize, must wait. The Famine, if it taught only the richer peasants the wisdom of eviction, made most of the rest chary of division. The western seaboard apart (where the old economy lived on), holdings usually passed from father to son intact, if not enlarged by neighbouring land cleared by death or emigration. Boys, needing land to marry, could no longer marry as they wished on plots pared from their fathers' land or won from the bog; they must, instead, put off their marrying until, by gift or inheritance, they acquired intact their family farm. One boy, traditionally the eldest, was thus established; one sister married the heir to a neighbouring farm. The rest of the family, chafing, as the Famine receded, at so inequitable an arrangement, might have pressed once more for a share of the land and a chance to settle at home; but family loyalty was stronger than brotherly jealousy—family loyalty supported, then overlain, by the pull of emigration, until today the peasant as likely as not envies his emigrant brother.

The Famine dramatized the risks of improvident marriage and halted the division that made it possible. Soon the land legislation made the peasant more ambitious and calculating—more ambitious because, as proprietor, tenant-at-will no longer, he yearned, peasant fashion, to establish his name at the land; more calculating because calculation, with no landlord to annex its fruits, became a rational proceeding. But his children's reckless marrying might bedevil his calculation: they must be restrained by a disciplined marriage geared to his ambition. An appropriate form was readymade in the 'snug farmer's' family, its success proven by their retaining their land while neighbouring holdings were divided

---

[1] The argument to this point is elaborated in Connell, 1950, op. cit.; that of the next stage in K. H. Connell, 'Peasant Marriage in Ireland after the Great Famine', *Past and Present*, 12 (1957), pp. 76–91; 'The Land Legislation and Irish Social Life', *Economic History Review*, 2nd Ser., xi, 1958, pp. 1–7, and 'Peasant Marriage in Ireland: its Structure and Development since the Famine', *Ec. Hist. Rev.*, 2nd Ser. xiv (1962), pp. 502–23.

and redivided. Much in this arranged marriage appealed to the new peasant. Disinheriting his other children, it preserved the land for his worthiest son. It saved land and son (if sober judgement could) from a lazy, thriftless wife, from the harder disgrace, a barren wife. With the father deciding not only whom, but when his son should marry, the land was not strained to support a second family before the first was dispersed; nor (for fathers put off their sons' marriage—and rivalry—and chose for them brides who were staid and mature) was the land burdened with families of maximum size, a material drain, but threatening also because the more numerous his brothers, the less secure the privileged heir.

By, perhaps, the end of the century, peasant marriage was usually 'arranged'; and then, more markedly than before, peasant children married little and late. They married late because a 'boy', not needing a wife until his mother could no more milk the cows, was not entitled to one until his father, at last, made over the land; and because the years had gone by before Lolita had the muscle and bone, the skill and dowry, sought in an old man's daughter-in-law. They married little because, though the normal family was large, only one of its boys and one of its girls married like their parents into peasant society: for the others (save in emigration) there was small chance of wife or husband.

This marriage, on the face of it, was gratifying less to its partners than to their fathers: well made, it reassured the old man, re-anchoring his line to the land; but his son knew more of its cost—in brides forgone when wanted; in decades' chafing at parental dominance, ended, ironically, as he came to terms with dependence and celibacy, by a bride complementary to the land, complementing him fortuitously if at all.

And this was the cost to the elect, the boy chosen to follow his father. Similarly (though for ten not twenty years) one girl waited, single and dependent, for the dowry that bought her match. For the other children, unless they travelled, lifelong celibacy was the rule; staying on at home, they became professional aunt or odd-job uncle, despised, a little ridiculous, working away for food, clothing and shelter and a shilling on fair day, never to work, accidents apart, for husband or wife of their own.

Few comparable communities have acquiesced in celibacy as has the Irish peasantry—taking almost for granted that a quarter of their number never marry; the rest, on the average, not until they are 38 if men, 30 if women. We have seen why old people wanted so unnatural an order; but why did their children submit? Initially, no doubt, young as well as old were shocked by the Famine; they shook off some of the old, easy-going ways and married with discretion. The land legislation, too, gratified young as well as old: the favourite son, with his father's reverence for the land, felt the folly of marriage before it brought so rich a prize: younger sons, such was their family loyalty, effaced themselves in America or as bachelors at home to strengthen their brother's 'hold of the land'. Then emigration was a safety-valve: probably still, in the 1950s, there were nearly six children in the average farming family in the Republic;[1] traditionally, fewer than two had followed their parents, and those, maybe, were the third most attracted by the life, least irked by the cost. No doubt, too, there was an element of compulsion: land qualified a boy for the customary marriage; fathers held the land, withheld it (if they wished), from a boy who burked at the match. But too much can be made of this: given the pressure, peasant marriage (as, say, in Poland)[2] might have allowed the heir to marry more normally: and many an Irish farm might have provided no less comfortably for a second, even a third, family: this, though no ultimate solution, would have allowed the heir of any generation to marry before his father's old age; and let a brother or two have families of their own, in their own country. Finally, young people in recent decades, though reared on Hollywood's ideas of marriage as well as their fathers', have complied with the match from a family loyalty different from their predecessors'. They have no vision of son and grandson drawing manure and planting potatoes; they yearn themselves for the Birmingham garage, the London office-site. Against this, life like their fathers' is all but intolerable, tolerated at all from a dread of forsaking their parents: one child, whatever the sacrifice, must look after the old people, pretending, if need be, that they are not the last of their line, that their land, when they go, will stay safe in the family, reverting neither to sheep nor alien hands.

But all this, however true, begs not the least, or least interesting,

[1] *Reports of the Commission on Emigration and other Population Problems* (Dublin, 1954), p. 96.

[2] William I. Thomas and Florian Znaniecki, *The Polish Peasant in Europe and America* (New York, 1927), i, 90–126; Sula Benet, *Song, Dance and Customs of Peasant Poland* (1951), pp. 145–55.

question: did the limitation of marriage imply comparable limitation of sexual activity? and if so, what reconciled the Irish to so much restraint? Continuously, it seems, the incidence of extra-marital relations has been relatively low in Ireland—astonishingly low for a people marrying so little and late. Few observers question this conclusion, whether they find it matter for praise or jest; it is confirmed, for what they are worth, by the statistics of illegitimacy. In Sundbärg's table, showing for the late 1890s the percentage of illegitimate to total births in fifteen countries, the Irish figure is lowest. More recently, Ireland still is favourably placed[1]—and, were figures available for the peasantry, they would probably be lower than those for the whole population. They might, of course, be deceptive: Irish seasonal labourers, it has been said, fathered more children in Glasgow or Liverpool than in the Rosses or Achill: abortion and infanticide were sometimes practised: priests, parents, and public opinion all did their bit to make legitimate births of illegitimate conceptions; and pregnant Irish girls, harshly regarded at home, sometimes have their babies in Britain. We know something of the number of Irish girls, pregnant before leaving home, whose babies are born in English Catholic institutions: their number, estimated in 1956 at some 20 per cent of the number of illegitimate births in the Republic,[2] would by no means have raised its illegitimacy rate to the level of Britain's. We know, too, for Ireland and England in 1911, the number of children born to couples married for less than a year. Of the Irish wives marrying in 1910–11 while under 20, fewer than 13 per cent had babies within the year: the corresponding figures for England and Wales was 34[3]—the discrepancy presumably reflecting the smaller proportion of Irish girls marrying 'because they had to'. But for all the treachery of the figures, the unmarried Irish are probably more, not less, chaste than is suggested by the international comparisons; for usually (certainly until recently), contraceptives are not available to the peasantry

[1] G. Sundbärg, *Aperçus statistiques internationaux* (Stockholm, 1908); *Reports of the Commission on Emigration and other Population Problems* (Dublin, 1954), p. 295. Sundbärg's percentages (as shown above, 'Illegitimacy before the Famine', pp. 82–3) range from 2·46 for Ireland to 12·10 for Portugal: that for England and Wales was 4·10 and that for Scotland 6·81.
[2] Ambrose Woods, 'Safeguards in England for the Irish Emigrant', *Christus Rex*, x (1956), p. 367.
[3] Censuses of Ireland and England and Wales, 1911.

in the south, and unfamiliar, at least to the Catholic peasantry, in the north.

Granted, then, that there are few extra-marital sexual outlets, the Irish tolerance of restricted marriage is the more puzzling. What compensations have been found? what barriers built around sexual indulgence?[1] Drink and dogs, cards, horses and gambling, religion, even the bombing and burning of Border posts, have been seen as the Irishman's way out. But the barriers to indulgence—his adaptation to continence—provide, I think, a more fruitful enquiry.

Migration and emigration make the problem more manageable. One child of every three born to peasant couples lives on in peasant society: not the least inducement to break away is the wish to marry and marry young: those left behind may be those less interested in marriage. Some years ago a Cambridge zoologist suggested that this point might be pressed farther[2]— dubiously far, indeed. On the assumption that the children of people more or less interested in marrying tend, in this trait, to resemble their parents, the Irish (he suggested), drained of their 'marriers' over three or four generations, are now genetically reluctant to marry—relieved, indeed, that their expectation of celibacy is so high. This hypothesis is not obviously compatible with the high fertility of the Irish when they do marry; but it is implausible also in its assumption that the degree of one's sexuality is determined by heredity, not environment.

Certainly, much in the peasant's environment made sexual gratification and marriage suspect. The volume of emigration is relevant yet again. In much of the country practically every peasant child has grown up to regard his own emigration as a real possibility: the worldly-wise, intending to travel light, uncluttered by wife and children, have been slow to marry while there was the chance of emigration.

A father's reluctance to name his heir tended, too, to keep his sons at home, uninclined as well as unable to marry: each, hoping for the land, waited for the match its succession would involve; each, reckoning to emigrate if his brother were chosen, was the

[1] To some degree, no doubt, the coincidence of little and late marriage and extra-marital 'chastity' implies neither 'sublimation' nor restraint, but the substitution of other sexual outlets for heterosexual intercourse: this is a matter I hope to consider elsewhere.

[2] C. B. Goodhart, 'Natural Regulation of Numbers in Human Population', *Eugenics Review*, xlvii (1955), pp. 173-8.

less likely to marry. Commonly, fathers so dilatory, with sons so irresolute, were denied a grandson to inherit the land. Two or three sons waited on into their thirties for their father to make up his mind. Their mother, perhaps, died meantime. With no boy designated heir, none was entitled 'to bring in a new woman'. A sister might stay on to do the housework. Then, eventually, when the old man died or named his heir, his children were jogging along happily enough, each as loath to disturb the rest of the family as to face what now was the ordeal of marriage.

Many a mother, too, though happy enough to see her daughters settle down—even the sons who had left home—resisted the marriage of the heir. Perhaps with justification, she pictured herself the object of his affection over 40 years and dreaded her relegation; she dreaded, too, the daughter-in-law, scheming not only for her son, but for the kitchen and yard she had ruled so long. By rousing a sense of sin, by ridicule, even by words unspoken, she kept her boy from girl-friends, leaving him awkward with women, perhaps incapable of courtship—a bridegroom, if at all, in a match made for him when her day was done.

But the peasant's Catholicism, it may be, was the most pervasive, the most persuasive, of the agencies reconciling the young to their curious marriage. This, looking at the Church's formal teaching, is an odd suggestion. The wildest critic can hardly maintain that the Catholic Church urges its lay members not to marry. 'Paul is no enemy of marriage. If he favours virginity, it is not because marriage is not good; it is only because virginity, accepted for the love of Christ is better.'[1] 'To abstain from marriage for supernatural motives and to dedicate oneself to a life of religious celibacy is . . . not merely good but a greater good than marriage.' But 'to avoid marriage for purely selfish reasons is indeed blameworthy.'[2] The argument hinges, not on the intent of the Church's teaching, but on its transmission, on whether the Catholic, coming from convent or Church school, from mission or confessional, was as convinced as the schoolmen wished of the propriety of marriage. Priests rarely (and briefly) challenged their Church's teaching: many, none the less, were ineffectual champions of marriage; their origin, training, and vows

[1] Alan Keenan, O.F.M., and John Ryan, *Marriage, a Medical and Sacramental Study* (1955), p. 222.
[2] C. B. Daly, 'Family Life: the Principles', *Christus Rex*, v (1951), p. 3.

of celibacy had made it a perplexing matter, too perilous, temporally as well as spiritually, to earn their whole-hearted advocacy.

'The greatest curse to the Irish nation has been Maynooth, because it has fostered the ordination of peasants' sons.'[1] Formerly, it was argued, the priesthood was small, and largely drawn from the more substantial families, those that could find the cost of sending a son to a Continental seminary;[2] but Maynooth, offering 200 scholarships from its foundation in 1795, allowed many a farmer, helped perhaps by generous neighbours, to shoulder the costs of ordination.[3] Early officers of Maynooth, however, denied that their student-body was of 'low order in society':[4] admittedly, they enrolled the occasional poor scholar, much as the Continental seminaries had their men living on the foundation, or, having been precociously ordained before leaving Ireland, on the fees they charged for religious offices:[5] Maynooth's 'free scholarships', moreover, merely reduced the financial obstacles to entrance; there remained, in particular, the cost of preparatory education, and initial expenses at college, estimated at £70 by the President, Dr. Crotty, in 1827.[6] His students, the President maintained, 'are generally the sons of farmers, who must be comfortable in order to meet the expenses . . .; of tradesmen, shopkeepers; and not a very small proportion of them are the children of opulent merchants, and rich farmers and graziers':

[1] [S. M. Hussey] Home Gordon (ed.), *The Reminiscences of an Irish Land Agent, being those of S. M. Hussey* (1904), p. 116.

[2] Ib.; Mrs. [M. C.] Houstoun, *Twenty Years in the Wild West* (1879), p. 79; L. Paul-Dubois, *Contemporary Ireland* (Dublin, 1908), p. 477; [Daniel O. Madden], *Ireland and its Rulers*, i (2nd edn. 1844), pp. 269–70.

[3] Eugene Francis O'Beirne, *A succinct and accurate Account of the . . . Popish College of Maynooth* (Hereford, 1840), pp. 2–3; *Report of Her Majesty's Commissioners appointed to inquire into the Management and Government of the College of Maynooth*, P.P., 1854–5, XXII, p. 23.

[4] *Eighth Report of the Commissioners of Irish Education Inquiry*, P.P., 1826–7, XIII, Very Rev. B. Crotty, President, in evidence, Appendix, p. 57.

[5] Ib. pp. 57–8.

[6] Ib. O'Beirne (a former student of Maynooth, though no longer a Catholic) thought that Dr. Crotty exaggerated in putting a student's expenses in his first year at £69: 'I verily believe that the average expenses of such students as enter on the "establishment"—that is to say, of such as partake of the Government grant, do not much exceed the odd £9. But the manifest object which the Doctor had in view, was to remove from the mind of the Commissioners the belief which they entertained, that the facilities afforded by the annual grant to Maynooth, rendered a place in the Roman Catholic Priesthood much more easy of access than formerly to persons of the humblest ranks of life' (O'Beirne, 1840, op. cit. p. 9).

from time to time, he claimed, the College enrolled a good many sons of the Roman Catholic gentry.[1]

Figures for 1808 (the only year for which they appear to be available) certainly bear out the President's contention that Maynooth's students came mostly from the land: of the 205 then in residence, 148 (or 72 per cent) were the sons of farmers, and another 11 of graziers. But there is less evidence than the President suggests of an opulent or land-owning background: the fathers of 17 students were recorded (ambiguously, in view of the Irish usage of the terms, or the disparity of income they may cover) as 'merchants', 'dyers', 'clothiers' or 'linen manufacturers', 'maltsters', 'corn or flour factors', 'architects', 'land-agents or surveyors'; and of the remaining students, a dozen came from grocery-shops or public houses, and single students from homes dependent on a wide variety of occupations, none of more seeming-comfort than those of the 'collector of taxes', the 'clerk of coal-mines', the 'ironmonger' or the 'ship's captain'.[2] Nor were other observers as sanguine as the President of the students' gentility (or as concerned that a Royal Commission, suspecting sedition, should be persuaded of it). The priests, according to O'Connell in 1825, are 'lowly-born' 'so generally as to partake in some measure of universality'[3]—and some two-thirds of those newly ordained were then coming from Maynooth;[4] fifteen years later 'no one . . . can deny, that the vast majority of the Maynooth students, for the twenty years past, has been composed of persons from the lowest grades of society'.[5]

Certainly, by the decades following the Famine, it was no longer presumptuous even for the peasant family to dream of seeing a

[1] *Eighth Report, Commissioners of Irish Education*, P.P., 1826–7, XIII, p. 58.
[2] *Papers relating to Maynooth College*, P.P., 1808, reprinted P.P., 1812–13, VI, pp. 6–27. The occupations not already specified were: chandler and tallow-chandler, ship- and house-carpenters, shoe-, boot- and truss-makers, baker, glover, tanner (two students), apothecary, wine-cooper, and nurseryman.
[3] O'Beirne, 1840, op. cit., p. 8.
[4] Of some 650 students reading in 1827 for the Irish priesthood, 391 were at Maynooth, about 120 in other Irish seminaries, and about 140 on the Continent. Maynooth thus accounted for 60 per cent of the student-priests, but probably for substantially more of the ordinands, for the other Irish colleges (some years earlier, at least) prepared many of their students, not for immediate ordination, but for entry to Maynooth (*Eighth Report of Commissioners of Irish Education Inquiry*, P.P., 1826–7, XIII, pp. 8–9; *Papers relating to Maynooth*, P.P., 1812–13, VI, p. 177).
[5] O'Beirne, 1840, op. cit., p. 3.

son 'with robes upon him':[1] more and more priests were being drawn from a dwindling laity;[2] Maynooth was offering more, and more valuable, scholarships,[3] and national schooling made entry easier; farms moreoever, were becoming larger, their dependents more prosperous and ambitious; and brothers and uncles, doing well 'in emigration', shared the cost and the glory of having a priest in the family. It was, indeed, a glorious prospect: '"Have a son a priest an' be shortenin' your time in purgatory!"';[4] immediately after the Famine there were few other ways of raising a son far above the peasantry, and always, to see a son 'emerge from Maynooth clothed in decent black' was 'a proud thing', ministering to a family's piety and prestige—even to its material well-being.[5]

The peasantry, then, by the second half of the nineteenth century, was able and eager to send its sons to Maynooth; but the more substantial families held back, deterred perhaps by nicer discrimination in detecting a vocation; by qualms about the manners[6] and education[7] acquired at Maynooth; by hopes of

[1] The phrase is Carleton's: David J. O'Donoghue, *The Life of William Carleton* (1896), i, 25.

[2] See Appendix, pp. 160-1, below.

[3] *Report, Maynooth Commission*, P.P., 1854-5, XXII, p. 67.

[4] Bryan MacMahon, 'Getting on the High Road Again', in John A. O'Brien (ed.), *The Vanishing Irish* (1954), p. 214.

[5] *Ireland and its Rulers*, i, 1844, op. cit., p. 254; Sydney Brooks, *Aspects of the Irish Question* (Dublin, 1912), p. 183; Liam O'Flaherty, *Skerrett* (1932), pp. 131-2. Fr. Burns, in Peadar O'Donnell's *The Knife*, was a 'fussy, self-important, conceited, good little man; like a clucking hen on the look for worms for her chicks, he was eyeing round for jobs for his family' (1930, p. 38).

[6] Charles Dillon, O'Donovan's Gaelic revivalist, seemingly of independent means, says 'I had a notion of becoming a priest myself once—I didn't. My mother was dead against it. . . . She'd cut off her right hand rather than eat meat on Fridays or miss mass, but the idea of a son of hers becoming a priest was unthinkable. . . . We had just had the parish priest to dinner, an awfully jolly chap, who sopped up gravy with a knife. She drew a lurid picture of the certain degeneration of my manners at Maynooth. She said she respected priests on the altar of course, but one could not have them to dinner except once a year or so, and then only by screwing up one's courage' (Gerald O'Donovan, *Father Ralph* (1913), pp. 70-1).

[7] 'Refined and deliberate study . . .', the Chancellor of the Exchequer told the Commons in 1812, 'was not necessary for Irish priests; they did not want more education, surely, than was possessed by the clergymen in distant parts of England and Wales.' 'He begged gentlemen to look at home, unless they wished, by an excess of grants, to make Maynooth College equal to Dublin, Cambridge or Oxford University.' Some measure of its inequality, it may be, lies in the enrolment of as many as forty Catholic students at Trinity College, Dublin, in 1807 (James Lord, *Maynooth College* (1841), pp. 188, 160, quoting Commons debates).

grander *'honours* and *emoluments'*[1] than its students might expect, and the chance of achieving them in a family business, in medicine or the law.[2] It is possible, too, that higher up the social scale, the irresistible vocation led to the regular, rather than the secular, priesthood.[3] The boy from the well-to-do family hardly relished the prospect of living 'by accepting half-crowns and shillings from the miserable people of Ireland';[4] of living, as a parish priest, 'upon a kind of charity obtained from very poor persons',[5] and 'inflaming their passions, and aggravating their prejudices' in his 'squabbling for fees'.[6] Maynooth, moreover (to its early critics), was no place for a gentleman: 'men of respectable families have mingled in the vulgar throng, which annually storms [its] gates', but most of them withstood only briefly the diet, the discipline, and the 'disgusting menial offices'.[7]

It is hard to come by statistical evidence of the priests' social origins: since the middle of the nineteenth century, however, observers are virtually agreed (whether they are galled or gratified) that many a peasant's son has found his way to the priesthood: they are 'the sons of persons in business and trade', a Catholic curate testified in 1853, 'and the sons of comfortable, middle, and humble farmers':[8] a more critical contemporary believed 'they

[1] Ib., p. 176, quoting Sir John Newport in Commons debates.
[2] *Ireland and its Rulers*, i, 1844, op. cit., p. 259.
[3] Fr. Ralph came from a well-to-do family. His mother had determined his vocation before he was born: her own and her household's life she ordered to further it: Ralph, while still a schoolboy, 'was no longer a son, but a sacred object dedicated to God which she regarded as a sort of fetish': she was dismayed, none the less, when, instead of joining the Carmelites, he entered Maynooth to prepare for the secular priesthood (Gerald O'Donovan, *Father Ralph* (1913), p. 234).
[4] Daniel O'Connell, quoted in *Letters from Ireland, 1886, by the Special Correspondent of 'The Times'* (1887), p. 172.
[5] *Ireland and its Rulers*, i, 1844, op. cit., p. 275; *Letters from Ireland*, 1887, op. cit., p. 172.
[6] Nassau William Senior, *Journals, Conversations and Essays relating to Ireland* (2nd edn., 1868), ii, 276.
[7] O'Beirne, 1840, op. cit., pp. 3, 12-13. 'I publicly and openly declare', said a former student, no longer a Catholic, 'that the College of Maynooth has never yet produced a gentleman or a scholar' (*The Popish College of Maynooth* (1839), p. 7).
[8] Rev. John Harold, before Maynooth Commission, P.P., 1854-5, XXII, *4*, 18. In the minutes of evidence heard by the Maynooth Commission each witness is given a number, and the questions put to him are numbered in a separate series: in references here the witness's number is italicized and precedes the number of the question,

are all taken from the humblest classes in society':[1] *The Economist* in 1881—and George Birmingham thirty years later—thought 'they are drawn, for the most part, from the peasant class';[2] Robert Lynd that they were usually the sons of farmers if not of publicans[3]—and the rare country publican was neither a peasant as well, nor the achievement and vindication of peasant virtue and prejudice.[4]

Now many a priest's attitude to marriage, whatever its veneer of learning, was that of the peasant society from which he sprang: that same society explains much of the quaintness and boisterousness of his teaching; and the obedience curiously accorded to teaching so unnatural.

'A young giant, whom nature had evidently cut out, mind and body, for a farmer; but who was doomed for the priesthood by

[1] *Ireland and its Rulers*, i, 1844, op. cit., p. 252.
[2] *The Economist*, 11 June 1881; 'George A. Birmingham' (J. O. Hannay), *Irishmen all* (1913), p. 178.
[3] Robert Lynd, *Home Life in Ireland* (1909), p. 124.
[4] One of the few dissentient voices was that of the Rev. P. J. Nowlan, a Catholic curate in Dublin. 'The Catholic clergy', he said, 'is recruited almost altogether from the great middle class of the town and country, principally from the towns: it is not a peasant clergy.' Nowlan, it may be, was generalizing from his own diocese: certainly in 1808 (the only year for which figures seem to be available) Maynooth students drawn from and destined for the archdiocese of Dublin came, more generally than their fellows, from urban and seemingly-comfortable homes (P. J. Nowlan, *An Irish Primer for English Statesmen* (Dublin, 1867), p. 12); *Papers relating to the Royal College of St. Patrick at Maynooth*, P.P., 1808, reprinted 1812–13, VI, pp. 6–27). More recently M. Blanchard has published the following table showing the proportion of student-priests drawn from various social classes:

Classe paysanne	30%
Classe ouvrière	20%
Classes moyennes (fonctionnaires, commerçants)	30%
Professions libérales	20%

These figures, if they can be accepted, suggest that in recent years the field from which the clergy are recruited has broadened markedly: M. Blanchard, however, stresses that they are based on no precise inquiry; and he contrasts them with the following (presumably accurate) figures relating to the student-priests from a rural diocese in the west:

Classe rurale	45%
Commerçants	27%
Instituteurs-professeurs	15%
Fonctionnaires	8%
Professions libérales	2,3%
Classes ouvrières	1,7%

(Jean Blanchard, *Le droit ecclésiastique contemporain d'Irlande* (Paris, 1958), p. 87).

family decree':[1] an anachronism so extreme might become a 'spoiled',[2] not a practising, priest: 'the clergy', none the less, 'share all the passions of their class':[3] 'the Irish priest looks at the economic problems of his parishoner from the point of view of the prejudiced peasant.'[4] To the priest's parents, in all probability, marriage was incidentally a source of its partners' happiness: lightly entered, indeed, it threatened acute unhappiness: essentially, marriage ensured labour for the land and an heir for the family: barring a parent's premature death or incapacity, every child was wise to postpone it, not a few to forgo it altogether.

This wisdom not only guided the teaching (or the silence) of the priest's parents on relations between the sexes: it was reiterated (as we shall see) by his teachers and spiritual advisers and exemplified by the marriages (or the celibacy) of his brothers and sisters—indeed of his responsible fellow-countrymen. So stern a view of marriage might, it is true, be challenged by his own emotions, or by a liking for the looser ways of the outside world: the man, however, taking vows of celibacy, was not powerless against the relevant emotion: his insular training instilled a scorn for laxity, un-Irish and un-Catholic; and the student, persistently perverse, might find his vocation in doubt.[5] Certainly his background and training left him ill-equipped for rational exposure, for logical approach to a less calculating marriage. Almanacks, newspapers, 'speeches from the dock': farmhouse reading, whatever it was, hardly spurred a boy to broaden or oppose his father's analysis of peasant society. At the age of 12 or 14 the intending priest probably left the farmhouse for the diocesan seminary, and from there, when he was 18 or more, he began his seven- or eight-year course at Maynooth.[6] The seminaries were 'manned by ill-educated young priests, fresh from Maynooth . . . whose main anxiety is to get promoted as quickly as possible to parish

---

[1] Patrick Kennedy, *The Banks of the Boro* (1867), p. 3.

[2] In Irish usage, a 'spoiled' priest is a former clerical student who left the seminary without taking his final vows. An ordained priest 'suspended from his priestly functions by his ecclesiastical superiors: "unfrocked"', is a 'silenced' priest (P. W. Joyce, *English as we speak it in Ireland* (1910), p. 323).

[3] 'Philippe Daryl' [Paschal Grousset], *Ireland's Disease* (1888), p. 229.

[4] E. B. Iwan-Müller, *Ireland: Today and Tomorrow* (1907), pp. 100–1.

[5] *Report, Maynooth Commission*, P.P, 1854–5, XXII, p. 39.

[6] Brooks, 1912, op. cit., p. 183.

work'.[1] Here, no doubt, is Protestant prejudice: continuously, nevertheless, from early adolescence into his twenties, the trainee-priest was impressed with Maynooth's view of social and economic problems, a view, implicit or formulated, which he questioned on pain of spiritual penalties, and questioned the more rarely because it coincided with the convictions of the class which reared teachers and students alike.

'You were the typical priest', one of George Moore's characters says, 'who looks upon women as the deadly peril and the difficulty of temporal life.' 'I remember', the priest replies, 'how at Maynooth the tradition was always to despise women.'[2] In the 1850s, according to the professors of theology, teaching on the sins against chastity was reserved until the students' last year: 'it is always treated of in a learned language, and every security taken, which piety and prudence can suggest, that it shall be handled with reverence and reserve, and in no spirit of licentious curiosity.'[3] 'Our students are taught to strengthen and fortify, by prayer and other pious exercises, their natural infirmity, and to regard and abhor as a soul-destroying sin, any wilful or deliberate complacency in an impure thought.'[4] They were instructed, as confessors, 'never to omit pointing out . . . the means of overcoming temptation; such as, avoiding the external occasions of sin, averting the mind instantly from the object of temptation and fixing it on some other object.' The young should be 'special objects of a most paternal solicitude': 'if, in early youth, the heart be preserved from the taint of corruption; if the virtue of chastity be firmly planted therein, resistance to temptation grows into a habit and becomes easy, and virtue strengthens with advancing years.' Priests, accordingly, must impress on parents the importance of watching over their children, 'of seeing the sorts of books they read; the sports they engage in; the places they frequent; and, above all, the companions with whom they associate'.[5] A former student of *De Matrimonio*, asked if his class had treated the subject lightly or with ribaldry, said that, on the contrary, 'it was a dirty or a dreadful matter—a horrible matter. They . . .

[1] Ib.
[2] George Moore, *The Lake* (1905), pp. 105, 250.
[3] *Report Maynooth Commission*, P.P., 1854-5, XXII, p. 65.
[4] Rev. J. O'Hanlon, D.D., Prefect of the Dunboyne Establishment and Librarian, ib., Answers to Paper K, p. 362.
[5] Rev. P. Murray, D.D., Professor of the First Class of Theology, ib., p. 377.

seriously thought it was filthy stuff altogether.'[1] Another looked back on it with much pain: 'I have known many of the young men, when studying certain parts of it, to have gone into the chapel, and to have read it on bended knees; I saw many young men that I conceived to be not of very strong passion, they thought it necessary to go in before what they believed to be the body and blood of Christ Jesus, on bended knees.'[2]

Teaching accepted with such sincerity and such turbulent emotion was transmitted with little less effect. It yielded, a Maynooth theologian believed, 'wonderful fruits of chastity and purity of heart . . . in every condition, and in every age of life': he had witnessed 'hundreds upon hundreds coming to confession under the weight of terrible passion . . . thenceforth, week after week, month after month, leading pure lives; struggling, as St. Paul had to struggle against the angel of Satan that buffeted him, and, like him, still victorious'.[3]

But a shadowy line divided godly chastity from sinful renunciation of marriage: the very success of this teaching—the stifling of 'impure thoughts', wresting the mind from 'objects of temptation', the avoidance of much social life, the wariness of mixed company—all this raised psychological (indeed, practical) barriers to marriage: all too readily the over-zealous confessor instilled in simple penitents not only a caution of marriage, but their reputed 'complete and awful chastity';[4] a perversion, of course, of the theologians' chastity, but sinless, even glorious, to the priest who slightly, perhaps unwittingly, twisted their teaching. Not surprisingly, to a liberal Catholic, it is 'partly through Maynooth, and the ideas it has spread, [that] the Irish popular mind has become poisoned and ashamed on the subject of love and marriage'.[5]

Marriage, to many a priest, was suspect on social and economic as well as on moral grounds. After the Famine, if the surviving

---

[1] Rev. D. L. Brasbie, in evidence before Maynooth Commission, P.P., 1854–5, XXII, *35*, 94. The former students quoted in this and the following sentences had both left the Catholic Church when they gave the evidence quoted here.
[2] Rev. W. J. Burke, ib. *36*, 10.
[3] Murray, Answers to Paper K, ib., p. 377.
[4] See below, pp. 137–8.
[5] William Patrick O'Ryan, *The Plough and the Cross* (Dublin, 1910), pp. 156–7.

population were to remain at home, marrying as men did in the outside world, the overriding problem was to increase agricultural productivity—and provide for more families. Traditionally, landlord and tenant had been laggardly improvers; landlords because they were preoccupied instead with immediate receipts and mounting debts; tenants, because they were deprived, in consequence, of the incentive, the knowledge, and the capital to improve. The old, ramshackle society, its population multiplying fast on a slovenly potato-culture, had been shaken by the Famine. By the fifties death and emigration had released the pressure on the land, but insufficiently to curb emigration. The treachery of the potato could never be forgotten; some other food must eke it out, if not take its place; but, whatever food replaced the potato, more land (or land more efficiently farmed) was needed to grow or buy it. And presently this insistence on a costlier standard of living was fostered by schools and newspapers, shops and advertisers, by emigrants' letters and visits and the seasonal labourer's dreams. To stay contentedly in Ireland, the peasant family must live more comfortably—its land be made more productive. In the generation after the Famine the peasant, suffering still a mercenary landlordism, still lacked incentive, knowledge, and capital. By the seventies, however, the landlord's exactions were being restrained, extra-legally and then legally. Increasingly, the means to improve lay within the peasant's grasp; and the incentive was more compelling as the land, in essentials, became his own. But convention, ignorance, laziness, a drive insufficient against the easier attractions of emigration—these all encouraged extensive rather than intensive improvement; they encouraged the peasant to add to the area, rather than the productivity, of his soil: and here, of course, there might be no lasting solution, for (certainly in the remoter parts of the country) their neighbours' progressive emigration might simply allow the remaining families to live more comfortably until, at last, loneliness drove them out.

In the peasant's religion, as in his tenure, discouragement to improvement was detected. 'Excessive and extravagant church-building in the heart and at the expense of poor communities':[1] the point has been made, too often and too carpingly:[2] plainer

---

[1] Horace Plunkett, *Ireland in the New Century* (popular edn. 1905), p. 107.
[2] See, for instance, Michael J. F. McCarthy, *Priests and People in Ireland* (Dublin, 1902).

churches, nevertheless—an affront to priestly or parochial pride more than to religious or aesthetic sensibility—, plainer churches might have spared Irish shillings and American dollars for richer grass and cleaner dairies—even for more welcoming schools, for 'we, the clergy . . . are very apt to forget that God has not one, but two houses in the parish, and that His interest in the second one is certainly greater than a comparison between the school and the church commonly suggests'.[1] More important, it was said also that the Catholic peasant's indifference or antipathy to improvement was heightened by 'the reliance of [his] religion on authority, its repression of individuality':[2] looking to the priest for guidance in business as in theology, the laity 'largely lost their capacity and their judgment in their own affairs'.[3] Authoritarianism in religion 'and its complete shifting of . . . the moral centre of gravity to a future existence . . . [these] appear to me calculated, unless supplemented by other influences, to check the growth of the qualities of initiative and self-reliance, especially among a people whose lack of education unfits them for resisting the influence of what may present itself to such minds as a kind of fatalism with resignation as its paramount virtue'.[4]

Improvement, then, there had to be, unless part of the population emigrated and much of the rest postponed or avoided marriage. But the peasant, having lived long under an unjust tenure, was slow to improve, and slower still for being sustained by a religion little concerned with material reform, the more inimical to it because of the solace it brought in hardship. Clearly, if the peasant were to resist emigration and marry young, he needed outside encouragement and guidance—advice based on knowledge beyond his reach of the technique and economics of farming efficiency. Now, however other-worldly their religion, there was some obligation on the priests to acquire such knowledge and offer such advice: souls were being lost in emigration and in marriage too long deferred: deprivation, moreover, was not simply of inessentials; priestly, even plain human, compassion —for hungry children and needless illness—must have made many a priest anxious to explain a better farming—the more eager, in

---

[1] Neil Kevin ('Don Boyne'), *I remember Karrigeen* (1944), pp. 60–1.
[2] Plunkett, 1905, op. cit., p. 102.
[3] 'Pat' [P. D. Kenny], *Economics for Irishmen* (Dublin, 1906), p. 147.
[4] Plunkett, 1905, op. cit., p. 102.

much of the country, because nobody would do it if he did not.[1]

But the priest, by and large, was poorly equipped to show the way to more productive farming. If he came from a country home (indeed, if he came from the town) he was probably disdainful already of peasant life; almost certainly he knew less than his brothers and sisters of its realities and potentialities. His training, far from giving him the knowledge, the capacity, the values to regenerate country life, sheltered him from it the more.

The course at Maynooth in the 1850s covered eight years: in the first two, to repair defects in the students' preparatory education, there were classes in classics, mathematics, English, and French;[2] thereafter the teaching was exclusively in theology, philosophy, and associated subjects, the authorities reputedly doing nothing to encourage students to retain or extend their general education.[3] They were forbidden (though without complete success) to read newspapers:[4] books they might possess, but nothing of 'immoral, infidel, or seditious tendency'.[5] The library was out-of-bounds to junior students, seniors made little use of it: although a new library building was available, that in use in 1855 was 'far too small even for the present collection of books, which is inadequate for a College of such extent and means'—something under £100 was spent annually on books; the catalogue was 'very defective and by reason of the books not being marked to correspond, it is . . . nearly useless'.[6] Students were 'absolutely prohibited' from visiting one another's rooms;[7] they spent their recreation periods almost exclusively with members of their own dioceses,[8] perhaps turning over, as their successors reputedly did, 'diocesan gossip and the possibilities of preferment'.[9] Professors, by college statute, must 'have their pupils modest and docile';[10] they were in touch with them, how-

[1] See below, pp. 150-1.
[2] *Report, Maynooth Commission*, P.P., 1854-5, XXII, p. 47.
[3] Ib., pp. 48, 61.
[4] Ib., p. 38.
[5] Ib.
[6] Ib., pp. 56, 64.
[7] Ib., p. 35.
[8] Ib., p. 36.
[9] Brooks, 1912, op. cit., p. 185.
[10] Very Rev. L. F. Renehan, D.D., President, in evidence before Maynooth Commission, P.P., 1854-5, XXII, *19*, 50.

ever, merely for the periods of lectures.¹ Infractions of college discipline were punished by admonition or expulsion; more effectively, by 'fear of an unfavourable report to their Diocesans and of exclusion from Orders'.²

Not surprisingly, with this education, the Maynooth priest, 'installed and isolated in his country presbytery, often showed very little intellectual activity and little taste for study . . .: his library [often] was poor and his pen unfruitful':³ his learning, it may be, had broadened little since O'Connell's speeches and the local newspaper were his 'literary aliment', *The Dublin Review* 'his most instructive reading'.⁴ 'Maynooth has not produced an economist in a hundred years';⁵ certainly until the present century she 'did not prepare her sons very efficiently for their role as leaders . . . [of] social progress'.⁶ Maynooth, whatever the quality of its theological training, was no substitute for a university: 'it has not given . . . that broader and more humane culture which only a university, as distinguished from a professional school can adequately provide.' 'Under the Maynooth system', Plunkett continued, 'young clerics are constantly called upon to take a part in the life of the lay community, towards which, when they entered college, they were in no position of responsibility, and upon which, so far as secular matters are concerned, when they

[1] *Report, Maynooth Commission*, ib., p. 39.
[2] Ib., pp. 38–9. *I remember Maynooth*, the friendly reminiscences of a student of the 1920s, shows the resilience of traditions established a century earlier. 'Maynooth', Fr. Kevin admits, 'is but Ireland drawn to a small scale': in seven years at college 'we had far less opportunities for the development of our political faculty, than we would have had in any other school or university with a roll-call of six hundred young men between the dream-swept years of eighteen and twenty-five'; 'the rule sternly forbade the reading of newspapers or other periodicals'; '[we lived] a very active life both in mind and body, finding little time for settling or even worrying about the affairs of the nation'; 'if a student went to the room next his own to ask (quite genuinely) for a class-book or a bottle of ink he was guilty of a rather serious breach of discipline' (Neil Kevin, *I remember Maynooth* (new edn. 1945), pp. 94, 93, 95, 173).
[3] Paul-Dubois, 1908, op. cit., p. 504.
[4] *Ireland and its Rulers*, i, 1844, op. cit., p. 268.
[5] Kenny, 1906, op. cit., p. 140.
[6] Paul-Dubois, 1908, op. cit., p. 504. But 'we should testify also to the progress which Maynooth has realized during the last twenty years, in the way of classical and scientific study. . . . Alike in the sciences and in literature, the standard of study has been raised and the number of professors increased. Laymen have been nominated to five or six chairs, and competent persons appointed to deliver series of lectures upon social and economic subjects' (ib.).

emerge from their theological training, they are no better adapted to exercise helpful influence. In my experience of priests I have met with many in whom I recognized a sincere desire to attend to the material and social well-being of their flocks, but who certainly had not that breadth of view and understanding of human nature which perhaps contact with the laity during the years in which they were passing from discipline to authority might have given to them.'[1]

Fr. Finlay (a Jesuit) was a leader in the co-operative movement, and, the pioneering over, more than 300 priests took the chair in their local societies:[2] Dr. O'Donnell—a Maynooth student, subsequently Bishop of Raphoe and Cardinal Archbishop of Armagh —was long a lively member of the Congested Districts Board; many a priest served on the local committees of the Board and of the Department of Agriculture. It may be doubted, however, whether priestly power has borne at all fully on the problem of agricultural productivity. 'How did the priests act?' Nassau Senior asked an improving agent in Kerry. 'Opposed me', he answered, 'to the utmost, as they do every improver and improvement.'[3] 'The priest', Senior himself felt, was 'the enemy of improvement, the enemy of education, the enemy of emigration'.[4]

The saintly priest, in the saintly parish, forbore 'preaching the thrift of money to the misers of grace':[5] 'Begor,' it was said of Sheehan's improving curate, 'Begor, he must be very fond of the money. He's always talkin' about it. Post offices and savings banks an' intherest! Why doesn't he spake to us of the Sacred Heart, or our Holy Mother, or say somethin' to rise us, and help us over the week?'[6] Usually, however, a priest's indifference to drains or co-operation showed neither disdain for things of this world, nor withdrawal from them: if riches and piety were doubtful partners, so also were riches and clerical power: 'many of our priests see that wherever the growth of industry develops the economic faculties, a lay life grows up that will not accept their

[1] Plunkett, 1905, op. cit., pp. 135–6.
[2] Ib., p. 119n.
[3] Nassau Senior, *Journals, Conversations and Essays relating to Ireland* (2nd edn., 1868), ii, 79.
[4] Ib., p. 245.
[5] P. A. Sheehan, *Luke Delmege* [1900] (1917), p. 458.
[6] Ib., p. 399.

dictation outside their sphere . . . and apparently they think it better to reign over ruin than to take their due and proper place in progress.'[1] But there is no such wily explanation of the laggardly leadership of many a priest: his 'horizon bounded, perhaps, by the thatched cabin on the one side and Maynooth on the other',[2] he was reared with the peasant's mistrust of technical change and had neither the training nor travel to re-appraise it; reared, moreover, to trace Irish ills to English oppression, he looked to political rather than technical renovation.

'In those immense ships which sail from Europe for America or Australia, everything has been provided for except the soul':[3] in emigration 'rosy-faced, fair young girls, so pure, so innocent, so pious', might be 'dragged down to shame and crime, and to an early and a dishonoured grave', 'stalwart youths were leaving the fresh fragrance of the meadows and the corn fields, and the friends of their youth, for the polluted air of the coal mine and the society of niggers and Chinese coal-heavers':[4] better, a third priest believed, 'better one meal a day of potatoes and salt in Ireland than face the sin and horrors of American city life.'[5] Much in emigration might alarm a priest. It offended his patriotism; it cost him his friends;[6] it endangered their souls and their Church's revenue.[7] Most of all, maybe, realizing that it was a self-generating movement, he feared it might get out of hand: when emigration in any parish became an everyday matter, its people came to reckon a good life their due, a life ready to be claimed in America, not laboriously achieved at home: the more from any townland already settled in America, the more tempting the remainder to follow suit, the more contributions towards their fare; the fewer left behind, the easier, admittedly, to acquire more land, but land lost its old mystique,

---

[1] Kenny, 1907, op. cit., p. 156.
[2] *Letters from Ireland, 1886, by the Special Correspondent of 'The Times'* (1887), p. 172.
[3] Adolphe Perraud, *Ireland in 1862* (Dublin, 1863), p. 242.
[4] 'A Country Curate' [Joseph Guinan], *Scenes and Sketches in an Irish Parish* (3rd edn., Dublin, 1903), p. 43.
[5] *The Irish Peasant*, 24 Feb 1906.
[6] Richard F. Clarke, S.J., *A Personal Visit to Distressed Ireland* (1883) p. 55.
[7] Ib.

it became poor compensation for the bleak life of a deserted countryside.[1]

However poor an economist, the priest with misgivings about 'improvements' and emigration was no thorough-going advocate of marriage: like his parishioners, he abhorred (if he contemplated) the artificial limitation of births: more marriage meant more children, children to whom a stagnant Irish farming had little to offer.

We have seen that the peasant student's almost instinctive suspicion of marriage might survive his priest's training and be confirmed by his view of improvements and emigration: it might, finally, be sharpened by personal conflict. Not every priest was serenely celibate, not, maybe, the man who 'had entered the Church without having any particular mission for the priesthood ... [who] had become a priest because his people, publicans and grocers in a small way of business, thought it was a good job for which they could afford to train their son'.[2] Kate O'Brien's Father Tom, finding his nephew with a country girl, 'thought that his [own] anger was all for God and the chastity God exacts. . . . But what he did not know was that a part of his violence was envy. Long fought and long controlled, buried now, as he thought, past all temptation or disturbance, the emotional fire in Father Tom was still awake, and had flickered piteously in spite of him, when he looked at last, unwillingly, at love.'[3] A sexual code,

[1] There are persistent suggestions that many a priest, for all his denunciation of emigration, tended to quicken its flow (and to facilitate, in consequence, the marriages of some of those remaining in Ireland). The priest's authoritarianism, his intolerance of criticism, crippled, it is said, 'the energies by which people might learn to work and to live at home instead of emigrating' (Kenny, 1906, op. cit., p. 154). Of more effect, no doubt, were priests, 'puritanically un-Irish, imposing strange austerities on a naturally jolly people, by a religion that is not austere' ('Pat' [P. D. Kenny], *The Sorrows of Ireland* (1907), pp. 91–2). The visitor, talking to emigrants at Queenstown, 'begins to suspect that the policy of dragooning the people in their homes and diversions, if it has helped to make the Irish the most continent of nations in the single matter of sex, has also done much to blast the innocent pleasures and gaiety of the countryside, and to invest the prospect of escape into life with a new attractiveness' (Sydney Brooks, *The New Ireland* (2nd edn., Dublin, 1907), p. 82). 'No man can get into the confidence of the emigrating classes without being told by them that the exodus is largely due to a feeling that the clergy are, no doubt from an excellent motive, taking innocent joy from the social side of home life' (Plunkett, 1905, op. cit., p. 117).
[2] Liam O'Flaherty, *The Martyr* (1933), p. 224.
[3] Kate O'Brien, *Without my Cloak* (1931), p. 336.

'twisted and bizarre', is not implausibly associated with 'compensation for thwarted instincts and suppressed desires'.[1]

It was seldom by flouting his Church's teaching on marriage that a priest gave effect to his own misgiving: but there was no commendation of marriage in its renunciation by a man of his power and prestige; nor in the emphasis many a priest laid on different parts of that teaching. His Church upheld, as firmly as it did the propriety of marriage, its monopoly of sexual pleasure: 'it is grievously sinful in the unmarried deliberately to procure or accept even the smallest degree of venereal pleasure.'[2] Now, by the years following the Famine, the Irish had long been familiar with youthful, impetuous marriage: they needed no insistence on its appeal or its propriety; such insistence, indeed, would have been heartless. In these years, if people abstained from marriage, it was not for the 'purely selfish reasons' the Church condemned. Their abstention was tolerable to Church and priests: the danger was that a people unexpectedly celibate and unversed in sexual restraint might anticipate the pleasures proper only in marriage. Many of the older priests, in these years, 'saw moral danger in the most innocent meetings of the young folk.... Their notions of woman recalled the fearful and wonderful pronouncements of some of the early Fathers. Love in the main was devilish, a subtle and odious poison designed to set young souls in the way of eternal perdition: ... sickly and melodramatic were the notions of it that they spread.'[3]

Nor, to many a priest, was love rehabilitated by the present century, when a smaller population, living more comfortably, was arguably postponing marriage for culpable, selfish reasons: the Church still 'thunders against the dangers of sex';[4] still, at mission after mission, there was the old emphasis upon the sins of the flesh.[5] Small wonder that teaching like this failed 'to inculcate a practical appreciation of the importance of marriage';[6] that

[1] Paul Blanshard, *Freedom and Catholic Power* (1951), p. 144.
[2] Henry Davis, S.J., *Moral and Pastoral Theology* (1938), ii, 210.
[3] W. P. Ryan, *The Pope's Green Island* (1912), pp. 78–9. The author of this work was the author also, under the name 'W. P. O'Ryan', of *The Plough and the Cross*, already cited.
[4] Sean O'Faolain, 'Love among the Irish', in John A. O'Brien (ed.), *The Vanishing Irish* (1954), p. 115.
[5] MacMahon, 1954, loc. cit., p. 213.
[6] John A. O'Brien, 'Disappearing Irish in America', in John A. O'Brien (ed.), *The Vanishing Irish* (1954), p. 98.

the peasant girl's chastity was variously described as 'remarkable',[1] 'ferocious',[2] 'complete and awful', a virtue no longer, but a 'blight', a 'dreadful evil':[3] small wonder that Catholics, trusting their priests, sometimes 'approach marriage with their minds full of prohibitions'. 'They feel that to enter the state poses a moral problem. They tend to think of the sins they might commit rather than of the holiness they might win.'[4]

There were priests who dissuaded their parishioners from marriage, not merely by creating the impression that it was 'a secondary and often imperfect state of life',[5] but by imposing rules of conduct that made courtship less likely. 'The bare thought of company-keeping or courtship filled them with horror. After several changes theologians had fixed the number of Deadly Sins as seven; Irish parish priests in practice made courtship an eighth. For lovers to walk the roadside in rural Ireland when the average priest was abroad was a perilous adventure. He challenged engaged couples, on occasion he challenged married people.'[6] In co. Cork, before the First War, 'the evils of company keeping were stormed from the pulpit';*[7] 'it was considered a disgrace to be seen walking with one of the opposite sex in broad daylight'.* An American tourist told of a Cork girl coming to a Protestant magistrate for a summons against her priest: 'he had impertinently interfered with her, "assaulted her", and told her to "go home", when he found her sitting in a lonely part of the road with her young man, rather late at night.'[8] The clergy in a western county 'used to arm themselves with sticks long ago, and go out by night and anywhere they'd meet a courting couple they'd work the stick on them'.* In the 1880s 'Father Collins was the custodian of Ramelton's morality. At ten o'clock every fair-night he used to walk through all the lonely lanes and by-ways, rounding up the lovers with his big stick. . . . His old eyes would strain into the darkness . . . "Denis McClure, is that you? . . . Be off home now, or

---

[1] 'A Guardian of the Poor', *The Irish Peasant* (1892), p. 133.
[2] Arland Ussher, *The Face and Mind of Ireland* (1949), p. 82.
[3] Filson Young, *Ireland at the Cross Roads* (1903), p. 76.
[4] Keenan and Ryan, 1955, op. cit., p. 213.
[5] Banning, 1954, loc. cit., p. 121.
[6] Ryan, 1912, op. cit., p. 79 .
[7] For the source of quotations marked with an asterisk, see above, p. 113 n. 1.
[8] William Henry Hurlbert, *Ireland under Coercion* (2nd edn., Edinburgh, 1888), ii, 32.

you'll feel the weight of this stick on your shoulders." [1]

In the novels, too, there are priests morbidly preoccupied with courtship: one, strangely, scoured the by-ways, snatching the hats of courting girls—and treasured in his presbytery a roomful of trophies:[2] another dwelt again and again on 'the dark lanes and lonely roads and boys and girls that follow hideous occasions of sin':[3] yet another 'came on us as we were walking peacefully on the shore road one night, and if he didn't up with his umbrella, and give her several licks of it on the head and shoulders'.[4] Father Tom

had kept the whole of his difficult bargain with the Church, and in the effort he had come by now, in middle life, to lay an over-emphasis on the horribleness of those sins of the flesh which he must never know outside of theological books, training himself to believe that the sensualities were an incomparably greater evil in the world than cruelty or dishonesty or greed. He was inclined to harp on the Catholic's Sixth Commandment, preaching sermons for which he was already locally famous on the horrors of night-walking and company-keeping and the loathsome goings-on in the lanes round Mellick after dark. On the subject of 'morality', which he seemed to take to mean exclusively man's conduct of his sexual life, Father Tom was fanatical. He could be hair-raising about the night life of cities he had never seen, and his hints as to the prevalence in Ireland of what he called 'the social evil' were nightmarish.[5]

Some priests wanted even young boys and girls kept apart—insisting (though at some cost to their education) that they were taught in separate schools,[6] that boys and men sat on one side

[1] 'Blackie' [Catherine Black], *King's Nurse, Beggar's Nurse* (1939), p. 15.
[2] O'Ryan, 1910, op. cit., Ch. 23, 'Love's captured hat', pp. 231–6. Elsewhere the author suggests the origin (possibly partly apocryphal) of this incident. The priest who patrolled the roads 'in our Boyne Valley days . . . generally made it a point to seize the young lady's hat before ordering her homeward, and by that period he was reputed to have a pretty stock of such spoils in a room of the presbytery'. Though 'this latter touch may have had no better foundation than local fancy . . . the full tale of the Irish clerical war on lovers would make a big, strange volume of repression and adventure' (W. P. Ryan, *The Pope's Green Island* (1912), p. 79).
[3] Michael McLaverty, *The Three Brothers* (1948), p. 219.
[4] But, the story continues, 'I made a grab at it ['his grand silk umbrella—silver handle and all'] and broke it across my knee' (Gerald O'Donovan, *Father Ralph* (1913), pp. 373–4).
[5] Kate O'Brien, 1931, op. cit., p. 36.
[6] Iwan-Müller, 1907, op. cit., p. 212.

of the church, girls and women on the other.[1] But the fiercer censure was reserved for meetings of adolescent and older boys and girls. To 'Sunday cyclist' and German tourist, it was 'a strange phenomenon', 'a depressing sight', 'to witness lads and lasses in the west walking on opposite sides of the road and incurring the ban of the priest if they talk to one another',[2] to see 'a normally light-hearted peasantry marshalled in male and female groups along the road, eyeing one another in dull wonderment across the forbidden space through the long summer day'.[3] 'So searing has this iron morality become that even the pleasant and wholesome social intercourse of young people has been banned and killed. In the old days . . . there were the 'quiltings', for example [girls making patchwork quilts, later joined by boys for a dance], . . . [and] at many a cross-road . . . the boys and girls would be dancing and playing games. . . . But such innocent festivities are now hardly known in Ireland. The mixing of the sexes, said the priests, was fraught with possibilities of mortal sin; and they set their faces against it.'[4] 'Keeping company is not

[1] Shane Leslie, 'Romance frowned upon', in John A. O'Brien (ed.), *The Vanishing Irish* (1954), p. 80.
[2] Iwan-Müller, 1907, op. cit., p. 212. [3] Plunkett, 1905, op. cit., p. 116.
[4] Filson Young, *Ireland at the Cross Roads* (1903), pp. 77–8. It would be wrong, of course, to blame the priests solely—even, perhaps, mainly—for the undoubted decline of dancing, 'quilting', and so forth, for the more restrained celebration of marriage, christening, and death. For years many a survivor of the Famine had little heart for merry-making: heavy mortality and emigration (increasingly of young people) made it harder to muster the minimum of merry-makers: the old social life, too, animated by cheap whiskey and the Irish language, disintegrated with mounting spirit-duties and with constabulary and Church adding to the risks, temporal and spiritual, of distilling poteen; with children learning English at school, and needing it to better themselves at home or 'in emigration'. 'The devil', it was once believed, 'cannot speak Irish': 'English was the language of heretics, and Irish that of saints' (Senior, 1868, op. cit., ii, 62, quoting Archbishop Whately). But later on '"Who has Irish, but the wretches of the world?"' (Maurice O'Sullivan, *Twenty Years A-growing* [1933] (1936), p. 318). 'It's a language only fit for spalpeens, it's that coarse and rough' (Gerald O'Donovan, *Father Ralph* (1913), pp. 62–3). 'Sure without English ye'll remain in misery and poverty and ignorance, same as ye always were. How can ye go to America without English? How can any of ye get a job like I have without English? It's English gave me bacon of a Sunday morning for my breakfast and gives me tea twice a day, while ye are all living on Indian meal, porridge, and potatoes and salt fish' (Liam O'Flaherty, *Skerrett* (1932), p. 11). '"When I was a boy"', in consequence, '"they tied a gobban into my mouth for the whole afternoon because I was heard speaking Irish"' (John M. Synge, *In Wicklow, West Kerry and Connemara* (Dublin, 1911), p. 69). '"I had a little board tied to my back, with these words written on it, "If you speak a word of Irish you will be beaten on back, and on flank"'' (O'Sullivan, 1936, op. cit., p. 224).

the custom of the country': the priest had spoken from the altar.[1]

'There is no harm in dancing', one of George Moore's priests said, 'but it leads to harm. If they only went back with their parents after the dance, but they linger in the lanes.'[2] 'I often seen the priest comin' to a house where there'd be a dance and huntin' them home at ten o'clock.'*[3] 'Any place there would be a dance in a house 'twas a regular custom for the local priests to raid it and . . . you'd see couples flying mad across the ditches and down off haystacks. . . . There was a dance over in —— one night, and in the middle of the night someone shouted that the priest was landed. There was a general rush for the door and one boy in his hurry went to jump the half-door and hit his forehead against the top jamb of the door. He was in need of the priest then in earnest but he had him on the spot.'*[4] More recently 'wooden roadside [dancing] platforms were set on fire by curates: surer still, the priests drove their motorcars backward and forward over the timber platforms; concertinas were sent flying into hill streams, and those who played music at dances were branded as outcasts.'[5] Writing in a Catholic journal, the Reverend Michael I. Mooney recalls (and justifies) clerical denunciation of small dance halls: they were 'dens of iniquity', 'haunts of the devil', 'vestibules of hell'.[6] Prompted (Fr. Mooney believes) by members of the hierarchy, the Irish Government introduced legislation on the licensing of dance-halls which 'completely destroyed the informal dances in private houses, which had been such a feature of country life during the winter months'; many a priest, moreover, had misgivings about the newly-built commercial halls, and opened, in rivalry with them, parochial halls 'controlled and directed by the parish priest or one of his curates'.[7]

It was not only in dancing that priests saw 'hideous occasions of sin': attempts to launch amateur theatricals sometimes

---

[1] George Moore, 'Home Sickness', in *The Untilled Field* (1903), p. 165.
[2] George Moore, 'Some Parishioners', ib., p. 59.
[3] But, this ninety-year-old farmworker added, 'there's none of that now and they can dance till midnight or after it, and a young girl can go to these dance halls without a brother or a friend to look after her and she is left to go home the roads at night.'
[4] Again, 'all that has stopped nowadays and the clergy don't ever molest anyone.'
[5] MacMahon, 1954, loc. cit., p. 212.
[6] Michael I. Mooney, 'The Parish Hall', *The Furrow*, 4 (1953), p. 3.
[7] Ib., pp. 3-4.

foundered on clerical disapproval:[1] priests, it is said, 'whip in hand, entered private houses and dispersed social parties'.[2]

Then there was the case of the Rory O'Moore branch of the Gaelic League at Portarlington, whose officers had been hushed, banned, blackguarded, and some of them beggared because they had insisted, against the obey-or-be-damned orders of the local clergy, on holding mixed classes for the teaching of Irish. The clergy had disowned them, and all of them withered away. The fig-tree had been cursed for bringing forth fruit. [The young Sean O'Casey] saw this odd thing himself in Moycally where he had gone on Sundays to teach Irish with a comrade, the two of them giving up their whole day of leisure to hasten the day of Ireland's deliverance. There the girls were forced to sit in the lower room of the local school, the men in the upper one, a local priest always present to see that this canonical rule was flagrantly obeyed. . . . And didn't the clergy fall flat with the weight of the denunciation they heaped on the proposal to send a caravan of artists round Ireland playing Irish plays in towns and villages, fearful of what would happen when the sun had set, and the artists were all asleep under the cedars and the stars. Hadn't he himself organized, in all innocence, Sunday evening summer gatherings between St. Margaret's and the Drumcondra branches of the League, each body marching half-way from their Club-room to meet at a pleasant crossroads, there to sing and dance an hour or two away to the sound of fiddle and fife; and on the second evening of the gatherings didn't the St. Margaret's curate come tearing on his bicycle, sent as courier from the parish priest, a red light on the top of his biretta, to tell them that these strange ways of men with maids wasn't, and never would be, recognized in Ireland; that it was an occasion of sin; that their conduct would embarrass the Irish saints above; and that they were showing a froward example to the Royal Irish Constabulary, the Royal Irish Academy, Trinity College, the Dublin Fire Brigade, the Grand Loyal Orange Lodge of Dublin, the Anti-taxi Association, and all those who constantly thought of the four lust things.

Convents as well as priests might inculcate or confirm reservations about marriage. 'The nuns who taught us did not tell us that marriage was a vocation from God just as much as their's was. Marriage was frowned on, and passed over rather as something to be ashamed of.' 'The male visitor [to this training college,

---

[1] Canon Rossiter, parish priest of Gorey, co. Wexford, objected to girls' taking part in a play: 'if he remained in the parish for 60 years he would be opposed to it' (*The Irish Nation*, 25 Dec 1909, p. 6).
[2] Ryan, 1912, op. cit., p. 78.
[3] Sean O'Casey, *Drums under the Window* (1945), pp. 166-9.

one of the largest in Ireland] was well-questioned before his admission if he were allowed in at all. He was frozen off the premises, and might not care to repeat his visits. He'd want a stout heart to do so. Even speaking to a male friend was considered a crime. . . . [When] we had passed our finals we were taken for a private talk with Rev. Mother in the parlour, who cajoled us to become nuns.'* In reality, maybe, as in fiction, some girls, fresh from the convent, might 'divide their time between doing up the altars in the cathedral, praying at the altar of St. Joseph for husbands, and philandering with Father Phil Doyle. Their idea of marriage, picked up from silly nuns in the fashionable convent they were at, is half a fairy tale and half a miracle. If they only burn enough candles at the statue of St. Joseph, Prince Charming is to come along and rescue them from the shop which they despise. Human nature has been so crushed out of them, that they would not recognize love if it came their way. The prince doesn't come . . . so they'll do as other girls of their class always do, enter a convent, and bring up other girls in the same make-belief.'[1]

But the farmer's daughter was probably less affected by explicit praise of the religious life and dispraise or distortion of marriage than by the nuns' example, and by a curriculum ill-attuned to farmhouse life—making distasteful, indeed, the life that marriage in Ireland was likely to entail. 'A nun with a true vocation . . . is the one person in a troubled world who tastes the security and bliss of Heaven in this life. She has given her life to God, once for all; nothing now can go wrong.'[2] Much went wrong in the farmhouse; and even the girl with no feeling for the veil might think twice before following her mother to the altar. Year after year 'our convent schools . . . are sending out young women eager to be ladies and utterly dissatisfied with a life spent in churning butter and baking cakes':[3] they are drawing-room ornaments,[4] 'pious, pleasure-loving and perfectly useless':[5] they 'contract an aversion for the squalid surroundings and homely manners of

[1] Gerald O'Donovan, *Father Ralph* (1913), pp. 167–8.
[2] Kathleen Norris, 'Muted Wedding Bells', in John A. O'Brien (ed.), *The Vanishing Irish* (1954), p. 146.
[3] Birmingham, 1913, op. cit., p. 217.
[4] Lynd, 1910, op. cit., p. 104.
[5] 'H– B–', *Letters from Ireland*, reprinted from *The New Ireland Review* (Dublin, 1902), p. 128.

their parents':[1] they 'look down with something like contempt on the marriageable young men of their own class'.[2]

The denunciation of dancing; the pillorying of courting couples; the devious disparagement of marriage: much of this was hardly to the taste of young men and women. Why, nevertheless, did they behave so generally as their priests advised? Partly because the rebels left the country and the conformists were rewarded with dowry or land; partly because parents and priests advised alike—the priest sanctioning and moralizing the peasant's sense of the exigencies of their society. But the peculiar authority with which the priest invested Malthusianism is not irrelevant to his parishioners' peculiar recourse to the preventive check—defined by Malthus as 'a restraint from marriage from prudential motives, with a conduct strictly moral during the period of this restraint'.[3]

Berkeley's was a prescient definition of the secular power of the Irish priests:[4] it has echoed into the present century, on an even sharper note: 'they enjoy a prestige and occupy a position among the majority of the people, which finds no exact parallel in any other section of the Christian clergy in the world'; 'their influence upon secular life', Plunkett continued, 'is of the most far-reaching character'; their opportunities 'in the economic field are surely far beyond any which were open to them a century and a half ago':[5] the priest, in Kerry, 'rules with more pomp than ever did any landlord';* in Connemara, he was 'practically tribal chief';[6] 'he's like a king over us' on O'Flaherty's Nara:[7] 'in no country in the world', an American priest believes, 'are the clergy so powerful and influential as in Eire.'[8]

For the last century (if not longer) the Irish priest's power has been broadly based. His religious office gave him the power to absolve sin; it made him the indispensable intermediary between

---

[1] Iwan-Müller, 1907, op. cit., p. 109.   [2] Ib., p. 110.
[3] T. R. Malthus, *Essay on Population* (Everyman edn., 1927), i, 14, n.1.
[4] 'No set of men upon earth have it in their power to do good on easier terms, with more advantage to others and less pain and loss to themselves. Your flocks are, of all others, most disposed to follow directions, and, of all others, want them most' (George Berkeley, *A Word to the Wise* . . . [1752], reprinted in *Tracts and Treatises illustrative* . . . *of Ireland* (Dublin, 1840–1), ii, 208).
[5] Plunkett, 1905, op. cit., p. 330.
[6] Stephen Gwynn, *A Holiday in Connemara* (1909), p. 285.
[7] Liam O'Flaherty, *Skerrett* (1932), p. 9.
[8] John A. O'Brien, 'The Road Ahead', in John A. O'Brien (ed.), *The Vanishing Irish* (1954), p. 233.

his flock and their God: 'it makes him', indeed, 'another Christ.'[1] 'Whatever occurs in a poor man's family, whether joyous or grievous, sickness or death, marriage or birth, the priest is a party; his presence and his office are required.'[2] His presence was felt, too, on more than religious and family occasions: 'in many parts of the country the priest is the match-maker, the arbitrator, the authority which decides whether a man shall buy or sell a farm, the price he shall pay for it, the market at which he shall deal, the manner in which he shall invest his savings, or in a word, the whole business of his life.'[3] With power so various it was a small thing (if a religious duty) to make one family rich, and another poor. 'Oh, a note from me will go a good way with the Board.'[4] 'When a person in a family has money, and grows old, the priest often becomes lawyer to him as well as spiritual adviser.'[5] 'Nothing is more firmly fixed in the minds of many shopkeepers and their peasant customers than that the prosperity or destruction of their business is at the will of the priest.'[6] Was the priest's ill-dowered niece a match for the heir to a prosperous shop? ' "Don't you know" ', the boy's mother ruminated, ' "that when they set up for themselves, he can bring the custom of the whole parish to them? It's unknown the number o' ways he can sarve them in. Sure, at stations, an' weddin's, wakes, marriages, and funerals, they'll all be proud to let the priest know that they purchased whatever they wanted from his niece an' her husband. . . . Faix, four hundher [pounds' dowry] from him is worth three times as much from another." '[7]

[1] Neil Kevin, *I remember Maynooth* (new edn., 1945), p. 136.
[2] 'Resident Native', *Lachrymae Hibernicae* (Dublin, 1822), p. 16. The point is more forcefully made: 'Observe the profound psychology of Catholicism in laying hold of us at all the vital points, especially the most vital, Birth, Love and Death. . . . The Catholic mother has no sooner returned to normal consciousness in the birth-couch than she is faced with possibilities of eternal damnation for her little treasure until she gets in the priest. His control over "the master-passion" is equally complete, placing him virtually in the position to give woman to man, to give man to woman, and to deny the gift . . . under pain of ostracism. . . . And then think of one man, a mere man, sometimes a drunkard, commonly a gossip, bound by his calling to know the innermost secrets, good and bad, of virtue and of vice, in every man and woman in his parish!' (Kenny, 1907, op. cit., p. 102).
[3] Iwan-Müller, 1907, op. cit., p. 94.
[4] 'George A. Birmingham' [J. O. Hannay], *Hyacinth* (1906), p. 110.
[5] Kenny, 1906, op. cit., p. 153.   [6] Ib., p. 151.
[7] W. Carleton, 'The Geography of an Irish Oath', *Traits and Stories . . .*, 1896, op. cit., iii, 135.

'Useful men, good Catholics, can have their dismissal dictated by the priest, and be driven out of Ireland for nothing more than uttering their opinions on lay matters peculiarly their own.'[1] 'A layman differs from the priest on a matter of butter, bacon or politics, and once it is known that "the priest is agin him", the mob is let loose.'[2] Some priests, it is said, waited until troublesome parishioners 'wanted favours, references for their children looking for jobs, etc., and then pounce on them, full of undying revenge and will not give what is being asked until the asker has humbled himself enough before the tyrant of a priest. . . . I have heard of such a priest who carried his revenge so far as to refuse to visit a dying man, and left him to die without the consolations of his religion. To die without the priest is looked upon by country people as one of the greatest calamities that can overtake a person and what must be the feelings of this poor man's family when he was left to die thus.'* Teachers lived more at the priest's whim (and with more effect) than most of their neighbours. They 'come under the lash of the parish priest in a more direct way than any other section of the people as he is their manager over their schools. They dare not offend him in any way, and they usually back him in his arguments with the common people.'* 'Every national schoolmaster . . . is the creature of the clerical manager, appointed, promoted, and dismissed by him at will':[3] with this 'elaborate enslavement' of teacher to priest, how can the teacher 'develop in young people . . . strength and honesty of character?'[4] Nor, in recent decades, is the priest without his say in determining what books may be circulated by libraries and booksellers; what plays and films be seen; what programmes

[1] Kenny, 1906, op. cit., p. 146.
[2] Ib., p. 153.
[3] Sydney Brooks, *The New Ireland* (2nd edn., Dublin, 1907), p. 71.
[4] Kenny, 1906, op. cit., p. 148. The priests 'don't want any independence or character in the laity'. 'We in the schools,' W. P. O'Ryan's young teacher continues, 'who are in the grip of clerical managers, can hardly call our souls our own, or if we try to do so it is with the prospect of dismissal before us. And then look at the efforts the clergy all round are making to prevent the establishment of a public library in Baile na Boinne. They've been to all the councillors, and when the question comes up next week all except one or two will be afraid to go against the wishes of the priests. So the people must remain without books. All the clergy—the young Irish Ireland priests, of course, excepted—are against knowledge for the people' (W. P. O'Ryan, *The Plough and the Cross* (Dublin, 1910), pp. 123–4). Priests, even the most scholarly, might bar their parishioners' access to books. Mr. Arland Ussher tells of a priest he knew in his boyhood, 'a man of deep learning and real culture',

broadcast: in the twenty-six counties, it is claimed, almost all the newspapers are 'wholeheartedly Catholic in their presentation of the news'.[1]

'The Dáil proposes; Maynooth disposes':[2] whatever the exaggeration here, there is no denying that political power has long been added to spiritual, economic, and educational. The eighteenth-century priests, trained on the Continent, imbibed in their seminaries 'the traditional spirit of passive obedience to established laws and authorities'. 'Loyalists and Conservatives', they 'suffered in silence for fear of provoking new tyrannies'.[3] Their successors, sons of humbler homes, smarted under grievances the national and agrarian struggles sought to mitigate; nor, trained in Ireland, were they long distracted from them: they were the more insistently drawn to politics by the rarity of other leaders and by their desire to control excesses. But for all their prominence in the popular movement, 'one of the most stalwart pillars of the Catholic Church in Ireland is Protestant England. . . . It is our system, our policy, our fatal trick of ignoring the Catholic laity in Ireland and of dealing over their heads with the Church direct that buttress and perpetuate the temporal power of Irish Catholicism.'[4] To the priest, then, accrued the prestige of popular leadership and credit for the concessions it won: nor was he lightly overruled when the benefits were apportioned—a dispensary doctor appointed; a slipway here or there; the public bull in this byre or that.

Three factors commonly underlay the accumulation of so much power in a priest's hands: his own wish; his parishioners' acquiescence, and the scarcity, in much of the country, of people able and anxious to share it. By the time a priest was entrusted with a parish, only an unusual humility saved him from feeling (or

---

'cynical and kindly' in conversation, his two-bottle cupboard ('port for ladies and "total abstainers", whisky for good Christians') opened for every visitor: in his own study there were 'dusty oil-paintings', 'the shelf of Latin books': but 'he strongly reprehended the establishment of a local public library.' ' "Teaching the latest ideas of blackguardism" he called it—though he had, in fact, virtual powers of veto over the books' (Arland Ussher, *The Face and Mind of Ireland* (1949), p. 82). Mr. Liam O'Flaherty has barbed this same lament: 'The parish priest himself has no education worth speaking of, so he dislikes others receiving one' (Liam O'Flaherty, *A Tourist's Guide to Ireland* (2nd edn., 1930), p. 41).

[1] Blanshard, 1954, op. cit., pp. 87, 88–121.
[2] Sean O'Faolain, 'The Dáil and the Bishops', *The Bell*, xvii (1951), p. 6.
[3] Paul-Dubois, 1908, op. cit., p. 477.   [4] Brooks, 1907, op. cit., p. 70.

at least professing) an implicit confidence in his judgement and a zeal to enforce it. People tend 'to make a priest of the family pet',* depriving themselves, perhaps disinheriting his brothers and sisters—even breaking the law—, to find him 'the best of everything that is going':*[1] 'the budding Levite has an easy time in his youth: he is spared the rough work of the farm':[2] from the moment he enters college he is 'the young God',[3] used 'to having the plain people bowing before him'.*

'Denis O'Shaughnessy going to Maynooth'[4] is the classic caricature of the country boy singled out 'to wear the robes as a clargy'.[5] It was drawn before the Famine; Denis, as presented by his priest to the bishop, was the son of 'a warm, respectable parishioner of mine':[6] but much later in the century many a humbler home still revolved on its Denis. 'The highest object of an Irish peasant's ambition is to see his son a priest.' At home the chosen boy 'was idolised—overwhelmed with respect and deference', and 'never asked to work, except it be his own pleasure to labour a day or two by way of amusement'. He 'becomes the centre in which all the affections of the family meet. He is cherished, humoured in all his caprices, indulged in his boyhood predilections, and raised over the heads of his brothers, independently of all personal or relative merit in himself.' In the neighbours' eyes, 'an incipient sanctity begins, as it were, to consecrate the young priest, and a high opinion of his learning and talents to be entertained, no matter how dull he may be so far as honest nature is concerned.' His own giddy dream was 'to

---

[1] 'In every house where a priest was being made, the kitchen door would be locked at meal times.' In the south of Ulster—so a former insurance agent told Patrick Kavanagh—'every house is insured and last year there was a hell of a row because one man burned out of his turn. Ye see the way it was, it wouldn't look [well?] if every house were burned on the one week, so there was a union formed and it was arranged that I'd burn this week, and you the next, and you else the next, and so on till yer turn would come round again. This fella had a bill to pay—he was makin' two priests and that no joke—so he burned out of his turn. . . . The man maintained that he didn't burn out of his turn, but the union had the books and it was lucky for him he didn't contest it in the law court for he'd be bet blind' (Patrick Kavanagh, *The Green Fool* (1938), pp. 159, 164).

[2] Brooks, 1912, op. cit., p. 183.
[3] MacMahon, 1954, loc. cit., p. 214.
[4] W. Carleton, *Traits and Stories of the Irish Peasantry* (ed. D. J. O'Donoghue, 1896), iv, 71–207.
[5] W. Carleton, 'The Hedge School', ib., ii, 233.
[6] Carleton, 'Denis O'Shaughnessy', 1896, op. cit., p. 166.

CENTURY AFTER THE FAMINE

be in the course of a few years a *bonâ fide* priest; to possess unlimited sway over the fears and principles of the people; to be endowed with spiritual gifts to he knew not what extent; and to enjoy himself, as he had an opportunity of seeing Father Finnerty and his curate do, in the full swing of convivial pleasure, upon the ample hospitality of those who, in addition to this, were ready to kiss the latchet of his shoes'. 'Buy me a knife and fork . . .', Denis directed his father, 'I'm not the man now to be placed among the other riff-raff of the family over a basket of potatoes'— and, sure enough, 'when the family were to be seen around the kitchen table at their plain but substantial breakfast, Denis was lording it, in solitary greatness, over an excellent breakfast of tea and eggs in another room.'[1]

Understandably, 'it is hard for a priest born under these circumstances and having special honours given to him from his early days to come off his soap-box and try to walk side by side with the common herd':* 'they are always given to understand they are superior beings, and as they have had very few chances of going through the ups and downs of ordinary people they often lack . . . brotherly sympathy':* 'the consequence', to Carleton, of over-indulging the priest-to-be, 'is that he gradually becomes self-willed, proud, arrogant, often to an offensive degree.'[2] The taste for authority, implanted by this boyhood cossetting might become more beguiling under the discipline of the priest's student-days,[3] and the submission expected then and later by his ecclesiastical superiors:[4] the repository, moreover, of so much

---

[1] Carleton, 'Denis O'Shaughnessy', op. cit., p. 72, 128, 94, 72, 89, 125, 103, 128.
[2] Ib., p. 72.
[3] *Report, Maynooth Commission,* P.P., 1854-5, XXII, pp. 35-9; Brooks, 1912, op. cit., pp. 184-5.
[4] 'There is no power in Ireland', one critic maintained, 'quite so autocratic as that of the bishop within the limits of his diocese; the most arrogant, bumptious and independent of priests is humility itself in its presence. The priest is even more the submissive bondsman of the bishop than is the school teacher of the priest. Against his ecclesiastical superior he has no rights; he must obey every order, however extravagant; he must pocket every insult and crawl for favours; the unforgivable sin is that he should hold opinions contrary to those of his bishop; and preferment goes to those who have most fully schooled themselves to judicious sycophancy' (Brooks, 1912, op. cit., p. 187). Power in the parish, if compensation for powerlessness in the Church, tanatalized the more, the more preferment was postponed: while the number of 'curates administrators and others' nearly doubled between 1849 and 1958, there was little increase in the number of parish priests and little lasting increase in the number of bishops (see Appendix, pp. 160-1).

spiritual power, he had less hesitation in trespassing on the trivialities of temporal life: his celibacy, too, may have some bearing on his 'restless pugnacity'.[1] So, also, may the uncertainty of the peasant's son raised to eminence.[2] 'I know no elevation in life so great or sudden as that which an Irish priest obtains, compared with his former one':[3] 'he finds himself in possession of a power which no tradition of the class from which he sprang has fitted him to use, which his education has in no way prepared him to endure nobly; the least opposition to his will, the mildest criticism of his action, makes him furious; his acts, like those of all bullies, are violent:[4] the 'disgusting arrogance' of many priests, a third commentator attributed to their using 'their suddenly acquired power, as the *parvenu* does his wealth for the purpose of idle display and offensive ostentation'.[5]

Why was the power sought by the priests so freely conceded by their parishioners? For long, in much of the country, few other people had the confidence of the peasantry, the capacity and will to act as their leaders. Resident landlords and agents, alien for the most part in race and religion, if not also in language, were the more suspect as instruments of political and economic power: native, Catholic landowners, reappearing after the Famine, were seldom kindlier or more respected,[6] and (with newly established dealers, lawyers, and teachers) might choose to rise in the wake

[1] Paul Blanshard, *Freedom and Catholic Power* (1951), p. 144.

[2] The Protestant rector, 'whatever his father may have been, does, in virtue of his office, dine with the landlord of the parish. . . . The State, indeed, no longer recognizes the Church of Ireland clergy, but "society" does, and the Irish Roman Catholic priest finds himself in the same sort of position as the English Dissenter. . . . Many of them are satisfied with the reality of political power and are willing to smile at the loss of the shadow of social recognition. . . . But others . . . are exceedingly touchy on the article of their gentility. . . . Are not their coats as black and their hats as glossy as those of any clergy in the world? Is the culture derivable from Maynooth less wide than that of the ordinary graduate of Trinity College, Dublin? Is not the horse in the Presbytery stable a superior beast to the rector's cob?' (Birmingham, 1913, op. cit., p. 176).

[3] O'Beirne, 1840, op. cit., p. 5.

[4] Birmingham, 1913, op. cit., p. 183. Birmingham here, of course, is describing only one kind of priest.

[5] *Ireland and its Rulers*, 1844, op. cit., i, 262.

[6] 'Never was English oppression more dreadful to the Irish than when its instruments were their fellow Catholics' (Seamus McCall, *Irish Mitchel* (1938), p. 106, quoting J. Godkin). Before the Famine, according to Carleton, 'The class most hateful to the people are those useless wretches who spring up from

of the priest rather than challenge his leadership.[1] A government, moreover, providing higher education for the priests, did little for their laity; and the hierarchy, scorning public money save on its own exacting terms, opted, in effect, for a laity little educated under its own control, rather than one more educated, partly by the State. Leadership, in consequence, when it needed formal education, fell to the priests; failing them, to the odd layman they had taught, and taught submission.

By and large, however, people yielded to the priest gladly; not grudgingly, for want of a better leader. They did so partly because of the quality of their faith. Observers, Irish and foreign, clerical and anti-clerical, are all but agreed on the firmness of religious conviction in Catholic Ireland: 'in no other country in the world, probably, is religion so dominant an element in the daily life of the people':[2] 'the faith of the Irish peasant is entire, unquestioning, absolute as that of a thirteenth century's serf':[3] not even in Spain were 'devotion to the church' and 'earnest piety' 'so deeply rooted in the hearts of the people':[4] well into the present century 'a maid seeking a situation will inquire how far the house of her employer is from the nearest church . . . a gardener or groom will accept lower wages for the sake of getting near a church which his children can attend and a school where

---

nothing into wealth accumulated by dishonesty and rapacity. . . . To such upstarts the poor classes are externally most civil, but such persons they most hate and abhor' (*Traits and Stories*, op. cit., iii, 261). When the Incumbered Estates Courts had increased the number of such upstarts, it was said by a western poor-law inspector to be 'the unanimous opinion' that they inflicted 'the greatest hardships, both as to evictions and exorbitant increases in rents' (*Reports from the Poor Law Inspectors . . . as to the existing Relations between Landlord and Tenant*, P.P., 1870, XIV, p. 74). 'Of all the landowning classes at that period [*c.* 1880] none were more hated and feared than the ex-Gombeen men who had invested their ill-gotten gains in the purchase of small insolvent estates coming up for sale in the Landed Estates Courts' (Henry Robinson, *Further Memories of Irish Life* (1924), p. 114).

[1] After Catholic emancipation 'the despised Popish priest was not only able to swing his Mass-bell without fear—he was able to appoint Popish judges, to return Popish members of Parliament, to nominate Popish magistrates. The electro-plated Catholic upper-class thus manufactured repaid in sycophancy the ecclesiastical dignitaries to whom they owed their patents' (William O'Brien, *When we were Boys* [1890], (Dublin, 1920), pp. 170–1).

[2] Plunkett, 1905, op. cit., p. 94.
[3] Daryl, 1888, op. cit., p. 227.
[4] Richard F. Clarke, S.J., *A Personal Visit to Distressed Ireland* (1883).

he can be sure that they will be taught their catechism.'[1] There is, no doubt, an intricate explanation of faith so firm. Living wretchedly, the Irishman certainly needed all the comfort religion might bring: irreligion was horrifying alike to parents, teachers, and priests; and the sceptic, shunned by his neighbours,[2] his livelihood endangered, more probably emigrated than spread his doubts at home. Under the Penal Laws the peasantry had cherished their Church for sharing their suffering;[3] and they respected afterwards its remarkable resilience. 'From the bosom of the darkness of the Penal days the Church seemed to have stepped into the dazzle of mediaeval Italy. . . . Religion was now coming out of the catacombs and marching on the seat of Empire. After the Fathers of the Desert, the founders of the Basilicas.'[4] Long deprived of its ancient edifices and permitted at last to replace them, the Catholic Church was the most grandiose builder in nineteenth-century Ireland: many a peasant member was impressed by the number,[5] the architecture, and the fitments of its buildings—by the realization that he and his emigrant children

[1] Birmingham, 1919, op. cit., p. 88. But, on the other hand, 'we have only to look at the extent of the "leakage" from Roman Catholicism amongst the Irish emigrants in the United States and in Great Britain, to realise how largely emotional and formal must be the religion of those who lapse so quickly in a non-Catholic atmosphere' (Plunkett, 1905, op. cit., p. 111).

[2] Brooks, 1912, op. cit., p. 189.

[3] John O'Driscol, *Views of Ireland* (1823), i, 139 ff.

[4] William O'Brien, 1920, op. cit., pp. 168–70.

[5] The following table, showing, for various dates, the number of Catholic churches and houses of religious orders, may much under-estimate the rate of new building; for it gives no indication of additions to existing churches or religious houses, of the proportion—presumably increasing—of new to old buildings, or of any tendency for new edifices to be larger either than those they replaced or than comparable buildings, newly completed.

Catholic churches and religious houses, Ireland, 1849, 1901, and 1958

	Catholic churches	Houses of religious orders and communities
1849	2152	207
1901	2418	587
1958	2508	980

(*Irish Catholic Directory*, 1851, p. 210; 1903, p. 414; 1960, p. 640. Note (a) to the table in the Appendix (p. 160) applies also to this table. The *Directory* for 1851 gives the number of churches in 24 dioceses, but not in the remaining three—Dublin, Tuam and Kilmacduagh, and Kilfenora: the figure given here for 1849 is the total for the 24 dioceses, increased by one-eighth.)

CENTURY AFTER THE FAMINE 153

(with the dealers their custom enriched) had largely financed them.[1] With a troubled parishioner, Gerald O'Donovan's saintly Fr. Ralph climbed the cliff looking down on the little town where he was curate. 'Would you tell me now', the cobbler asked, 'what buildings you can make out from here?' 'The cathedral', Father Ralph replied, 'the two convents, the monastery, the asylum, the workhouse, the bishop's palace, the parochial house, and, I think, the Emporium.' Spreading buildings, 'the garish brasses surrounding the altar, the vulgar lamps, the gorgeous vestments of the priest . . ., the purple robes of the bishop': to the peasant, these were the marks, proper and unforgettable, of the Church's pomp and power, seldom prompting him to ask, with Fr. Ralph, 'Was his God the God of all this tinsel magnificence, who bedecked himself at the expense of hungry children and toiling underfed men and women?'[2]

The people's piety, the Church's grandeur: these were no bad base for priestly power. But the Irish priest was esteemed for more than his office. 'He was zealous and untiring in the discharge of religious duties.'[3] Sometimes a gormandizer,[4] rarely a drunkard (more rarely, if he were, retaining his cure), what popular criticism there was bore mostly on his arrogance[5] and eagerness for fees: there was talk of his 'almost insane craving for money';* of his 'hysterical fits of rage over paltry little coins';* of his bargaining so hard for marriage fees that matches were postponed or abandoned.[6] Catholic peasants, it is said, showed a 'universal preference' for banks with Protestant managers; they looked and lived

---

[1] Jean Blanchard, *Le droit ecclésiastique contemporain d'Irlande* (Paris, 1958), pp. 101–2; Arnold Schrier, *Ireland and the American Emigration* (Minneapolis, 1958), p. 120; Gerald O'Donovan, *Father Ralph* (1913), pp. 110, 314, and *passim*.
[2] O'Donovan, 1913, op. cit., pp. 313, 317.
[3] Daryl, 1888, op. cit., pp. 221–2.
[4] Ib.   [5] See above, p. 147–50.
[6] In the diocese of Elphin, early in the present century, 'a bargain was always struck [with the priest] in the "fortune" matches and the holy sacrament was often prefaced by such a conversation as "Do it for £13, father"—"No; I won't marry you under £16"—"Split the difference, father", etc. etc.' (*Irish Nation*, 19 June 1909, p. 7). 'In his calm, pleasing way, he argues that he has two curates who immediately take half of the fee and that times have been improving recently. Then he gives them a goodly measure from the bottle'.* How do the very poor 'find the bright coin? The Church will refuse to tie the knot until it is forthcoming' (*Irish Nation*, 19 June 1909, p. 7). 'Long ago', in co. Cork, 'poor people went from house to house to make up a little for the priest's money to get a girl married' (I.F.C., MS. 939, p. 214).

below their means because of the priest's as well as the landlord's exactions.[1] No doubt the seeming greed of many a priest was the mark of peasant stock,[2] hardened by his, and his Church's, dependence on the people's offerings; no doubt, either, that it indulged his relations or Church more often than unpriestly leaning to luxury or avarice:[3] it sustained, nevertheless, the very real comforts of Irish clerical life—comforts enjoyed by few of the laity, by few, indeed, of the clergy abroad. Paschal Grousset, touring Ireland in the 1880s, shared a car for a few days with a party of 'village and parish priests': 'their black coat has all the softness of first quality cloth; their travelling bag is of good bright leather; their very umbrella has a look of smartness'; 'they . . . would on no account stop at second-rate inns'; 'the appetite of the reverend fathers is excellent, and . . . the *carte* of the wines is a familiar object with them. They each have their favourite claret: one likes Léoville, another Château Margaux, while the third prefers Chambertin. . . . After dessert they remain last in the dining room, in company with a bottle of port. At ten o'clock that night, entering it to get a cup of tea, I find the three seated round glasses of smoking toddy.'[4] More recently, another French observer has stressed that the Catholic Church in Ireland, poorer in property than elsewhere, is freer of financial worry, '*et son clergé a le niveau de vie le plus élevé parmi ceux observés en Europe*'. In general, M. Blanchard concludes, 'la condition des prêtres est aisée, comparée du moins à celle des ecclésiastiques de France. Les fidèles sont généreux et les pourvoient largement de moyens d'existence. Curés et vicaires ont une garde-robe correcte, voire soignée, des maisons biens entretenues. *Ils portent sur leur visage et leur personne un air de prospérité. Ils n'ont pas de soucis matériels.*'[5] But, for all the muttering against clerical greed, ordinary

[1] Brooks, 1912, op. cit., pp. 196–7.
[2] Lynd, 1909, op. cit., pp. 125–6.
[3] But when the will of a Munster priest who 'craved for money, money, all the time . . . was published he had nearly four thousand pounds. . . . [Christ struggled] to prevent His disciples from falling victims to avarice and it is a sad reflection that after almost two thousand years continual teaching of the opposite virtue the clergy themselves have not yet learned it.'*
[4] 'Philippe Daryl' [Paschal Grousset], *Ireland's Disease* (1888), pp. 217–20.
[5] Blanchard, 1958, op. cit., pp. 159, 140–1. The passages I have italicized are ignored in the unattributed translation of M. Blanchard's study published '*Permissu Ordinarii Dioec. Dublinen. die 16 Aug. 1962*' by Clonmore and Reynolds in Dublin and Burns and Oates in London (Jean Blanchard, *The Church in Contemporary Ireland* (Dublin, 1963), pp. 90, 79, iv).

clerical indulgence bred respect rather than bitterness. The Irish priest, too, was exculpated from 'the vices of the Italian and Spanish priests' and commended for his 'exemplary purity'.[1] He was, moreover, one of the peasantry: they paid him: he was 'laden with the prejudices' of his class:[2] 'the most brilliant thing ever done by the Irish priests was the invention of the legend that they had always been on the side of the people':[3] rightly or wrongly, they wore much of the patriot's glory.

But there was fear as well as love in the people's submission to the priest, the prospect of material as well as spiritual reward. Ignorance of theology as well as devotion to religion made people exaggerate the sphere in which disobedience to the priest incurred spiritual penalties. And not every priest, however precise his theology, eagerly enlightened them: some ('throwing into the scale [their] sacerdotal emblems')[4] enforced their advice on secular matters with spiritual pains and penalties:[5] 'one of the first economic necessities of Ireland today is to teach the priest ... how to draw the line at making a secular instrument of his sacred privilege.'[6]

There were Irishmen, too, pagan as well as pious, who credited their priests with magical as well as spiritual power. If the backslider lost his cow, 'Sure, he couldn't have any luck, he never goes to Mass.'[7] When Liam O'Flaherty's Skerrett opposed the priest, the people of Nara 'would not be surprised if he had suddenly been turned into a goat before their eyes, or if the ground had opened up and swallowed him': 'Until we shun this devil . . .', Father Moclair laid down, 'God will turn His divine face away from us. He will be deaf to our prayers and our land shall be barren. Our seas will refuse us fish. Disease will destroy our cattle. Brother will turn against brother and son against father. We'll be visited by all the horrors that are foretold with the coming of Anti-Christ.'[8] Carleton, a century before Moclair's time, had 'no hesitation in asserting that the bulk of the Irish peasantry really believe that the priests have ... power'

---

[1] Daryl, 1888, op. cit., p. 221; Ryan, 1912, op. cit., p. 90.
[2] John O'Driscol, *Views of Ireland* (1823), ii, 115; see also pp. 126-7, above.
[3] W. P. Ryan, *The Pope's Green Island* (1912), p. 41.
[4] Arthur Lynch, *Ireland: Vital Hour* (1915), p. 129.
[5] Iwan-Müller, 1907, op. cit., p. 94.
[6] Kenny, 1906, op. cit., p. 146.
[7] Brooks, 1912, op. cit., p. 189.
[8] Liam O'Flaherty, *Skerrett* (1932), pp. 214, 266.

'to translate all the Protestants into asses'.[1] '"It's wonderful how soon a priest can clear up a quarrel." . . . "Doran [the priest said], if you rise your hand more, I'll strike it dead on your body, and to your mouth you'll never carry it while you have breath in your carcass. . . . Clear off, you Flanagans, you butchers you, or by St. Dominick, I'll turn the heads round upon your bodies in the twinkling of an eye, so that you'll not be able to look a quiet Christian in the face again."'[2]

Clearly, the teaching of the priests, whatever its burden, has not been lightly disregarded in the Catholic countryside; but in all that pertains to marriage there may be even more than the customary correspondence between teaching and practice. Many a priest (we have seen), drawn by his own emotions as well as by spiritual and material considerations, dwelt on marital matters with unusual persistence and emphasis. The Church sought, too, to preserve its members from lay advocacy of marriage less disciplined, or differently disciplined. Parents—if they thought instruction seemly—respected the priest, and were the more likely to reiterate his advice because it coincided with their interest and prejudice. But teachers, doctors, welfare-workers, none of these, with the priests' consent, gave advice on relations between the sexes:[3] the priest alone might instruct: with the whole weight of his authority, in pulpit, confessional, and conversation, with spiritual and secular sanctions, he regulated marital and

[1] Carleton, 'The Station', *Traits and Stories*, op. cit., i, 163 and n.
[2] Carleton, 'Shane Fadh's Wedding', ib., i, 90.
[3] According to Mr. Paul Blanshard, 'an important corollary to the Catholic sexual code is that all sexual education should be under priestly control' (*Freedom and Catholic Power* (1951), p. 126). This contention seems to underlie the celebrated letter sent by the Secretary to the Hierarchy to the Taoiseach (the prime minister) during the discussion in 1950 of the Government's ill-fated proposals for a mother-and-child health service.
  Education in regard to motherhood [the Hierarchy's spokesman maintained] includes instruction in regard to sex relations, chastity and marriage. The State has no competence to give instructions in such matters. We regard with the greatest apprehension the proposal to give to local medical officers the right to tell Catholic girls and women how they should behave in regard to this sphere of conduct, at once so delicate and sacred.
  Gynaecological care may be, and in some other countries is, interpreted to include provision for birth limitation and abortion. We have no guarantee that State officials will respect Catholic principles in regard to these matters. Doctors trained in institutions in which we have no confidence may be appointed as medical officers under the proposed services, and may give gynaecological care not in accordance with Catholic principles.
(Paul Blanshard, *Ireland and Catholic Power* (1954), pp. 76–7.)

CENTURY AFTER THE FAMINE 157

pre-marital relations[1]—down, indeed, to matters the lay mind might mistake for the minutiae.[2] Latterly, no doubt, there has been some invasion of this clerical preserve. But during the early decades of the new State, while widespread literacy and easier travel, the radio and the cinema, familiarized a looser marriage, the priest's ideal, sheltered by the critic's emigration, was increasingly buttressed by the law. Divorce, permitted until 1925, is forbidden by the Constitution of 1937.[3] In 1929, in its initial legislation against birth-control, the Dáil merely made it an offence to advocate or advertise methods and materials.[4] Six years later, however, it forbade the import and sale of 'any appliance, instrument, drug, preparation or thing designed, prepared or intended to prevent pregnancy resulting from sexual intercourse between human beings'.[5] A doctor, in consequence, giving his patient a contraceptive—though neither is a Catholic—is liable to be imprisoned.[6] At least one couple, it is said, has been fined for kissing;[7] a 19-year-old girl was fined for

[1] 'In Ireland, everything connected with marriage and sex comes within the scope of the Church's power. Courtship is the business of the Irish priest, and petting is the business of the Irish priest, and even the etiquette of the marriage bed is the business of the Irish priest—as well as birth-control, abortion, mixed marriage, illegitimacy, sodomy, masturbation, divorce, separation, sex education, and "keeping company". Every Irish Catholic is trained to accept the rule of his Church in all these areas as a matter of course' (ib., p. 148).

[2] On the meticulousness of the Church's oversight of sexual matters see, for instance, the discussion of the sacrament of marriage and the sixth and ninth commandments in *Problems in Theology* (Dublin, 1960), i, *The Sacraments* (pp. 342-430) and ii, *The Commandments* (pp. 194-263), by the Very Reverend Dr. John McCarthy, sometime Professor of Moral Theology at University College, Dublin, and of Moral Theology and Canon Law at St. Patrick's College, Maynooth. Among the matters Dr. McCarthy discusses are: 'The morality of kissing', 'The morality of the use of tampons', 'Liceitas lotionum vaginalum post copulam' and the lawfulness of 'procuring seminal specimens for fertility tests' by 'the use of a punctured condom in marital intercourse, provided always, we repeat, that the puncture is large enough. . . .' (ib., i, 430-3; ii, 205-8, 225-7, 259-63).

[3] Blanshard, 1954, op. cit., p. 162; *Bunreacht na hÉireann: Constitution of Ireland* (Dublin, 1945), Article 41, 3, 2°: 'No law shall be enacted providing for the grant of a dissolution of marriage.'

[4] Censorship of Publications Act, 1929, sec. 16.

[5] Criminal Law Amendment Act, 1935, sec. 17.

[6] Ib.; Blanshard, 1954, op. cit., p. 162.

[7] 'Blackrock was a seaside resort near Dundalk, afterwards to achieve fame as the place where kissing wasn't allowed. A boy and girl were brought up on the local court and fined for kissing on the beach at Blackrock' (Kavanagh, 1938, op. cit., p. 320).

courting.[1] The Irish Republic, indeed, 'is probably the only place of any considerable size in the world today where the entire Catholic sexual code is accepted at its face value'.[2]

But, for all the power of Church and State, so formalized a code would hardly have been adopted so generally if it were at variance with social and economic needs: indeed, the peasant's respect for the Catholic code as transmitted to him has sprung, not least, from its compatibility with his patriarchal and material ambition. He hardly dissociated the disasters of the Famine from the marriage customary in his class—for early marriage, laxly 'arranged', perhaps romantic, had plausibly aggravated both the growth of population and its dependence on the potato. And later, when living standards might be improved, when the land legislation gave reality to the peasant's dream of establishing his family on land of its own, a prudent marriage was desired the more, a marriage, shrewdly arranged by the boy's father and the girl's in the interest of 'land' and 'family'; in the interest, too, of old men's authority and their wives'.

Now a father who hesitated to play the patriarch because of the cost of the arranged marriage to his children might be heartened by the priest's example: it was the finicky layman, still troubled by mercenary marriage, when his spiritual leader was ready to make as well as solemnize a match; when he bargained on behalf of his sister or niece, added to her dowry and took his percentage of her neighbour's.[3] The priests, too, helped to reconcile the young to the costs of the match. The boy, chosen to inherit the

[1] *Irish Times*, 24 June 1967. The proceedings (at Limerick District Court) were brought under the Criminal Law Amendment Act, 1935, sec. 18, which forbids the commission in a public place of any act that might 'offend modesty or cause scandal or injure the morals of the community'. Proceedings against the girl's companion were delayed while his address was being confirmed.

[2] Blanshard, 1954, op. cit., p. 162. This statement needs qualification to take account, not least, of some divergence between the tendency of the Irish Church's teaching on marriage and the letter of Catholic doctrine (see above, pp. 121–44).

[3] 'How far are the clergy to be blamed for the dearth of marriages? They acquiesce in matchmaking' (*Irish Nation*, 19 June 1909, p. 7). 'The priest who performs the service ascertains the amount of the "fortune" and charges a high figure. Often he regulates it in ratio to the number of acres or stock the parties possess' (ib.). In a Cork report, 5 per cent of the dowry might be earmarked by the priest. Similarly in the west—where, to whittle down his levy, some (it is said) paid half the dowry openly, half in secret. A priest in *Knocknagow* expected the equivalent of half the annual rent of the bride's father (I.F.C., MS. S355, Cork, p. 109; Terence McGrath, *Pictures from Ireland* (1880), p. 115;

land, and the girl, to be 'fortuned off', must normally remain single unusually long, and marry eventually on their fathers', rather than their own, initiative; their brothers and sisters, if they remained in the Irish countryside, were unlikely ever to marry. It was easier for the peasant's children to postpone or renounce their own marriage when they knew and respected so many examples of religious celibacy; when marriage was so beset by prohibitions that it seemed a perilous venture; when, in so much seemly social activity, the sexes were segregated. And this same segregation of the sexes, culminating in the priests' 'making courtship an eighth deadly sin', left the boys and girls who tolerated it disinclined (perhaps unable) to make their own matches, acquiescent instead in their fathers' choice. 'If you do not let them walk about the lanes and make their own marriages, they marry for money.'[1]

'We agreed' [Canon Sheehan's Father Dan and his sometimes dissident new curate],

We agreed in thinking that the Christian ideal of marriage was nowhere so happily realized as in Ireland, where, at least up to recent times, there was no lurid and volcanic company-keeping before marriage, and no bitter ashes of disappointment after; but the good mother quietly said to her child: "Mary, go to confession tomorrow, and get out your Sunday dress. You are to be married on Thursday evening." And Mary said: "Very well, mother", not even asserting a faintest right to know the name of her future spouse. . . . Married life in Ireland has been, up to now, the most splendid refutation of all that the world and its gospel, the novel, preach about marriage, and the

---

Charles J. Kickham, *Knocknagow* [1879] (Dublin, 1953), p. 75). Many a priest, naturally enough, helped to dower his sister or niece. 'A priest's marriage', however, 'is never lucky'—for in the popular mind (Carleton explained) 'priest's money . . . "is the price of sin" ' (the price, that is, of absolution). The more worldly, none the less, chanced their luck: 'It'd be a great back to you entirely to have the priest for a relation'; 'It would be a gorgeous thing to . . . have your brother-in-law with power in his hands to help you out of many a difficulty' (Katharine Tynan, 'The Irish Priests', *Fortnightly Review*, N.S. lxxxii (1907), 466; William Carleton, 'The poor Scholar', in *Traits and Stories of the Irish Peasantry* [1830–3] (1896), iii, 188n.; Gerald O'Donovan, *Waiting* (1914), p. 72; Brinsley MacNamara, *The Valley of the squinting Windows* [1918] (Tralee, co. Kerry, 1964), p. 93). (On the supposed ill-luck of 'priest's marriages'— those whose partners he brought together as well as those he financed—see also: I.F.C., MSS. 939, Cork, p. 199; 1022, Longford, pp. 72–4; Michael MacDonagh, *Irish Life and Character* (1899), p. 205.)

[1] George Moore, 'Some Parishioners', in *The Untilled Field* (1903), p. 59.

most splendid and complete justification of the supernaturalism of the Church's dogmas and practices.[1]

[1] P. A. Sheehan, *My New Curate* [1899] (Boston, Mass., 1900), pp. 387–8.

APPENDIX

Population, Catholic population and proportion of Catholics to total population; numbers of Catholic clergy, regular and secular (distinguishing bishops and archbishops, parish priests, and administrators and curates); and the number of Catholics per priest and per secular priest; Ireland (thirty-two counties), 1849–1958

	Total population (000)	Catholic population (000)	Percentage of Catholics to total population	Archbishops and bishops	Parish priests	Administrators, curates and others	Total secular clergy	Regular clergy	Total priests	No. of Catholics to one secular priest	No. of Catholics to one priest (secular and regular)
	(1)	(2)	(3)	(4)	(5)	(6)	(7)	(8)	(9)	(10)	(11)
1849	6552(b)	5092(c)	—	27	1010	1371	2408	193	2574(d)	2115	1978
1861	5799	4505	78	34	1041	1489	2564	567	3131	1757	1439
1901	4459	3309	74	27	1021	1932	2980	588	3568	1110	927
1946	4305	3257(e)	76	29	1068	2481	3578	1398	4976	910	655
1958	4332(f)	3257(e)	75	28	1092	2713	3833	1776	5573	850	585

(a) *The Irish Catholic Directory*, from which these figures are taken, does not indicate the year to which they relate: I have presumed that the figures for a given year are to be found in the *Directory* dated two years later.

(b) 1851.

(c) The religious distribution of the population was officially returned only from 1861: the figure given here (for 1851) has been determined on the assumption that the Catholic population bore the same proportion to the total population as it did in 1861.

(d) The figures in this column are the sum of those in columns (4), (5), (6), and (8): for the years from 1861 slightly different totals are given in *The Irish Catholic Directory*.

(e) 1946, 26 counties; 1951, 6 counties.

(f) 1951.

(Column (1), from *Reports of the Commission on Emigration and other Population Problems* (Dublin, 1954), p. 281; columns (2), (4), (5), (6) and (8), from *Irish Catholic Directory*, Dublin, 1851; 1863, p. 210; 1903, p. 414; 1948, p. 680; 1960, p. 772.)

This table, by taking no account of Irish priests serving abroad, underestimates—in recent years seemingly by some 25 per cent—the number of priests drawn from the Irish Catholic population: 'With more than 2000 priests, 4000 sisters, and 400 brothers, Ireland gives more missionaries to the world than does any other country except Holland' (Jean Blanchard, *The Church in Contemporary Ireland* (Dublin, 1963), p. 86). But, in spite of this, as the following table shows, there are more priests per thousand of the Catholic population in Ireland than in most other predominantly Catholic countries in Europe.

Number of Catholic population to one priest (secular and regular)

Ireland, 1958	585
Belgium	530
Italy	690
France	718
Austria	940
Spain	970
Germany	1000
Portugal	1630

In countries where Catholics are a minority their number per priest is smaller, ranging (in the figures M. Blanchard quotes) from 50 in Iceland to 440 in Switzerland.

(Ireland, from table above; other countries from Blanchard, 1963, op. cit., p. 106, n.148, quoting *Le Monde*. M. Blanchard does not indicate the years to which these figures refer.)

INDEX

Abortion, seemingly strong appeal of to prospective father and mother of illegitimate child and to girl's parents, 62; but apparently rarely practised, 62–3; possible reasons, 63–4.

Bastard, harshness of popular attitude towards, 61; sometimes mitigated by his good conduct or by acquisition of property, 61–2; little prospect of marrying well unless he had property, 62. *See also*, Fathers of illegitimate children; Mothers of illegitimate children; Illegitimacy; Desertion; Foundling Hospital, Cork; Foundling Hospital, Dublin; Foundlings; Infanticide.
Begging, as a resource of mothers of illegitimate children, 57–8.

Catholicism, doctrine on marriage, 121, 137: *see* Convents, Priests.
Celibacy, prevalence of, 113, and n.4; reasons for, 120–1.
Chastity of peasant girls, 137–8.
Convents, influence of on pupils' attitude towards marriage, 142–4.

Desertion of illegitimate children, how and where deserted, 65–6; belief that restriction of entry to Dublin Foundling Hospital reduced, 73. *See also*, Foundlings; Foundling Hospital, Cork; Foundling Hospital, Dublin.
Distillation, illicit, in England, 14, 20–22; influence of immigrant Irish, 21; urban location, 21; demand from industrial users of spirit, 22; decline of, 22, 23;

Distillation, illicit, *cont.*
in Ireland, prevalence of, 10, 49; in Ireland compared with England and Scotland, 23, Fig. 5, pp. 42–3; reasons for greater prevalence in Ireland, 23–30; factors encouraging, late eighteenth, early nineteenth centuries, 1, 2; site, choice of, 8–11; location of, Fig. 2, p. 31; 30–34; concentrated north of line from Limerick to Newry, Fig. 2, p. 31, 30–44; possible reasons for concentration and relative absence elsewhere, especially in mountainous districts of west Cork and Kerry, 32–44, smuggling, 33–4, butter-making, 34–5, preference for beer, 34 and n., shortage of grain, 35, concentration of lawful distilling in south, 36–44; personnel, 11–12; inducements to engage in, 25–30, poverty and need of supplementary income, 25–7, source of rent, 26–7, means of disposing of grain where communications poor, 27, natural features, 28, sympathy for among general public, clergy, landlords, magistrates, juries, 28–30; profits of, 19–20; fluctuations in amount of Fig. 5, pp. 42–3, 44; possible reasons for, movements in price of grain, 44–5, fluctuations in yield of potatoes, 44n., facility of saving turf 44n., variations in spirit-duty, 45–6; decline of, as measured by number of detections, 23, Fig. 5, pp. 42–3; reasons for decline, 46–8, transformation of old economy, 46–7,

Distillation, illicit, in Ireland, *cont.* opposition of Catholic church, 47 and n., more effective opposition by State, 47, 48, stronger competition from licensed distillers, 47–8, deterioration in quality of poteen, 47, increased consumption of beer, 48; implications of, 49–50, fiscal, 50, crime, 50, bribery, 10, 50, violence, 10–11, 15, population, 50 and n., economic and social, 49–59, tended to increase rent, 27. *See also* Poteen;
  in Scotland, 14, 22–23; prevalence of, early nineteenth century, 22; landlords' opposition, 23; decline of, 23.
Distillation, licensed, concentrated in south and east, Fig. 4, p. 40, 36; largely because of excise legislation, 36; progress of concentration, 1777–1822, 37–8; evasion of duty in 1770s, 36; legislation, 1779 and 1791, to lessen evasion by concentrating industry, 36–7; continuing evasion of duty in 1820s, 41; impediments to progress of, 23–5.
Duty, spirit, introduction of, 1; frequent variations in 24, 45; level of in England, 21n.; level of in Ireland, 1, 19, 21, Fig. 5, pp. 42–3; level of in Scotland, 21n., 23.

Emigration, facilitated diffusion of arranged marriage, 116, 117, 118, 120.
Ether, chemical composition of, 93–4, 87n.; early use of as inebriant, 87–8.
Ether-drinking, reasons for spread of in various countries in later nineteenth century, 88; by 1890s morphia displacing ether among well-to-do, but taste for ether descending social scale, 89; ether-drinking in peasant communities in East Prussia, Russia, Norway, France and Hungary, 89, in working-class families in Britain, 89–90;

Ether-drinking, *cont.*
  in Ulster, nature and reliability of evidence, 91 and n.; general description, 90–1; use of poteen, methylated and rectified spirit as adulterants, 94; cost of ether, 102; method of drinking, 91; amount drunk, 91–2; unpleasantness of process of drinking, 92, followed by more agreeable sensations, 92; cycle of intoxication quickly completed and readily repeated, 93; most drinkers small farmers, labourers or members of their families, 93; source of ether, 94, some may have been locally distilled, 94, but most brought from Britain, 94, to order of local chemists or wholesalers in Irish ports, 95; distributed by publicans and shebeen-keepers, doctors, shopkeepers, hawkers and beggars, 95–6; sold for money or exchanged for goods, 96; area affected, Fig. 6, p. 98, 97; accounts of introduction, 99; time of diffusion, 97–100; possible reasons for diffusion, 100–3, ether's supposed medicinal properties, 100, temperance, campaigns, 100–1, 88, decline of illicit distillation, 101–2, favourable publicity and wider distribution of ether as it facilitated advances in surgery, 102, cheapness of ether after Methylated Spirit Act, 102, offered novel sensations, 102–3; possible reasons why little ether drunk beyond relatively restricted area, 103–5, continuing availability of poteen until, with rising incomes, people could afford lawful spirit, 103, availability of methylated spirit and other substitutes for poteen, 103–4, spread of ether-drinking from one or more centres interrupted by opposition of Church and State, 104–5; opposition to ether-drinking, 105–8, Catholic clergy seem continuously to have

INDEX

Ether-drinking, in Ulster, *cont.*
denounced it, though initially with little success, 105, opposition in press, Parliament and by clergy and General Synod of Church of Ireland, 105, 106, 'scheduling' in 1890 under Poisons Act, 1870, 106, 107, practice criticised by coroners' juries, 107, legislation against by Parliament of Northern Ireland, 1923, 1927, 107–8; decline of, 107–8; physical and mental troubles attributed to, 108–9; though extent probably exaggerated, 110; risk of being suffocated by ether fumes or of dying from an overdose, 111; risk of fire, 111; apparently responsible for little social evil, 111.

Faith of Irish, firmness of, 151–2; reasons for, 152–3.

Fathers of illegitimate children, social origins of, 53; no statutory obligation to provide for child, 58–9; usually father evaded responsibility, 58; though sympathetic court might try to enforce contribution from him, 59–61.

Foundling Hospital, Cork, 73–6; Act establishing, 1735, method of financing and objects of, 73, 74, 75, 76; accepted children annually at Easter, 73; put out to nurse, 73–4; then maintained in hospital and put to service or apprenticed, 74; statistics of admissions, deaths, discharges, 1820–33, 74, 76; reasons for heavy mortality, 74–5; criticised for high mortality, for children's ill-equipment to face world, for immorality, for spreading venereal disease, for inflating price of coal, for taking in children not, or improbably, of Cork parentage, 75–6; vested in Poor Law Commissioners, admissions cease, 1838, 76.

Foundling Hospital, Dublin, 66–73; establishment and objects of, 66–7; initially children sent to foster-mothers in country until 7 or 8 years of age and then kept in Hospital until old enough to be apprenticed, 67; crisis of 1797 and high mortality preceding, 67–8, reasons for, 68; reform in 1798, 68; nursery department introduced, with wet-nurses, 69–70, neglect of children in, ib.; children might be brought to hospital by 'child-cadgers', 68–9; their hardships on journey, ib.; might be left anonymously at hospital, 70; figures for admissions, deaths and discharges, 1796–1826, 70–1; condition and future of children discharged from hospital, 71; entry restricted, 1820, ended, 1829, 72; numbers of admissions, 1820–30, 72–3; belief that restricted entry increased infanticide and reduced desertion, 73; vested in Poor Law Commissioners, 1838, 72.

Foundlings, formal responsibility for with churchwardens of Established Church, 66; their powers, formal and assumed, 66, 77; probably most until 1830s sent to Foundling Hospitals in Dublin or Cork (q.v.), 66; fate of others, 76–8; precariousness of their lot after 1833 when parochial cess ceased to be levied, 77–8; responsibility for foundlings sometimes assumed by Catholic priest, 78; how he disposed of children, 78–9; fate of those quite unprovided for, 79.

'Gentleman's miss', 53–4.

Illegitimacy, method of collecting information bearing on by Poor Inquiry Commissioners, 1835–6, 51–2n.; inadequacy of evidence bearing on incidence of before Famine, 79; literary evidence and contemporary and later statistics suggesting low incidence, 79–83; possible reasons

Illegitimacy, *cont.*
for low incidence, 83–6, early and general marriage, 84, equable family life and relatively strong attachment between parents and children, 83–4, relatively few resident servants, 84, no bastardy or poor law, 84, popular disapproval of illegitimate child and mother and bleakness of their lives, 84–5;
   apparently low level of after Famine, 82–3, 119 and n.1; reliability of figures, 119.
Improvements, agricultural, needed if postponement of marriage to be avoided, 129–30; tenants deterred from, 130–1; priests' attitude towards, 131–5.
Infanticide of illegitimate children, evidence of prevalence, 64–5.

Marriage, 'arranged', structure of, 116–7, appeal of to peasant, 117; cost of to his children, 117; why children submitted to, 118.
Marriage, age at, 113 and n.3, 114 and n.5; youthful in late eighteenth and early nineteenth centuries, 114 and n.5, reasons for, 115; postponement of, in eighteenth century, 114 and n.5, after Famine, 113, 114–8; reasons for, 114, 115–8, 129–30; whether implied limitation of sexual activity, 118–20.
Mathew, Fr Theobald, 100n.; possible tendency of his temperance campaigning to restrict illicit distillation, 44n.
Maynooth, St. Patrick's College, whether foundation of facilitated ordination of peasants' sons, 122–3; course of training in, 132, 133; discipline in, 132–3; teaching on marriage, 128–9, tendency to encourage 'chastity and purity of heart', 129, and to raise psychological and practical barriers to marriage, 129.
Methylated spirit, drinking of, 103–4.
Methylated Spirit Act, 1855, tended to reduce illicit distillation in England, 22, in Scotland, 23; tended to reduce price of ether and to encourage ether-drinking, 102.
Mothers of illegitimate children, many servants, and reasons for, 52–3; number reduced by marriage of pregnant girl to child's father, 54; pressures in this direction from public opinion, priests, magistrates, etc., 54–5; mother's difficulty in marrying otherwise, 55, sometimes overcome by her seemly conduct, by money, land or stock provided most probably by her seducer, 55–6; harshness of popular attitude towards unmarried mother, 51–2; greater tolerance in Wales, 85; harsher attitude in Ireland associated with Irish Catholicism, 85–6; likely future, domestic or other service, begging or prostitution, 56–8; unlikely to secure help from child's father, 58–61.

Poteen, raw materials, traditionally malt and raw grain, 2; potatoes and other substitutes increasingly used as production declined, 3 and n.; hops, yeast, soap, nitre and charcoal also used, 4 and n.; sources of raw materials, 14–15; how made, 3–6; malting, 3; brewing, 4–5; distilling, 5–6; 'singlings', 'first-shot', 5; 'doublings', 5–6; 'double refine', 6; equipment for making, malting, 3–4, brewing, 4, 7, distilling, 5, 7–8; cost of stills, 7–8, hiring of stills, 11–12; maturing, 6; adulteration, 6; by-products, 6 and n.; methods of distilling poteen, 13–17; extent of distribution in Ireland and Britain, 13–14; middlemen, 14–17, 18; established markets, 14–15; entrepôt trade in Aran Islands, Portstewart, Ballycastle, 15–16; sale of in shebeens, 17–18; sale of as

INDEX

Poteen, *cont.*
resource of widows, 18; how transported, 16–17; price of, 18–19, 48; consumers of, 17–18, 24–5.
See also Distillation, illicit.

Priests, Roman Catholic, social origins of, before foundation of Maynooth, 122, immediately afterwards, 122–3, 148–9, in later nineteenth and twentieth centuries, 123–6, 148–9; desire of peasantry to send sons to Maynooth, 123–4; substantial families probably more reluctant, 124–5; education of, 127–9, 132–3;
attitude to agricultural improvement, 131–5, to emigration, 135–6; whether, though denouncing it, their actions tended to encourage it, 136, n.1;
attitude to illicit distillation, 29, 47 and n.; to ether-drinking, 105;
attitude to marriage, 121–2; their tolerance or approval of arranged 'match' and the postponement or abandonment of marriage it implied, 158–9; their attitude to marriage in harmony with social and economic 'needs', 158; influenced by peasant origin of many priests, 121–7; confirmed by education, 127–36, by their attitude to agricultural improvement and emigration, 129–36, and by their vows of celibacy, 136–7; why their attitude towards marriage of great influence, 144; meticulousness of their supervision of matters concerning sex and marriage, 156–7; their attitude supported by legislation in 26-counties, 157–8; their intolerance of other advice on marriage and associated matters, 156; priests tended to make laity tolerant of celibacy by their own example, 137, by emphasising certain parts of

Priests, Roman Catholic, attitude to marriage, *cont.*
Church's teaching on marriage, 137–8, by attitude to courtship, 138, by insisting on segregation of sexes, 138–40, by discouraging 'quilting', dancing, amateur theatricals etc., 140–2;
extent of priests' secular power, 144–7; reasons for, social origins, 155, 126–7, religious office, 144–5, association with popular movements, 147, 155, and with British government, 147, their own desire to exercise secular power, 147–50, their laity's acquiescence, 150–6, rarity of rival contenders for power, 147, 150–1;
conscientiousness of priests in discharge of duties, 153, their 'exemplary purity', 155; standard of living, 154; criticism of, 153–5, for arrogance, 153, suggested reasons for arrogance, 147–50; for eagerness for fees, 153–4;
statistics of, numbers in various categories, and proportion to Catholic population, 1849–1958, pp. 160–1; proportion to Catholic population in other European countries, 161.

Prostitution, as resource for mothers of illegitimate children, 57–8; tendency of girls discharged from Foundling Hospitals to resort to, 71–2, 75.

Roman Catholic Church; *see* Catholicism; Priests, Roman Catholic.

Sexual activity, whether limitation of marriage implied limitation of, 118–20, 120, n.1; compensations for, 120; adaptation to continence, 120–1, 113–61.

Spirit, illicit, *see* Poteen.

Spirit, 'parliament' (lawful), price of, 1815, 1, 19; ill-repute of and reasons for, 24–5.